AQA History

AS Unit 2

A Sixties Social Revolution? British Society, 1959–1975

Exclusively endorsed by AQA

Sally Waller

Published in 2008 by:
Nelson Thornes Ltd
Delta Place
27 Bath Road
CHELTENHAM
GL53 7TH
United Kingdom

08 09 10 11 12 / 10 9 8 7 6 5 4 3 2 1

A catalogue record for this book is available from the British Library

978-0-7487-8268-0

Illustrations by Beehive Illustration, David Russell Illustration and Graham-Cameron Illustration

Page make-up by Thomson Digital

Printed in Croatia by Zrinski

Contents

AQA introduction

Nelson Thornes and AQA

Nelson Thornes has worked in collaboration with AQA to ensure that this book offers you the best support for your AS or A level course and helps you to prepare for your exams. The partnership means that you can be confident that the range of learning, teaching and assessment practice materials has been checked by the senior examining team at AQA before formal approval, and is closely matched to the requirements of your specification.

Blended learning

This book forms a blend with electronic resources: this means that links between topics and activities between the book and the electronic resources help you to work in the way that best suits you, and enable extra support to be provided online. For example, you can test yourself online and feedback from the test will direct you back to the relevant parts of the book.

Electronic resources are available in a simple-to-use online platform called Nelson Thornes learning space. If your school or college has a licence to use the service, you will be given a password through which you can access the materials through any internet connection.

Learning activity

These resources include a variety of interactive and non-interactive activities to support your learning.

Progress tracking

These resources include a variety of tests that you can use to check your knowledge on particular topics (Test yourself) and a range of resources that enable you to analyse and understand examination questions (On your marks…).

Research support

These resources include WebQuests, in which you are assigned a task and provided with a range of web links to use as source material for research.

Study skills

These resources support you to develop a skill that is key for your course, for example planning essays.

When you see an icon, go to Nelson Thornes learning space at www.nelsonthornes.com/aqagce, enter your access details and select your course. The materials are arranged in the same order as the topics in the book, so you can easily find the resources you need.

How to use this book

This book covers the specification for your course and is arranged in a sequence approved by AQA.

The features in this book include:

Timeline

Key events are outlined at the beginning of the book. The events are colour-coded so you can clearly see the categories of change.

Learning objectives

At the beginning of each section you will find a list of learning objectives that contain targets linked to the requirements of the specification.

Key chronology

A short list of dates usually with a focus on a specific event or legislation.

Key profile

The profile of a key person you should be aware of to fully understand the period in question.

Key term

A term that you will need to be able to define and understand.

Did you know?

Interesting information to bring the subject under discussion to life.

Exploring the detail

Information to put further context around the subject under discussion.

A closer look

An in-depth look at a theme, person or event to deepen your understanding. Activities around the extra information may be included.

Sources

Sources to reinforce topics or themes and may provide fact or opinion. They may be quotations from historical works, contemporaries of the period or photographs.

Cross-reference

Links to related content book which may offer more detail on the subject in question.

Activity

Various activity types to provide you with different challenges and opportunities to demonstrate both the content and skills you are learning. Some can be worked on individually, some as part of group work and some are designed to specifically "stretch and challenge".

Question

Questions to prompt further discussion on the topic under consideration and are an aid to revision.

Summary questions

Summary questions at the end of each chapter to test your knowledge and allow you to demonstrate your understanding.

AQA Examiner's tip

Hints from AQA examiners to help you with your study and to prepare for your exam.

AQA Examination-style questions

Questions at the end of each section in the style that you can expect in your exam.

Learning outcomes

Learning outcomes at the end of each section remind you what you should know having completed the chapters in that section.

■ Web links in the book

Because Nelson Thornes is not responsible for third party content online, there may be some changes to this material that are beyond our control. In order for us to ensure that the links referred to in the book are as up-to-date and stable as possible, the web sites provided are usually homepages with supporting instructions on how to reach the relevant pages if necessary.

Please let us know at **webadmin@nelsonthornes.com** if you find a link that doesn't work and we will do our best to correct this at reprint, or to list an alternative site.

Introduction to the History series

When Bruce Bogtrotter in Roald Dahl's *Matilda* was challenged to eat a huge chocolate cake, he just opened his mouth and ploughed in, taking bite after bite and lump after lump until the cake was gone and he was feeling decidedly sick. The picture is not dissimilar to that of some A level history students. They are attracted to history because of its inherent appeal but, when faced with a bulging file and a forthcoming examination, their enjoyment evaporates. They try desperately to cram their brains with an assortment of random facts and subsequently prove unable to control the outpouring of their ill-digested material in the examination.

The books in this series are designed to help students and teachers avoid this feeling of overload and examination panic by breaking down the AQA history specification in such a way that it is easily absorbed. Above all, they are designed to retain and promote students' enthusiasm for history by avoiding a dreary rehash of dates and events. Each book is divided into sections, closely matched to those given in the specification, and the content is further broken down into chapters that present the historical material in a lively and attractive form, offering guidance on the key terms, events and issues, and blending thought-provoking activities and questions in a way designed to advance students' understanding. By encouraging students to think for themselves and to share their ideas with others, as well as helping them to develop the knowledge and skills they will need to pass their examination, this book should ensure that students' learning remains a pleasure rather than an endurance test.

To make the most of what this book provides, students will need to develop efficient study skills from the start and it is worth spending some time considering what these involve:

- Good organisation of material in a subject-specific file. Organised notes help develop an organised brain and sensible filing ensures time is not wasted hunting for misplaced material. This book uses cross-references to indicate where material in one chapter has relevance to material in another. Students are advised to adopt the same technique.

- A sensible approach to note-making. Students are often too ready to copy large chunks of material from printed books or to download sheaves of printouts from the internet. This series is designed to encourage students to think about the notes they collect and to undertake research with a particular purpose in mind. The activities encourage students to pick out information that is relevant to the issue being addressed and to avoid making notes on material that is not properly understood.

- Taking time to think, which is by far the most important component of study. By encouraging students to think before they write or speak, be it for a written answer, presentation or class debate, students should learn to form opinions and make judgements based on the accumulation of evidence. These are the skills that the examiner will be looking for in the final examination. The beauty of history is that there is rarely a right or wrong answer so, with sufficient evidence, one student's view will count for as much as the next.

Unit 2

Unit 2 promotes the study of significant periods of history in depth. Although the span of years may appear short, the chosen topics are centred on periods of change that raise specific historical issues and they therefore provide an opportunity for students to study in some depth the interrelationships between ideas, individuals, circumstances and other factors that lead to major developments. Appreciating the dynamics of change, and balancing the degree of change against elements of continuity, make for a fascinating and worthwhile study. Students are also required to analyse consequences and draw conclusions about the issues these studies raise. Such themes are, of course, relevant to an understanding of the present and, through such an historical investigation, students will be guided towards a greater appreciation of the world around them today, as well as develop their understanding of the past.

Unit 2 is tested by a 1 hour 30 minute paper containing three questions. The first question is compulsory and based on sources, while the remaining two, of which students will need to choose one, are two-part questions as described in Table 1. Plentiful sources are included throughout this book to give students some familiarity with contemporary and historiographical material, and activities and suggestions are provided to enable students to develop the required examination skills. Students should familiarise themselves with the question breakdown, additional hints and marking criteria given below before attempting any of the practice examination-style questions at the end of each section.

Answers will be marked according to a scheme based on 'levels of response'. This means that the answer will be assessed according to which level best matches the historical skills displayed, taking both knowledge and understanding into account. All students should have a copy of these criteria and need to use them wisely.

Table 1 *Unit 2: style of questions and marks available*

Unit 2	Question	Marks	Question type	Question stem	Hints for students
Question 1 based on three sources of c.300–350 words in total	(a)	12	This question involves the comparison of two sources	Explain how far the views in Source B differ from those in Source A in relation to…	Take pains to avoid simply writing out what each source says with limited direct comment. Instead, you should try to find two or three points of comparison and illustrate these with reference to the sources. You should also look for any underlying similarities. In your conclusion, you will need to make it clear exactly 'how far' the views differ
Question 1	(b)	24	This requires use of the sources and own knowledge and asks for an explanation that shows awareness that issues and events can provoke differing views and explanations	How far… How important was… How successful…	This answer needs to be planned as you will need to develop an argument in your answer and show balanced judgement. Try to set out your argument in the introduction and, as you develop your ideas through your paragraphs, support your opinions with detailed evidence. Your conclusion should flow naturally and provide supported judgement. The sources should be used as 'evidence' throughout your answer. Do ensure you refer to them all
Question 2 and 3	(a)	12	This question is focused on a narrow issue within the period studied and requires an explanation	Explain why…	Make sure you explain 'why', not 'how', and try to order your answer in a way that shows you understand the inter-linkage of factors and which are the most important. You should try to reach an overall judgement/conclusion
Question 2 and 3	(b)	24	This question is broader and asks for analysis and explanation with appropriate judgement. The question requires an awareness of debate over issues	A quotation in the form of a judgement on a key development or issue will be given and candidates asked: Explain why you agree or disagree with this view	This answer needs to be planned as you will need to show balanced judgement. Try to think of points that agree and disagree and decide which way you will argue. Set out your argument in the introduction and support it through your paragraphs, giving the alternative picture too but showing why your view is the more convincing. Your conclusion should flow naturally from what you have written

Marking criteria

Question 1(a)

Level 1 Answers either briefly paraphrase/describe the content of the two sources or identify simple comparison(s) between the sources. Skills of written communication will be weak. *(0–2 marks)*

Level 2 Responses will compare the views expressed in the two sources and identify some differences and/or similarities. There may be some limited own knowledge. Answers will be coherent but weakly expressed. *(3–6 marks)*

Level 3 Responses will compare the views expressed in the two sources, identifying differences **and** similarities and using own knowledge to explain and evaluate these. Answers will, for the most part, be clearly expressed. *(7–9 marks)*

Level 4 Responses will make a developed comparison between the views expressed in the two sources **and** own knowledge will apply to evaluate and to demonstrate a good contextual understanding. Answers will, for the most part, show good skills of written communication. *(10–12 marks)*

Question 1(b)

Level 1 Answers may be based on sources or on own knowledge alone, or they may comprise an undeveloped mixture of the two. They may contain some descriptive material which is only loosely linked to the focus of the question or they may address only a part of the question. Alternatively, there may be some explicit comment with little, if any, appropriate support. Answers are likely to be generalised and assertive. There will be little, if any, awareness of differing historical interpretations. The response will be limited in development and skills of written communication will be weak. *(0–6 marks)*

Level 2 Answers may be based on sources or on own knowledge alone, or they may contain a mixture of the two. They may be almost entirely descriptive with few explicit links to the focus of the question. Alternatively, they may contain some explicit comment with relevant but limited support. They will display limited understanding of differing historical interpretations. Answers will be coherent but weakly expressed and/or poorly structured. *(7–11 marks)*

Level 3 Answers will show a developed understanding of the demands of the question using evidence from **both** the sources **and** own knowledge. They will provide some assessment backed by relevant and appropriately selected evidence, but they will lack depth and/or balance. There will be some understanding of varying historical interpretations. Answers will, for the most part, be clearly expressed and show some organisation in the presentation of material. *(12–16 marks)*

Level 4 Answers will show explicit understanding of the demands of the question. They will develop a balanced argument backed by a good range of appropriately selected evidence from the sources and own knowledge, and a good understanding of historical interpretations. Answers will, for the most part, show organisation and good skills of written communication. *(17–21 marks)*

Level 5 Answers will be well focused and closely argued. The arguments will be supported by precisely selected evidence from the sources and own knowledge, incorporating well-developed understanding of historical interpretations and debate. Answers will, for the most part, be carefully organised and fluently written, using appropriate vocabulary. *(22–24 marks)*

Question 2(a) and 3(a)

Level 1 Answers will contain either some descriptive material which is only loosely linked to the focus of the question or some explicit comment with little, if any, appropriate support. Answers are likely to be generalised and assertive. The response will be limited in development and skills of written communication will be weak. *(0–2 marks)*

Level 2 Answers will demonstrate some knowledge and understanding of the demands of the question. They will either be almost entirely descriptive with few explicit links to the question **or** they provide some explanations backed by evidence that is limited in range and/or depth. Answers will be coherent but weakly expressed and/or poorly structured. *(3–6 marks)*

Level 3 Answers will demonstrate good understanding of the demands of the question providing relevant explanations backed by appropriately selected information, although this may not be full or comprehensive. Answers will, for the most part, be clearly expressed and show some organisation in the presentation of material. *(7–9 marks)*

Level 4 Answers will be well focused, identifying a range of specific explanations backed by precise evidence and demonstrating good understanding of the connections and links between events/issues. Answers will, for the most part, be well written and organised. *(10–12 marks)*

Question 2(b) and 3(b)

Level 1 Answers may **either** contain some descriptive material which is only loosely linked to the focus of the question **or** they may address only a limited part of the period of the question. Alternatively, there may be some explicit comment with little, if any, appropriate support. Answers are likely to be generalised and assertive. There will be little, if any, awareness of different historical interpretations. The response will be limited in development and skills of written communication will be weak. *(0–6 marks)*

Level 2 Answers will show some understanding of the demands of the question. They will either be almost entirely descriptive with few explicit links to the question **or** they contain some explicit comment with relevant but limited support. They will display limited understanding of differing historical interpretations. Answers will be coherent but weakly expressed and/or poorly structured. *(7–11 marks)*

Level 3 Answers will show a developed understanding of the demands of the question. They will provide some assessment, backed by relevant and appropriately selected evidence, but they will lack depth and/or balance. There will be some understanding of varying historical interpretations. Answers will, for the most part, be clearly expressed and show some organisation in the presentation of material. *(12–16 marks)*

Level 4 Answers will show explicit understanding of the demands of the question. They will develop a balanced argument backed by a good range of appropriately selected evidence and a good understanding of historical interpretations. Answers will, for the most part, show organisation and good skills of written communication. *(17–21 marks)*

Level 5 Answers will be well focused and closely argued. The arguments will be supported by precisely selected evidence leading to a relevant conclusion/judgement, incorporating well-developed understanding of historical interpretations and debate. Answers will, for the most part, be carefully organised and fluently written, using appropriate vocabulary. *(22–24 marks)*

Introduction to this book

Fig. 1 *Progress in the general election is broadcast from the ITN newsroom on 7 March 1959*

In 1940, George Orwell wrote that 'Only revolution can save England.' Propelled by the outbreak of war a year earlier, Orwell believed Britain to be on the verge of a dramatic transformation that would level down Britain's traditional class structure and transform British society. He was wrong. The revolution he expected never happened. What did happen was that Britain emerged from the dark years of war to experience a major economic boom, which bred a content that was far from inducive to revolutionary change. Yet war did alter Britain, as did the years of post-war prosperity, and it was during the 1960s – or at least the 'long 1960s', which can be identified as the period 1959–75 – that something akin to the social and cultural revolution

Orwell was thinking of can be discerned. Maybe 'revolution' is too strong a term. Certainly the changes were nothing like as cataclysmic or all-embracing as Orwell's predictions. Yet, changes there were and the lives of those born just before or since the beginning of the 1960s have been very different from those of a generation earlier as a result. As you read this book, try to make up your own mind as to whether there really was a '1960s social revolution'.

After the experience of war, when people of different social backgrounds were thrown together in the fight against a common enemy, a new Labour government was elected in July 1945. Furthermore, for the first time in the history of that party, Labour commanded sufficient parliamentary support to carry through a massive programme of welfare reform. Responding to the findings of the 1942 Beveridge Report, which had identified the 'five giants' – want, disease, ignorance, squalor and idleness – as the major problems needing to be tackled in Britain, Attlee's Labour government created a 'cradle to the grave' welfare state. Following the Family Allowances Act of 1945, which gave five shillings a week to all mothers for each child after the first born, it included, from 1948, a new scheme of National Insurance and National Assistance to provide for the unemployed and needy and a National Health Service that provided free health care for all (although charges for spectacles and dental care treatment were reintroduced in 1951). This Labour government also pursued an economic policy that made full employment a priority and key industries, such as coal and railways, were nationalised to bring them under direct state control. The school leaving age was raised to 15 in 1947 and, thanks to the Butler Act, passed in 1944 by the wartime coalition government, the provision of education and the opportunities for bright youngsters from lower-class backgrounds to advance themselves were increased.

It is sometimes suggested that it was the creation of this welfare state that helped avert the revolution that Orwell had anticipated. Certainly, with the spread of the 'nanny state', some of the causes of poverty disappeared and the division between the 'haves' and 'have nots' lessened. Although Labour's nationalisation measures were partly reversed by the subsequent Conservative governments that dominated politics between 1951 and 1964, the commitment to the welfare state remained. Although Britain's two leading political parties might differ on the detail, both Labour and Conservative politicians accepted that society had an obligation to provide its members with health services, houses and education and the 1950s were, consequently, a period of stability and broad consensus in politics.

However, this is only part of the story. In line with the rest of Europe, Britain enjoyed high growth rates in the post-war decade. Economic boom, coupled with relatively low inflation and a very low unemployment level of 1–2 per cent through the 1950s, also encouraged stability by bringing enormous improvements to average standards of living. Scientific advances – for example the spread of penicillin, which was developed in the war years, better understanding of nutrition and technological breakthroughs and productivity improvements that permitted the spread of affordable cars, TVs and electrical goods – all helped to transform lives. The purchase of non-essentials such as household appliances, clothing, transport and holidays increased. Mundane tasks that had made a drudgery of so many lives in previous decades were eased by new innovations and more leisure time resulted with which to enjoy the fruits of this progress. In 1958, the opening of the Preston bypass heralded a new age of motoring for the masses, while the steady growth of the TV helped create a new common culture – and one that was as much part of the factory worker's council flat as the aristocrat's mansion.

The economic boom meant that women could emerge from their traditional status as stay-at-home housewives to enjoy new opportunities. They were particularly sought in the expanding labour market created by the service industries, although many did still give up work on the birth of their first child. Young people were also affected as they experienced a collective wealth unknown before this era and they found in the 1950s rock scene a new cultural identity that crossed traditional class divides. Wealth was still relative but it not only helped avert Orwellian revolution, it also brought about the conditions in which a different, and less obvious, type of revolution would take place. By 1959, many signs of change were already firmly in place.

Nevertheless, the underlying political stability of the 1950s is indicative of the continuity that remained within British society. 'Traditional' class divisions and attitudes remained strong and the public-school educated ruling elite of the 1950s was no different from that of the pre-war era. Despite being the 'party of the working class', Labour was led by the middle-class intellectual Hugh Gaitskell from 1955, while the Conservative governments under Winston Churchill (1951–5), Anthony Eden (1955–7) and Harold Macmillan (1957–63), were dominated by 'Edwardian' aristocrats whose lifestyles were far removed from the mass of middle-class voters who helped put them in power. Class divisions did not melt away and indeed were reinvigorated after the blurring of the war years. The upper class remained in place, while the middle classes did well out of the 1950s, rising in confidence and determination, and the working classes, while benefiting from much of what was going on around them, still retained traditional patterns of behaviour within the family, community and at work.

The 1960s witnessed no major political upheaval; no one event that can be said to have brought about a revolution. Indeed, the developments of the 'long 1960s' of 1959–75 were, in many respects, a continuation of changes heralded in the 1950s. However, they have been singled out by social commentators, historians and even by the general public as having a rather deeper significance. To many who lived through the era, the 1960s seemed unique. In 1958, it would have been hard to predict the degree to which attitudes, behaviour and outlook would be changed in the next 10 years. The year 1968 saw widespread student unrest with violent protests against the Vietnam War in Grosvenor

Square, London. It witnessed the opening night of the musical *Hair* on the London stage, celebrating sex, drugs and nudity. It was the year of Enoch Powell's 'Rivers of Blood' speech predicting imminent disaster from continued immigration into Britain and it was the first birthday of the BBC's new youth radio station, Radio One, which was celebrated with a stream of popular British music, dominated by the Beatles – who had received MBEs for their working-class assault on traditional British culture.

The 'long 1960s' were marked by a number of fundamental changes. Some of these were shared with other countries of the developed western world. These included the growth of youth culture, the emancipation of women and the spread of feminism, the collapse of the Christian moral framework and the spread of drugs and sexual liberation. However, there were other, more specifically British, changes too. There was the consumer culture of the Beatles, Mary Quant and Carnaby Street that gave rise to notions of 'Swinging London' and there was the undercurrent of challenge to Britain's traditional social barriers and cultural divide. This change manifested itself in a number of ways. In 1963, John Lennon invited members of the audience 'in the cheap seats' at the Royal Variety Show to clap, while those in the expensive ones were to 'rattle your jewellery'. (His original dressing room threat to say 'rattle your f – – – – – jewellery' was vetoed by the Beatles' manager, Brian Epstein.) The Conservative Party decided, the same year, that after the co-opted Alec Douglas-Home, the last aristocrat to head the party, they really needed a democratic system of election to choose their leader. The political leaders of the 'high 1960s' – Harold Wilson (Labour Prime Minister 1964–70 and 1974–6) and Edward Heath (Conservative Prime Minister 1970–4) – both came from similar working/lower-middle class backgrounds and helped break the tradition of aristocratic governance, while around them the by-word of the 1960s seemed to be 'liberation'.

'Liberation' was reflected in the disappearance of 'old-fashioned' manners and unwritten rules about acceptable behaviour and lifestyles, as well as a new sexual freedom encouraged by the availability of the oral contraceptive pill. Under Wilson, and to a lesser extent, Heath, a stream of liberalising legislation from the relaxation of censorship to the decriminalisation of homosexuality, the legalisation of abortion and the provision of equal pay for women found its way on to the statute books. Such 'liberation' did not go unchallenged, but the impact of economic and technological change forced the re-evaluation of traditional moral codes. In an era of the mass media, scandals like the Profumo affair of 1963 could no longer be hushed up. Economic freedom bred social freedom and, in legislating to enshrine such freedom in law, the politicians were primarily responding to change rather than creating it.

Fig. 2 *1960s fashion*

The 1960s also saw changes to the British landscape and people. Cars transformed urban communities and new roads ran riot through the countryside. Slum clearance and the provision of new housing, often in tower blocks, altered cities and created vast suburbs of functional buildings. It was, perhaps, to escape such surroundings that increasing numbers began to take holidays abroad, widening their horizons and bringing back glimpses of other cultures. Aspirations were also raised by the continued expansion of education and the growing student population. Decolonisation and economic prosperity brought an inflow of immigrants into Britain, many of whom were coloured and whose 'alien' ways of behaviour gave a new dimension to life. New food, new music but also new tensions entered British society and immigration became a politically sensitive issue. Tensions were also increased as some industries like coal mining struggled against change and the 1970s began with a spate of strikes and embittered industrial relations that ended Heath's career.

By 1975, the optimism and excitement that had marked the mid-1960s had begun to fade away and the era ended quietly, rather as it had begun. The years of sustained prosperity had passed and deep-seated problems within the British economy had become more evident. The political stability that had resulted from the 1950s affluence had disappeared in the wake of growing unemployment while declining labour relations dampened the enthusiasm for further social change. The student activities of the later 1960s made taxpayers more hostile to the 'indolent youth', and the Beatles' involvement in drugs and mysticism tarnished their sheen and hastened their split in 1970. The years 1970–5 were in some ways an epilogue to an already passing era – with governments showing a determination to halt what was seen as the rising tide of permissiveness and to restore order and control.

The 1960s saw both change and continuity. The old social structures were never destroyed and, with a population of around 55 million, it is perhaps not surprising that there was a huge diversity of individual experience. Reaction to the 1960s can range from unduly romantic sentimentality to outright repulsion and from ecstatic enthusiasm to a failure to see what the fuss was about. Reflect on such reactions as you read this book and try to form your own view as to whether there was a 1960s social revolution. Ask your parents, grandparents and other older friends and relatives what the 1960s meant to them. Challenge those who romanticise or demonise the decade and try to build up your own profile of the years 1959–75 based on your collection of photos, memorabilia and reminiscences, as well as the fruits of your personal reading and research. Keep an eye on today's newspapers where there are frequent references to the 1960s as parallels or contrasts to more recent developments and tune into TV and radio programmes which feature 1960s issues or personalities. Watch the films, see the plays, read the novels and listen to the music of the 1960s. Using the following pages as your guide, it is hoped that you will be able to understand, empathise with and evaluate some of the developments of this emotive period.

Fig. 3 *There was a last-minute rush of Commonwealth immigrants before the Commonwealth Immigrants Act 1962 came into effect*

■ Timeline

The colours represent categories of change during the 1960s: Red: Political, Black: Economic, Blue: Social, Green: International/Britain's place in the world

1944	1945	1945	1945	1945	1946	1946
Butler Act provides for education appropriate to 'age, abilities and aptitudes'. (A tripartite structure of grammar, secondary technical and secondary modern schools based on an 11 plus system, is developed)	7 May War with Germany comes to an end	**Family Allowances Act** introduces child benefits to parents	**July** Labour government is elected, with Clement Attlee as Prime Minister	15 August War with Japan comes to an end	**National Insurance Act, National Health Service Act** and **National Assistance Act** help create a welfare state 'from the cradle to the grave'	**New Towns Act** designates areas where new towns are to be built under development corporations (government bodies)

1952	1952	1953	1954	1954	1955
6 February King George VI dies; accession of Elizabeth II	4 October Britain successfully explodes its first atomic bomb	Iron and steel industries are denationalised	**July** End of food rationing	Opening of Kidbrooke School, the first purpose-built comprehensive school	**April** Anthony Eden replaces Churchill as Conservative Prime Minister

1957	1958	1958	1958	1960	1961	1961
Macmillan's 'Never had it so good' speech. Conservative government is re-elected	Campaign for Nuclear Disarmament (CND) is founded. The first Aldermaston March takes place	First 13 km (8 mile) stretch of motorway opens	Race riots break out in Notting Hill, London	Compulsory National Service ends. Production of the contraceptive pill	Britain begins negotiations for membership of European Economic Community (EEC)	Demonstrations against nuclear weapons in London. Staging of play *Beyond the Fringe* and launch of *Private Eye* magazine establish the satire movement

1947	1947	1948	1948	1950	1951	1951	1951
Nationalisation of coal industry begins	School leaving age is raised to 15	**British Nationality Act** permits free entry into Britain for all Commonwealth citizens	National Health Service, National Insurance and National Assistance are implemented	**February** Labour government is re-elected	Nationalisation of iron and steel industry	Aneurin Bevan resigns from the Labour cabinet over the introduction of charges in the NHS. The Labour Party is split over the issue	**October** Conservative government is elected. Winston Churchill becomes Prime Minister

1955	1955	1956	1956	1956	1956	1957
May Conservatives win the general election	ITV, a second (and an independent, commercial) television channel, is launched	Suez Crisis reveals Britain's limited world status	Colleges of Advanced Technology are created	First nuclear power station is commissioned at Calder Hall	John Osborne's play *Look Back in Anger* symbolises the attack of the 'angry young men' on the Establishment	Harold Macmillan replaces Eden as Conservative Prime Minister

1962	1962	1962	1962	1963	1963	1963
Commonwealth Immigrants Act introduces entry voucher scheme, restricting Commonwealth immigration	Local education authority provides mandatory grants for university students	Establishment of National Economic Development Council encourages economic cooperation between government, business and trades unions	*That Was The Week That Was* TV programme brings satire to the BBC	Britain's entry to the EEC is refused	The Beatles have three No. 1 hits	The Robbins Report calls for the expansion of higher education

1964	1964	1964	1965	1965	1965	1965	1965
A Labour government is elected with Harold Wilson as Prime Minister	BBC2 is launched	The mini-skirt arrives on the cat walk	The government announces a five-year national plan for economic growth and creates the Department of Economic Affairs	The establishment of the Prices and Incomes Board to regulate wage and price increases	**Race Relations Act** aims to reduce discrimination and the Race Relations Board is set up	Circular 10/65 encourages local education authorities to reorganise secondary schooling on comprehensive lines	The Labour Prime Minister, Harold Wilson, nominates the Beatles for MBEs

1967	1967	1967	1968	1968	1968	1968
Family Planning Act allows local health authorities to provide a family planning service	The legalisation of homosexuality in private between consenting males over 21	The National Front is formed from a number of extreme-right, anti-immigration parties	Public expenditure cuts are implemented; NHS prescription charges are re-imposed	**Commonwealth Immigrants Act** aims to exclude Kenyan Asians	Enoch Powell's 'Rivers of Blood' speech warns about the results of unlimited immigration	Widespread student unrest; large anti-Vietnam War demonstrations take place in Grosvenor Square, outside US embassy in London

1970	1970	1970	1971	1971	1971
A third British application to join the EEC is made	Margaret Thatcher's circular 10/70 is intended to reverse the 1965 policy on the comprehensivisation of secondary education	First national conference of the Women's Liberation Movement takes place	**Immigration Act** introduces a clause demanding self or close relative birth connections, which effectively ends non-white immigration	**Industrial Relations Act** gives the government broad powers of intervention in industrial disputes but is widely opposed by the trades unions	The decimalisation of currency: £ s d replaced by £ p

1973	1974	1974	1974	1975	1975	1976
Miners, power workers and railway workers ban overtime. A three-day working week is introduced from the end of December because of power shortages	**February** Heath calls general election; the miners' strike begins. Labour forms a minority government under Harold Wilson	Miners' strike and three-day week end in March	**October** General election. The Labour Party gains a majority and forms a government	Referendum gives clear majority for staying in EEC	**Equal Pay Act** comes into force; **Sex Discrimination Act** establishes the Equal Opportunities Commission	Wilson resigns and is replaced by James Callaghan as Labour Prime Minister

1965	1966	1966	1966	1967	1967	1967	1967	1967
The death penalty is abolished	Labour wins the general election with an increased majority	National Assistance is renamed Supplementary Benefit	Colour TV begins	Britain applies for membership of the EEC (again). The application is vetoed by France	The £ is devalued from $2.80 to $2.40	Radio One is launched as a channel for popular music	Student unrest occurs at the London School of Economics	**Abortion Act** legalises the termination of pregnancy

1968	1968	1969	1969	1969	1970	1970
The musical *Hair* opens in London revealing nudity on stage (following the abolition of the Lord Chamberlain's powers of theatre censorship)	Pope Paul VI issues the encyclical *Humanae Vitae* condemning artificial contraception	The voting age is lowered from 21 to 18 years	The first polytechnics are created: Hatfield, Sheffield, Sunderland (30 more follow between 1969 and 1973). The Open University is established	The divorce law is liberalised by allowing 'irretrievable breakdown' in a marriage as grounds for divorce	**Equal Pay Act** is passed to prevent discrimination in pay between men and women; implementation is on a voluntary basis until 1975	Conservatives win the general election and Edward Heath becomes Prime Minister

1972	1972	1972	1973	1973	1973	1973
The miners' strike leads to a state of emergency with large-scale power cuts	The imposition of a statutory incomes policy	First publication of *Cosmopolitan* and *Spare Rib* magazines	Britain becomes member of EEC	The school leaving age is raised to 16	The first local commercial radio stations are launched	OPEC raises the price of oil

1 The age of affluence

In this chapter you will learn about:

- why Macmillan was so satisfied in 1957

- the state of the British economy at the end of the 1950s and its position in comparison with other nations

- the optimism of the British public and its significance

- the significance of the 1959 general election for both the Conservative and Labour parties.

Fig. 1 *Harold Macmillan, Conservative Prime Minister*

The effect of post-war prosperity by the end of the 1950s

On 20 July 1957, the Prime Minister, Harold Macmillan, addressed 1,500 people at Bedford Town's football ground. The meeting had been called to mark 25 years' unbroken service from Mr Lennox-Boyd, the colonial Secretary, but Macmillan used it as an opportunity to consider the state of the British economy and delivered the oft-quoted words of Source 1.

Key profile

Harold Macmillan

Harold Macmillan (1894–1986) was an Eton/Oxford-educated intellectual, who had served under Churchill during the war years. In 1920, he married Lady Dorothy – a member of the aristocratic Cavendish family. By 1958, 35 members of his government were related to him by marriage, including 7 of the 9 members of his

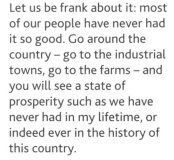

Let us be frank about it: most of our people have never had it so good. Go around the country – go to the industrial towns, go to the farms – and you will see a state of prosperity such as we have never had in my lifetime, or indeed ever in the history of this country.

1   *Harold MacMillan, 20 July 1957*

cabinet. He deliberately cultivated a distinctive serious-minded and gentlemanly 'Edwardian' image. He wore a top hat and white tie, was a member of five clubs and frequently appeared on the grouse moors. He was courteous but astute and his contribution to British affluence led to nicknames like 'Macwonder' and 'Supermac'. He resigned in 1963, suffering from ill health.

Why was Macmillan so satisfied?

Fig. 2 *Post-war Britain remained dreary as rationing continued. This is often referred to as a time of 'austerity'*

Fig. 3 *After years of restraint, the supermarket proved a shopper's paradise. What do you notice about these shoppers?*

To understand some of the economic terms in this section, look at the 'Exploring the detail' boxes on the right.

Table 1 *The UK balance of trade, 1946–60, in £m*

	Balance of visible trade	Balance of invisible trade	Overall trade balance
1946–50	−160	+104	−56
1951–55	−345	+326	−19
1956–60	−94	+226	+132

Activity

Statistical analysis

Study Table 1.

1. What has happened to the UK's overall trade balance?

2. What would this suggest?

3. What has caused the overall trade balance to change in this way?

4. Do you think politicians would have been pleased with these trade figures? Explain your answer.

Exploring the detail

Visible and invisible trade

Countries like Britain make money through trade. Visible trade provides income through the direct buying and selling of goods, while invisible trade includes money made through services such as shipping, banking and insurance. When a country imports more than it exports, there will be a trade deficit. Sometimes a deficit in visible trade can be offset by invisible trade. The difference between the value of imports and exports is known as the trade balance.

Exploring the detail

Inflation and deflation

Inflation occurs when people have more money to spend than there are goods available. Consequently, prices go up. If controls are brought in which curbs their spending, prices go down. This is deflation. Controls can include 'freezing' wage rises, increasing taxation and making borrowing harder so that goods cannot be bought on credit. Nevertheless, some inflation can help an economy because it encourages manufacturers to expand their businesses and employ more people. Conversely, deflation can lead to unemployment and reduce exports. The problem for governments is to avoid excessive inflation while keeping the economy growing (see Figure 4 on page 12).

Although it took some time for Britain to adjust back to a peacetime economy after the disastrous years of war, the general pattern of the 1950s was one of continued economic improvement. The last ration books were thrown away in July 1954 and, as wartime austerity was finally brought to an end, the British people were set to enjoy a higher standard of living than ever before.

The population was growing fast, thanks to an acceleration in the birth rate at the end of the Second World War. By 1961, there were 51 million people in Great Britain, which was 5 per cent (two million) more than in 1951. Thanks to a boom in the post-war global economy, a sustained increase in overseas trade brought high levels of earnings from exports and investments. This, together with the rising demand at home, ensured plentiful employment. Although the numbers employed in the traditional 'basic' occupations, like agriculture, fishing, coal mining and ship building, fell during this period, there was a huge expansion in electrical and engineering work along with cars, steel and other metals, and the service industries that ranged from financial and professional services to transport and sales. Nearly 5 million people were employed in service industries by 1960, one in five of the population and roughly the same number as in all heavy industry. (This figure becomes one in four if national and local government employees are included.)

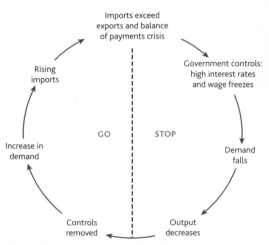

Fig. 4 *The stop-go economic cycle*

Economic growth brought rising wages and, in a state of nearly full employment, most people enjoyed a spectacular rise in income. No wonder Macmillan felt the British had 'never had it so good'. The later 1950s were a period of unprecedented affluence and rampant consumerism. However, although 'Supermac', as he was affectionately termed, could afford to be reasonably self-satisfied, this rosy picture hides some less positive developments. The growth in wages was outstripping the rate of increase in production and this brought inflation. The Prime Minister was constantly faced with the task of how to maintain growth and employment but keep prices steady.

Macmillan referred to it as the '64,000-dollar question' and his answer was partly in an appeal to industry and the public:

> What we need is restraint and common sense – restraint in the demands we make and common sense in how we spend our income.

Urging workers to forgo wage rises was all very well, but individual trades unions did not always see matters in the same light, particularly those unions representing industries such as coal, which were struggling to retain their pre-war position. Government controls had to be used to curb excessive inflation and taxation remained high, both to control excessive spending that would lead to an unwanted increase in imports and to pay for the rising costs of social services.

As Macmillan explained:

> To maintain the British economy at the right level, between inflation and deflation, balancing it correctly between too much and too little growth, is a delicate exercise. It is not a subject to be solved by mathematical formulae, or exact calculation. It is like bicycling along a tightrope.

2 *From the 'Conservative Campaign Guide, 1964' – referring to the later 1950s*

The economy was characterised by a pattern known as **stop-go**.

Although high salaries created a large internal consumer demand, they failed to give manufacturers any stimulus to increase their export trade and reduced workers' inclination to work overtime, which would have helped bolster the export industries. Thus, whilst there was a feeling of buoyancy in the country, the inflationary situation did cause concern. As the trades unions demanded ever higher wages, an inflationary spiral seemed to have set in.

Britain enjoyed a higher income per head than any other major country, except for the United States. However, this does not mean that the UK's growth rates exceeded those of elsewhere.

Table 2 *A comparison of the industrial production 1952–59, using 1950 = 100 as a baseline*

	1952	**1955**	**1957**	**1959**
West Germany	126	179	204	225
France	110	131	156	170
Italy	117	153	177	202
Netherlands	103	134	143	158
USA	111	124	127	133
UK	101	121	123	129

Table 3 *A comparison of shares in world trade in percentages, 1950–62*

	1950	**1951**	**1959**	**1962**
UK	25	22	17	15
USA	27	26	21	20
West Germany	7	10	19	20
Japan	3	4	7	7

 Activity

Statistical analysis

In pairs, study the data in Tables 2 and 3, and Figures 5 and 6. Using the information in these tables, and your own knowledge, prepare a report on the state of the British economy in 1959. In your report you should:

- outline the position, as you see it – with suitable factual support
- offer your own explanation for this state of affairs.

Present your report to the rest of the class and, as a group, consider whether economic intervention by the government is necessary and, if so, what measures you would recommend.

Macmillan was certainly concerned about the state of the economy. He reminded his listeners of this in that memorable speech of 1957 (Source 1), which continued:

> What is beginning to worry some of us is 'Is it too good to be true?' Or perhaps I should say 'Is it too good to last?'

However, for a population that had more money in its pockets than ever before, the warnings tended to fall on deaf ears. Bolstered by an improvement in the terms of world trade in the later 1950s,

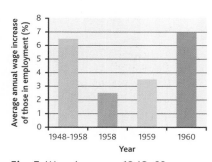

Fig. 5 *Wage increases, 1948–60*

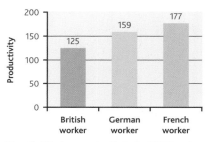

Fig. 6 *Worker productivity by 1960, using 1950 = 100 as a baseline*

which enabled Britain to import about 29 per cent more goods than it had in 1951 for the same number of exports, there was little reason to question the belief that Britain was changing, and for the better.

So the late 1950s were an age of optimism. The British enjoyed more jobs, more money, more goods, better housing and the provisions of the new welfare state. The adults, who had been used to wartime deprivation, suddenly found themselves with money to spend on cars, new appliances, luxuries and entertainment, while the younger generation, growing up amid plenty and oblivious to past shortages and fears, sought to enjoy life to the full.

Such were the circumstances that heralded the arrival of the 1960s.

■ The 1959 general election and its significance

Since 1951, Britain had been ruled by Conservative governments. The Liberal Party, led by Jo Grimmond from 1956, had never recovered from a split in 1916 and the Labour Party, after six successful years in government, 1945–51, remained in opposition, torn apart by continuous arguments about the direction of the Party and its commitment to Marxist ideas.

■ Questions

1 Explain why Macmillan could claim that the British people at the end of the 1950s had 'never had it so good'.

2 Explain why Macmillan's statement cannot be considered entirely accurate.

Fig. 7 *How did the Conservative Party try to win the electorate's support in the 1959 election campaign?*

On 8 October 1959, the country went to the polls. The results (from a turnout of 78.7 per cent) are shown in Table 4.

Table 4 *General election results, 1959*

Party	Votes	Seats	Change	UK vote share (%)
Conservative	13,750,875	365	+20	48.8
Labour	12,216,172	258	−19	44.6
Liberal	1,640,760	6	No change	6.0
Others	254,845	1	−1	0.6

Key profiles

Hugh Gaitskell

Hugh Gaitskell (1906–63) was a Winchester/Oxford educated academic from an upper-middle class background. He had served in Attlee's government as Chancellor of the Exchequer where he had made his mark as a man of great sincerity. He had strong convictions and much strength of will and purpose but, despite his talent he was not a good communicator. He inspired respect rather than devotion and could appear intellectually arrogant and inflexible. Nevertheless, he managed to heal some of the Labour Party divisions and he proved a modernising influence. His death, at the age of 57, shook the party.

Jo Grimond

Jo Grimond (1913–93) was an Eton/Oxford educated lawyer who became Liberal leader in 1956. He was a charismatic speaker whose good looks and charming manner won him much public admiration. He came over well on television and he helped to raise the national profile of the Liberals. He gave the party a new vision and drive, so that by the early 1960s they had started winning some by-elections, e.g. Torrington in 1958, which was its first success since 1928. As well as taking local government seats, Grimond aimed to create a radical, non-socialist left-wing party and, by 1966, he had increased the number of Liberal MPs from 6 (in 1956) to 12. Nevertheless, when he resigned in 1967, the party was still a minor parliamentary force.

Manifestos

Labour

We welcome this election; it gives us, at last, the chance to end eight years of Tory rule. In a television interview, Mr Macmillan told us that the old division of Britain into the two nations, the Haves and the Have Nots, has disappeared. In fact, the contrast between the extremes of wealth and poverty is sharper today than eight years ago. The business man with a tax-free expense account, the speculator with tax-free capital gains, and the retiring company director with a tax-free redundancy payment have indeed 'never had it so good'. It is not so good for the widowed mother with children, the chronic sick, the 400,000 unemployed, and the millions of old age pensioners who have no adequate retirement income. Instead of recognising this problem as the greatest social challenge of our time, the Prime Minister blandly denies it exists.

3   *Adapted from party election manifesto for 1959*

Conservative

Eight years ago was a turning point in British history. The Labour Government had failed in grappling with the problems of the post-war world. Under Conservative leadership this country set out upon a new path. It is leading to prosperity and opportunity for all. The British economy is sounder today than at any time since the First World War.

Key chronology
Political leaders

Prime minister	Leader of the opposition
Clement Attlee (Labour) (1945–51)	Winston Churchill
Winston Churchill (Cons) (1951–5)	Clement Attlee
Anthony Eden (Cons) (1955–7)	Hugh Gaitskell
Harold Macmillan (Cons) (1957–63)	Hugh Gaitskell

Activity
Group activity

Divide the class into three groups and allocate a different political party to each group.

Each group will need to study the election posters in Figure 7 and manifestos in Sources 3, 4 and 5, as well as looking back over the earlier section of this chapter. Each group should prepare a suitable election speech for their party and a spokeperson should be chosen to deliver it to the class. A mock election might be held, with voting according to the persuasiveness of the speakers.

Our exports have reached the highest peak ever. We have cut taxes in seven budgets, whilst continuing to develop the social services. We have provided over two million new homes and almost two million new school places, a better health service and a modern pensions plan. We have now stabilised the cost of living while maintaining full employment. We have shown that Conservative freedom works. Life *is* better with the Conservatives.

4   *Adapted from party election manifesto for 1959*

Liberal

We must have more Liberals in Parliament for the sake of honest, above-board politics. The Conservative Party is clearly identified with employers and big business and they cannot deal objectively or fairly with the problems continually arising between employer and employee. The Labour Party is in the hands of the Trade Union Leaders. The whole nation is the loser from this crazy line up of power politics. A Liberal vote is a protest against the British political system being divided up between two powerful party machines, one largely financed by the employers and the other by the Trade Unions.

5   *Adapted from party election manifesto for 1959*

Question

Use Sources 3, 4 and 5 and your own knowledge.

a   Explain how far the views in Source 4 differ from those in Source 3 in relation to the economic position of the British people in 1959.

b   How important were economic issues in the 1959 election? You may like to read to the end of this chapter before answering this part.

AQA Examiner's tip

For a source comparison question (Question (a)), draw up a table with three columns. As you are asked 'how far' the sources differ, note their differences and similarities. Do not waste time writing out what each source says, but work through the points of comparison, supporting them with reference to the sources. End with a conclusion in which you answer 'how far' they differ by explaining any similarities too.

Difference (or similarity)	First source evidence	Second source evidence

The significance of the results

The victory of 1959 was the third for the ruling Conservative Party and the Labour Party was bitterly disappointed. They indulged in lengthy post-election analysis. Although it was accepted that Gaitskell had made one rather foolish mistake in campaigning – suggesting that the Labour Party could raise pensions without increasing income tax – there were far deeper issues that had prevented Labour gaining the success it craved. It was revealed, for example, that although Labour had gained slightly more votes among women and older people, it had lost among working men. A survey was commissioned and conducted by Mark Abrams and Richard Rose for the monthly journal the *Socialist Commentary*.

This discovered:

■ Labour was identified with the working class rather than the 'nation as a whole'.

■ Voters (including Conservative supporters) were generally happy with the nationalisation (undertaken by Labour) of the electricity, gas, atomic energy and airline industries, but they thought public ownership of coal and the railways had been a failure and there was little enthusiasm for further nationalisation.

■ Macmillan was favoured over Gaitskell as a leader 'strong enough to make unwelcome decisions', which was considered the most important quality in a Prime Minister.

■ Labour was seen as the party most likely to prevent a nuclear war.

The problem was that 40 per cent of manual workers now considered themselves middle class and commentators were left wondering whether Labour could ever get back into government and whether its traditional values could have any appeal as the lives of its core voters changed.

Fig. 8 *Progress in the general election is broadcast from the ITN newsroom on 7 March 1959. How does this scene compare with coverage of elections today?*

Douglas Jay (Labour) wrote:

> I believe myself that the party in 1959 had allowed itself to get a bit out of date in the sense that there was still the cloth cap image. There was a sort of idea that the ordinary Labour supporter was an unemployed miner, living on unemployment benefit and that the Labour Party stood for nationalisation and almost nothing else. I think these two things were harmful. There was a sense of phoney prosperity which was somehow associated with Harold Macmillan's moustache. The fundamental thing was to get away from the cloth cap image, the cloth cap talk and realise that the Labour Party had to move into being a left-centre majority party.

6

■ Key term

Clause Four: the section of the Labour Party Constitution of 1918 that declared that public ownership of the means of production, distribution and exchange was necessary 'to secure for the workers by hand or by brain, the full fruit of their industry'. This clause committed the party to opposing capitalism and carrying out a programme of nationalisation but by the 1960s it was outdated and the party leaders chose to ignore it.

■ Cross-reference

To learn more about concerns regarding **nuclear weapons** and **nuclear disarmament**, see pages 71–2.

Harold Wilson's government is discussed on pages 94–8.

■ Activity

Source analysis

Explain how far the views in Source 7 differ from those in Source 6 in relation to the reasons for the Conservative victory of 1959.

There was talk of a new name for the party and of changing the Labour constitution, which was committed to 'common ownership of the means of production' (**Clause Four**), but Gaitskell failed to carry his party with him on this. He did, however, go on to succeed in resisting the attempts of the left-wing of the party to commit Labour to unilateral nuclear disarmament in 1961 and, by the time of his death in 1963, he had done much to establish Labour as a credible party of government. The benefits of his leadership were eventually to be reaped by Harold Wilson in 1964.

Lord Butler (Conservative) provided another commentary on the 1959 election:

> I think the 1959 election was successful for the Conservatives because Macmillan was proving himself a very able and competent Prime Minister. He was very powerful in the House of Commons. He was able to control debates with very carefully prepared speeches and I think the economy was encouraged to expand and was at its very best shape when the '59 election came along.
>
> There was a certain amount of criticism of 'You've never had it so good' even in the mind of Macmillan. At one stage he attempted to go back on it. He didn't exactly say 'I didn't say it' because he had said, it but he did feel in his own mind that it presented too materialistic a conception.

Whatever Butler's view, the Conservatives had certainly benefited from the economic growth that had allowed them to make tax cuts of around £350 million in April 1959, before the election. They were able to remind the electorate that under the Conservatives from 1951, economic growth had been over 3 per cent a year, that wages had risen while inflation remained low, that house prices were steady and everyone was in work. Macmillan had effectively been able to compare his party's record with the 'nightmare' of Labour Party socialism. He played on concerns about Labour's policies of nationalisation and central planning and the Party's record when in government following the Second World War, when 'rationing, shortages, inflation, and one crisis after another in our international trade' spread anxiety. In short, the Conservatives heavily relied on the fact that the voter was also the consumer and, delighted by Labour's post-election admission that they could no longer depend on 'working class' support, regarded their future as secure.

■ Summary questions

1. How far do problems with the Labour Party explain the outcome of the 1959 general election?

2. 'In 1959, all types of British people shared a sense of optimism.' Explain why you agree or disagree with this view.

The Establishment

Fig. 1 *A cartoon by 'Vicky' (Victor Weisz) for the* Evening Standard

The leadership of Harold Macmillan and Sir Alec Douglas-Home to 1964

The pictures in Figure 1 illustrate the Conservative Prime Ministers between 1951 and 1964.

1 Winston Churchill (1951–5)
2 Anthony Eden (1955–7)
3 Harold Macmillan (1957–63)
4 Alec Douglas-Home (1963–4)

Key profiles

Winston Churchill

Winston Churchill (1874–1965) was born into an aristocratic, military family and educated at Eton and Oxford. Churchill had accumulated much authority and prestige from his leadership of Britain during the Second World War, when his rousing speeches and determination had helped Britain through its 'darkest hour'. He was bitterly disappointed not to be returned to power in 1945, but came back in 1951 at the age of 77, the oldest Prime Minister since Gladstone. He was then past his prime and admitted that he found the detail of government business tiresome. He suffered from a stroke in 1953 (which was kept from the public) but he recovered and continued in power until 1955.

Anthony Eden

Anthony Eden (1897–1977) came from a landed family and was educated at Eton. He was a brilliant linguist and a highly cultured man who had enjoyed a good deal of experience as a minister and diplomat, but suffered from frequent bouts of ill health with a

Activity

Thinking point

Study Figure 1. What do you think the cartoonist is trying to say about a) the Conservative Party, and b) leadership and politics in Britain at this time?

Cross-reference

Harold Macmillan is profiled on pages 10–11.

biliary duct problem which had been made worse by poor surgery. His ascent to power had been blocked by Churchill, and Macmillan later said that he was like a racehorse that had been trained to win in 1938 but was only let out of the starting stalls in 1955. He miscalculated when authorising a British invasion of Suez in 1956 and was forced to resign through ill health a year later.

Alec Douglas-Home

Alec Douglas-Home (1903–95), another ex-Etonian, had succeeded as the 14th Earl of Home in 1951 but he renounced his title under the Peerages Act of 1963 so that he could serve as an MP in the Commons. He was Foreign Secretary under Macmillan from 1960 to 1963 and an unexpected choice to succeed him in 1963. Chosen by the outgoing Prime Minister, he was often teased for his aristocratic bearing. He was amiable enough and not at all stupid although unskilled in economics, but he was derided for what he represented even more than what he was. Variously described as 'an old Etonian cricket-loving laird', a 'cadaverous-featured drawling aristocrat' and a 'tweedy and remote figure', he seemed to appear more at ease in a grouse shoot than on the floor of the Commons. In 1965, Wilson accused him of an 'Edwardian establishment mentality'.

The Establishment

In 1959, the Oxford historian Hugh Thomas edited a collection of essays that went by the title of *The Establishment*. Thomas wrote:

Fig. 2 *The Establishment at home. Harold Macmillan and his wife, Lady Dorothy, with their grandchildren on the steps of their home, Birch Grove, Chelwood Gate, Sussex*

It is Victorian England, with all its prejudices, ignorances and inhibitions, that the Establishment sets out to defend. The Establishment is the present-day institutional museum of Britain's past greatness. To those who would desire to see the resources and talents of Britain fully developed and extended, there is no doubt that the fusty Establishment, with its Victorian views and standards of judgement, must be destroyed.

By the 'Establishment', Thomas was referring to the comparatively small but powerful group of people who governed Britain. This was not just the politicians but included civil servants, judges, bishops, university vice chancellors and leaders of business and the army. Henry Fairlie, a journalist who contributed to the book went still further referring to:

the whole matrix of official and social relations within which power is exercised including such lesser mortals as Chairman of the Arts Council, the Director General of the BBC and even the editor of *The Times Literary Supplement*.

2

Whatever their political persuasion, these figures all came from the same 'class' and shared the same aspirations. Even more than this, they had been through the same classical education at public schools and Oxford or Cambridge and had either joined the same regiments or become members of the same clubs. They understood and supported one another through the 'old school tie' network.

Thomas's view found ready support. Forward thinkers believed the nation was being held back by the snobbery and outdated morality of its ruling elite. The Establishment was charged with putting a snobbish emphasis on arts education in preference to science, blocking the advance of talent and hiding misdeeds from the public. In 1955, for example, government attempts to cover up the activities of two foreign office officials, Guy Burgess and Donald Maclean, who had fled to Russia in 1951 after spying for that country, became public knowledge. Anthony Eden's disastrous handling of the Suez crisis in 1956 also added to the arguments of those who felt the ruling establishment was incompetent.

The attack on the Establishment came from various quarters. In the late 1950s, a group of writers, who came to be known as the 'angry young men', led the way in using the arts to attack the behaviour and attitudes of the established upper and upper-middle classes, while social scientists, among them Richard Hoggart (*The Uses of Literacy*, 1957) and Anthony Sampson (*The Anatomy of Britain*, 1961) provided evidence of Britain's 'class-ridden' society, its entrenched attitudes and the lack of social mobility. Films such as *I'm All Right Jack* (1959) began a new type of social satire, while cartoonists poked fun at Macmillan's government (which included a duke, the heir to a barony, a marquess and three earls). Sir Alec Douglas-Home, Prime Minister from 1963, was often lampooned by his Labour opponents as the '14th earl', but even the most prominent spokesmen in the Labour Party came from an 'elitist' background, in terms of education if not family connections, until the mid-1960s. What Britain needed, it was argued, were leaders who had earned their positions through their personal merit and understood the modern, technical age in which they were living.

A closer look

Angry young men and rebel literary figures

The 'angry young men' is a term given to a group of writers who rebelled against traditional theatre and literature and produced plays and books that, they felt, reflected contemporary society. Their writing was sarcastic, bitter, intense and often bleak. Mundane settings and everyday language were used to parody contemporary Britain. The first of the genre was John Osborne's play, *Look Back in Anger*, shown in 1956. Other playwrights who tried to address social issues, include John Arden who wrote *Live Like Pigs* (1958) and Harold Pinter who wrote *The Birthday Party* (1958) and *The Caretaker* (1960). The novelists included Angus Wilson, who wrote *Anglo-Saxon Attitudes* (1956); William Golding, *Lord of the Flies* (1954); John Braine, *Room at the Top* (1957), which was made into a film in 1959; Alan Sillitoe, whose novel *Saturday Night and Sunday Morning* (1958) was also made into a film; David Storey, *This Sporting Life* (1960); and Stan Barstow who produced *A Kind of Loving* (1960).

 Exploring the detail

The Suez crisis

Anthony Eden (Conservative) ordered an attack on Egypt after its leader, Nasser, nationalised the Suez canal. It soon became clear that such an attack could not succeed without support from America, to whom the action smacked of colonialism. World opinion was hostile and the United Nations demanded a ceasefire. Britain was forced to withdraw.

 Cross-reference

To remind yourself of some of the **political figures** who made up the late 1950s Establishment, see Chapter 1.

Activity

Revision exercise

Look back at the profiles of the politicians you have read about. Were they all members of the Establishment?

Activity

Preparing a presentation

Try to see some of the plays or films, or read some of the novels mentioned here. They will increase your understanding of this era and provide new insight into society in the late 1950s/early 1960s. Remember, however, that changes in 'high' culture do not always reflect the views of the masses. *Look Back in Anger*, for example, was badly received and some of the audience even walked out, but Kenneth Tynan (theatre critic for the *Observer*) praised it and it gained status and was televised.

Prepare a class presentation based on what you have seen or read and share with your group your own reactions and feelings about what it has taught you about society in this period.

Fig. 3 *The Prime Minister Harold Macmillan in action, 1960*

■ Cross-reference

The government's **stop-go policies** are described on page 12.

Details of **Beeching's actions** regarding the railways can be found on page 51.

■ Key term

EEC: the European Economic Community came into being in 1957 when France, West Germany, Italy, Belgium, the Netherlands and Luxembourg signed the Treaty of Rome. It provided for the free movement of goods between the participating nations, whose economies prospered relative to that of Britain.

The leadership of Harold Macmillan

With a Commons majority of over 100 after the 1959 election victory, Macmillan was at the height of his power. 'Supermac' showed that he could cope with a variety of issues while still retaining an appearance of calm 'unflappability'. His motto for the cabinet room was 'quiet calm deliberation disentangles every knot', but it took considerable commitment and effort to juggle the conflicting requirements of economic stability at home and the maintenance of Britain's status overseas. In some respects he still lived in the past, believing unemployment a greater concern than inflation and acting as though Britain was still a major world power. Nevertheless, he was flexible enough to attempt some new initiatives and he understood that the Conservative Party might need to change its image. In 1962, Macmillan surprised the country by demanding the resignations of seven senior ministers. The changes were largely the result of personal pique over policy failures but 'Mac the knife', as the media nicknamed him, also ensured that some of his new appointments came from outside the Establishment. The non-landed Reginald Maudling became Chancellor of the Exchequer; Sir Edward Boyle, a youngster of 38, became Minister of Education; and the 44-year-old Sir Keith Joseph was made Minister of Housing.

Macmillan's biggest internal problem concerned the economy. This may seem odd, given that in 'real' terms the British economy, which had been growing since 1945, was at its peak between 1960 and 1964. However, the government became trapped in a cycle of stop-go policies in an attempt to maintain economic stability.

As the economy began to enter the 'stop' phase of the economic cycle in 1961, Selwyn Lloyd, Macmillan's first Chancellor of the Exchequer, set up the National Economic Development Council (NEDC, known as Neddy). This consisted of government representatives, academics, employers and the trades unionists, and it was made responsible for long-term planning. A National Incomes Commission (known as Nicky), to keep an eye on wages and prices, was added in 1962. Reviews were undertaken and new policies towards nationalised industries agreed, including 'Beeching's Axe' of railway lines. Despite their efforts, Britain's economic troubles did not go away, but the idea of the 'managed economy' with future planning by consultation and consent represented a change of strategy and was an indication that, under Macmillan, the processes of government were beginning to change.

Macmillan also appreciated that Britain's future lay with the Common Market or **European Economic Community (EEC)**. He believed participation would be good for Britain, both economically and politically, and in July 1961 it was announced that Britain would apply for membership. Edward Heath was chosen as Britain's determined negotiator, but in January 1963 the French President, General de Gaulle, vetoed British entry. He claimed that Britain was different from the other countries of Europe and too attached to its own Commonwealth, although his fear that Britain and its ally America might dominate the EEC at France's expense probably had more influence on his opposition.

The problems of the Establishment including the Profumo affair

The Profumo affair

In March 1963, the trial of the West Indian, John Edgecombe, opened at the London Criminal Court, the Old Bailey. He was under prosecution for an incident three months earlier when he was accused of firing two shots at a flat belonging to Stephen Ward in Wimpole Mews, London. Inside had been his intended victim, Christine Keeler, who, at just 21, was described as a 'long-legged, dark-haired beauty'. She had subsequently fled abroad leaving no contact details and was not present at the trial.

The *Daily Express* published a large photograph of the missing Christine Keeler on its front page, adjacent to an article announcing that John Profumo, Secretary of State for War, had offered his resignation to the Prime Minister 'for personal reasons'. The coincidence of information was no accident. The journalists were well aware of the link between the two stories, but libel law prevented them from exposing it directly. They were effectively inviting their readers to draw their own conclusions. Edgecombe and Ward were not the only men Keeler had shared a bed with. Following an enquiry in May and June, John Profumo was exposed as one of Keeler's former lovers. Despite his initial denials, on 4 June 1963 Profumo announced 'with deep remorse' to the House of Commons that he had misled its members about his relationship with Keeler and would resign both his government position and his parliamentary seat. Such admissions shook Conservative confidence and Lord Hailsham thundered that 'a great party is not to be brought down because of a scandal by a woman of easy virtue and a proved liar'.

Profumo left politics and devoted himself to social work in the East End of London while Keeler, who was tried and imprisoned on related charges, did well out of telling her story to the *News of the World*. While the public enjoyed all the intimate details, Macmillan was nearly 'driven out of office by two tarts', as Julian Critchley put it, referring also to Keeler's friend, Mandy Rice-Davies.

In fact, Macmillan had done little more than to be too trusting, but in the atmosphere of the early 1960s this was crime enough. Labour, somewhat reinvigorated under the leadership of Harold Wilson following Gaitskell's death in January 1963, used the affair to attack the government and climb to a 20 per cent lead in the opinion polls. Two months later, there were queues to buy Lord Denning's report into the security aspects of the Profumo affair, but it added little. It laid most of the blame on Stephen Ward and merely criticised the government for failing to deal with the affair more quickly.

The Conservatives' fall in the opinion polls was not just a reaction to the Profumo affair. The government's stringent economic policies of 1961–2, which had frozen pay rises, had not been popular and in a by-election at Orpington March 1962 a Conservative majority of nearly 15,000 had been turned into a majority of 7,800 for the Liberal, Jeremy Lubbock. Nevertheless, by October 1963 there were signs of economic recovery and Labour's opinion poll lead was cut back to 13 per cent. However, just as his party seemed to be recovering, Macmillan was struck down by a misdiagnosed medical condition. He was suffering prostrate trouble and, following an operation, the temporarily bedridden premier decided to resign.

Fig. 4 *The political career of John Profumo, pictured here in 1964 with his wife Valerie and their two children, was abruptly ended after his lies to the Commons over his relationship with Miss Keeler were exposed*

Cross-reference

To learn about **Harold Wilson**, look ahead to page 95.

Cross-reference

To learn more about *That Was The Week That Was*, read pages 42 and 80–1.

A closer look

The Profumo affair

The Conservative politician John Profumo and his wife Valerie had spent the weekend of 8–9 July 1961 at the country estate of Lord Astor, at Cliveden in Buckinghamshire. Here, they had met the guests of Stephen Ward, who rented a small cottage on the estate. Profumo's eye had been caught by Christine Keeler (whom he first spotted naked in a swimming pool) and a brief but indiscreet affair had followed. Profumo not only visited Keeler at Ward's flat in Wimpole Mews, where she lived, he also took her for a drive in a car belonging to another member of the government and met her at his own house while his wife was away.

Captain Eugene Ivanov, the naval attaché at the Soviet Embassy, was one of Ward's close acquaintances and Keeler's many lovers. Like all 'official' Russians serving in Britain at the time, his job involved some spying. Consequently, when the British Security Service discovered Profumo's link with Ward, they warned him of the potential security risk. Profumo took heed, believing, wrongly, that the security services were aware of his liaison with Christine Keeler. He ended the affair, although rather unwisely sent a letter of explanation that began 'Darling' and continued in affectionate terms.

The whole episode might have been forgotten but for the unfortunate shooting incident and Christine Keeler's own indiscretion in talking about her 'affair'. Media interest grew and late on the night of 21 March 1963 Profumo was urgently summoned to the House of Commons, where he denied any misconduct. He told the House that, although he had been on friendly terms with Miss Keeler, he had not seen her since December 1961 and had nothing to do with her non-appearance at the Old Bailey trial. This was all true. However, he then told a lie. He claimed that there had been 'no impropriety whatever' in his relationship with Miss Keeler and he threatened to sue those who made scandalous allegations.

The statement failed to silence the rumours. The *Daily Express* found Christine Keeler in Madrid and by the end of March she was back in London, ready to expose her relationship with Profumo. Ward, who had initially tried to shield the minister, also made a statement. The press enjoyed every minute of Profumo's embarrassment. The American *Time* magazine reported: 'Britain is being bombarded with a barrage of frankness about sex.' The *Daily Herald* asked: 'Are we going sex-crazy?' The satirical TV programme *That Was The Week That Was* hosted by David Frost produced a parody of the music-hall song, 'She Was Poor But She Was Honest':

See him in the House of Commons
Making laws to put the blame
While the object of his passion
Walks the streets to hide her shame

Fig. 5 *Christine Keeler, the cause of John Profumo's disgrace in 1963*

Activity

Talking point

1. Why did Profumo resign his position and seat? Was he right to do so?

2. 'A peer in Lord Astor, a cabinet minister in Profumo, a Soviet agent in Ivanov, a procurer in Ward (who turned out to be a vicar's son) and a brace of good-time girls.' (Moynahan). Why did the Profumo affair cause such a sensation?

Key profiles

John Profumo

John Profumo (1915–2006) was a high-ranking Tory who had been educated at Harrow and Eton. He married the film actress Valerie Hobson and mixed in high society. He was one of the most promising politicians in Macmillan's cabinet where he was Secretary of State for War (1960–3), but his affair brought his political career to an end. He spent the next 40 years raising money and supporting a charity, Toynbee Hall in the East End of London. On his death, Tony Blair said: 'He was a politician with a glittering career who made a serious mistake, but who underwent a journey of redemption and who gave support and help to many, many people.'

Christine Keeler

Christine Keeler (born 1942) had spent her childhood living in a badly converted railway carriage, on the edge of a gravel pit in Berkshire, where she was brought up by her unmarried mother and stepfather. She left home at 16 after an unhappy childhood and found work at Murray's cabaret club in London, where she met and befriended Mandy Rice-Davies and became part of the circle surrounding Stephen Ward. Although she made some money out of her affair with Profumo, it soon disappeared, and after her time in prison she never found a stable relationship or job. She married twice and, after a number of jobs, became a dinner lady at a school in London. When the headmaster discovered who she was, she was dismissed without explanation. She abandoned job-hunting and instead wrote a biography telling her side of the story.

Exploring the detail

Spies

To understand Macmillan's premiership, the context within which he governed is important. This was the time of the Cold War, of 'McCarthyism' in the USA and of a desperate fear of Communism. The USSR had constructed the Berlin Wall in 1961 and in 1962 the Cuban Missile crisis had brought the world close to extinction in nuclear war. In Britain, a series of revelations that British officials had acted as Russian spies followed. In 1961, George Blake was given a 42-year sentence for spying but escaped after serving 5 years. In 1962, John Vassall, a foreign office bank clerk, was jailed for 18 years. He had been blackmailed into spying for the Russians after being caught indulging in illegal homosexual practices. In January 1963, Kim Philby, the former head of the Soviet section of Britain's secret intelligence service, fled to the USSR and it was revealed he had been working for the USSR for many years.

The leadership of Sir Alec Douglas-Home

Macmillan named his foreign secretary, Sir Alec Douglas-Home (pronounced Hume), as his successor. Rejecting more obvious candidates such as Butler and Lord Hailsham, Macmillan and his 'inner circle' of advisers believed that the Earl of Home (who, under recent legislation had been able to renounce his peerage and become Sir Alec Douglas-Home) was likely to cause the least division in the party. However, he could hardly have chosen a more Establishment figure. Apart from being an earl himself, when Home announced his cabinet of 23 members, 10 were old Etonians and only 3 had not been to public schools. He was an easy target for the satirists, although he proved a more effective leader than might have been expected.

Fig. 6 *Sir Alec Douglas-Home (Conservative) being interviewed after the election of 1964. Harold Wilson (Labour) can be seen by his side and Jo Grimond (Liberal) is in the background*

Under his premiership, Edward Heath, at the Board of Trade, repealed the law that forced shopkeepers to sell goods at standard prices set by suppliers, while Reginald Maudling, Chancellor of the Exchequer, pushed the economy into a 'go' phase by lowering the bank rate to encourage consumer spending. Britain's growth rate rose from 4 per cent in 1963 to nearly 6 per cent in 1964. Nevertheless, while exports rose just over 10 per cent between 1961 and 1964, imports remained nearly 20 per cent higher.

By 1964, the Conservatives found themselves under intense attack from Labour. They were accused of economic mismanagement and perpetuating an outdated class system.

The middle-class Harold Wilson, who could truly claim to have risen by his own merit, declared that the last 13 years of Conservative rule had been 'wasted' and that only the Labour Party could lead Britain in the 'modern' age. Even in the Conservative Party, middle-class and ambitious Tories like Iain MacLeod and Enoch Powell were uncomfortable with the way Alec Douglas-Home had been named as their leader. Their opposition led to a new system being put in place whereby any future leader would have to be elected by the whole parliamentary party.

Given the extent of discontent, it is surprising that the election, in October 1964, turned out to be close-run. Nevertheless, Labour won and this marked the end, not only of Conservative rule, but also of what it had come to represent. It symbolised the victory of the forces of modernisation over the Establishment. Whether Wilson really swept the Establishment away or simply replaced it with a new version will be considered in Chapter 9. Nevertheless, when, in July 1965, the Conservatives replaced Alec Douglas-Home with Edward Heath, who like Wilson was a middle-class, grammar-school boy, it seemed to confirm the death of the old-style Establishment.

Cross-reference

Enoch Powell is discussed in more detail on pages 128–30.

For details of the **1964 election** and its result, as well as the related **'anti-Establishment' satire,** refer to page 94.

Learning outcomes

This section has provided you with the political context within which major social and cultural changes were beginning to occur. Such changes do not, of course, start and stop with changes of government, but it is important to appreciate the circumstances from which the 'Swinging 60s' were born. The continuing political context will be found in Chapter 9.

AQA Examination-style questions

1 Read Sources A, B and C and answer the questions that follow.

[Eleven] years of Conservative rule have brought the nation to a low point. The hopes and eager expectations of 1959 have been dashed. Nothing else, the Conservatives seemed later to think, mattered, compared with the assertion that the nation had never had it so good. Today they are faced with a flagging economy, an uncertain future and the end of illusions about Britain's greatness. There are plenty of earnest and serious men in the Conservative Party who know that all is not well. Popularity by affluence is finished because it has rested on a very insecure basis.

A
From **The Times,** *'It's a moral issue', 11 June 1963*

The legacy of the Conservative governments from 1951 to 1964 is mixed. While vulnerable to the charge that their economic and domestic policies were too much preoccupied with short-term considerations to the detriment of Britain's long-term future, nevertheless they presided over a period of limited inflation and little unemployment. There was real progress under the Conservatives.

B
Adapted from Andrew Boxer,
The Conservative Governments 1951–1964, 1996

Harold Macmillan was a high-minded Victorian reformer. He was vague and paternalistic in his thinking. He was the ultimate master of staying in the saddle and was good at retaining power, but without ideas. The country continued to be run by cliques – public school, Oxbridge and family provided the fusebox of power. But this Britain failed. The symbols of that failure were the spy scandals, the Profumo affair and the rising froth of satirical laughter. Macmillan himself finished it off, bloodily, in the 'Night of the Long Knives' in 1962 when he removed a third of his cabinet ministers without notice.

C	

*Adapted from Andrew Marr, **A History of Modern Britain**, 2007*

(a) Explain how far the views in Source B differ from those in Source A in relation to the record of the Conservative governments from 1959.   *(12 marks)*

Pick out phrases in both sources that provide a contrast of views. For example, Source B speaks of 'real progress' and of a society that was less prone to the ravages of inflation and high unemployment than later became the case. Source A, on the other hand, suggests the country was at a 'low point', hopes had been 'dashed' and there was an 'uncertain future'. You should be able to make both general and more–specific comments about the different views. Don't forget that 'how far' also requires you to look at the similarities. Both sources accept, for example, that economic and domestic policies can be criticised and that the Conservative policies were too much preoccupied with the short term.

(b) Use Sources A, B and C and your own knowledge. How successful was Harold Macmillan's premiership between 1959 and 1963?   *(24 marks)*

Make a two-column table with examples of Macmillan's successes on one side and failures on the other. Next, decide where to cite evidence from the sources and consider in what order you will make your points. Your answer should make a balanced argument and lead to a well-supported conclusion.

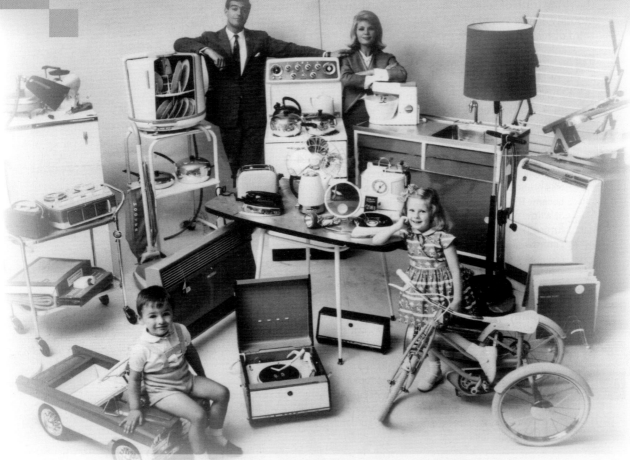

Fig. 1 *It is 1962 and the consumer age has arrived. How many 'new' household appliances can you identify here?*

In this chapter you will learn about:

- how increased purchasing power came about and why people felt more affluent in the 1960s

- what is meant by 'consumerism' and consider the impact of living in an affluent, consumer society

- how new scientific and technological developments contributed to change in the 1960s.

The growth in consumer spending

The 1960s were a time when ordinary people were buying more of the types of goods previously regarded as luxuries, novelties and non-essentials; cars and the latest fashionable clothes are just two examples. Shopping became a leisure activity that offered different sectors of the population, and particularly young people, the chance to buy themselves a particular lifestyle and identity. The unique ingredient that helped the 1960s to 'swing' was the rise in general wealth, which narrowed the gap between the rich and middle classes as well as that between the middle incomes and the poor. Economic security, as well as economic opportunity, created a society generally referred to as 'affluent'.

Despite the weaknesses of the British economy and the misguided economic policies of the governments of the period, most people living at this time felt they were living in an age of affluence. This was not a purely British phenomenon. In line with almost everywhere in the western world, technological change, investment, improvements in efficiency and productivity and the growth of international trade had led to a growth in real wages, which increased the purchasing power of the average citizen. In Britain, this meant that by 1965 the necessities of food and clothing absorbed just 31 per cent of consumer spending. There was more money to spare and more money to spend.

Table 1 *Prices and wages compared with 1955 (the year 1955 is provided with a base rate of 100)*

Year	Retail price index	Weekly wage rates	Weekly earnings	Real wage rates	Real earnings	Registered unemployed
1955	100	100	100	100	100	232,000
1960	114	124	130	109	114	360,000
1965	136	151	175	112	129	329,000
1970	170	202	250	119	147	579,000

Activity

Statistical analysis

Study Table 1.

1 Look at the weekly wage rates and compare these with the weekly earnings, which take overtime into account. Then compare these with the increase in retail prices. What do you observe?

2 Columns 5 and 6 give an indication of the 'real' wage rates and earnings, allowing for inflation. Wages cover standard pay, while earnings include overtime and additional payments. Do these confirm your observations so far?

3 Given that the UK population in the 1960s was between 53 and 55 million, what do the unemployment figures suggest?

4 What, in real terms, would have happened to the cost of consumer goods like cars and clothes between 1955 and 1970?

There was also a variety of other reasons why people felt more affluent in the late 1950s and 1960s:

- Improved welfare services, education and housing enhanced the quality of life.
- Working hours had been reduced in the 1950s and most employees were able to take two weeks' paid holiday a year.
- Reductions in income tax, which fell five times between 1957 and 1964, from 9s. 6d. (47.5p) to 7s. 9d. (39p), in the pound inspired confidence.
- Reductions in purchase tax, which had been 100 per cent on items such as electric fires, cosmetics and cars in 1951, had fallen to 25 per cent on such goods by 1963.
- A growing range of goods in the shops offered tempting and accessible consumer choice.

Although opinion polls during the 1950s had suggested that few Britons were convinced that their standard of living was rising. From June 1960, views started to change. The old memories of war, rationing and austerity were finally laid to rest. Traditional anxieties, particularly among the working class, about the need for thrift and careful management, were

Cross-reference

You will find details of **economic policies** on pages 12–14 and 96–7.

replaced by a growing feeling that it was better to spend and enjoy the pleasures that modern technology was helping to bring than to worry about the future. Thus it was that more people became sufficiently confident about their personal finances and future prospects to take on the responsibility of a mortgage with a building society loan. In 1960, building societies provided 326,125 new mortgages involving advances of over £544 million. Home ownership almost doubled – from 27 per cent to 50 per cent between 1950 and 1970 – with nearly 6 million new homes being built.

Since the price of a small car and that of some of the other 'new' products, such as TVs and washing machines, was steadily falling, material aspirations, encouraged by advertising, grew. Consumer spending rose from under £16 million at the end of 1959 to nearly £16.75 million by the end of 1960. Standards of living were lifted as the working class, in particular, benefited from the ever-growing range of consumer products and domestic appliances. In Mark Abrams's survey, conducted after the 1959 election, 40 per cent of manual workers already considered themselves to be 'middle class'. It was the demands of this expanding middle class that encouraged still further production and ever more imports, forcing prices down and so creating a 'consumer cycle'.

■ **Cross-reference**

Mark Abrams's survey is introduced on pages 16–17.

■ **Did you know?**

The Consumers' Association became the fastest growing association of the decade and, in 1957, it launched the magazine *Which?* to help people find their way through the daily mass advertising with which they were bombarded. In 1967, *Which?* celebrated its 10th anniversary with a special edition devoted to washing machines, with contributions from the Prime Minister Harold Wilson and leader of the opposition, Edward Heath.

Table 2 *Percentage of new household goods found in British homes, 1955–75*

	1955	1975
Vacuum cleaner	51	90
Washing machine	18	70
Refrigerator	8	85
Freezer	n/a	15
Television	35	96
Telephone	19	52
Central heating	5	47
Dishwasher	1	2

Adapted from Derek Murphy (ed.), **Britain 1914–2000**, *2000*

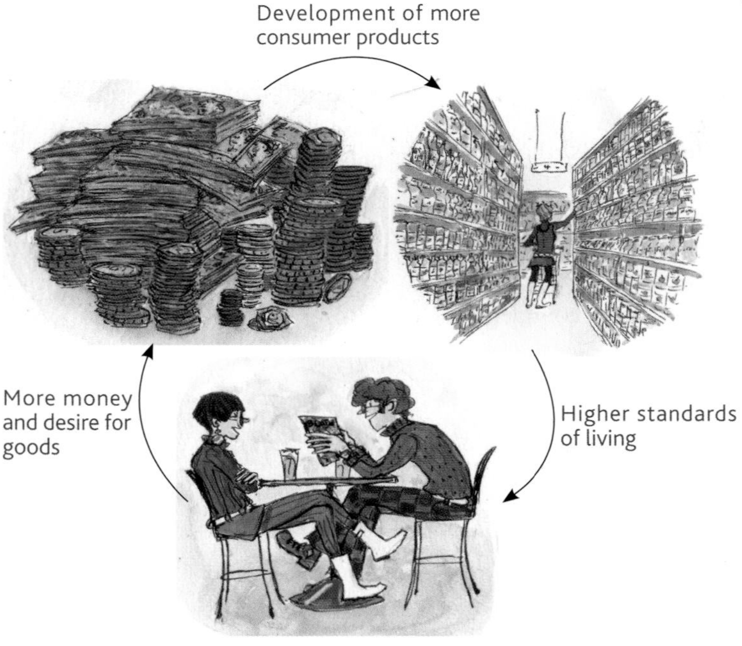

Development of more consumer products

More money and desire for goods

Higher standards of living

Fig. 2 *Consumerism*

Consumerism meant different things to different people. For some, it was simply the availability of sliced bread, fish fingers and crisps from the new supermarket; for others, a television, washing machine and better heating; for the better off, a car and maybe a holiday abroad; for the young, records, film and fashion. Perhaps its defining feature was that it meant an opportunity to possess or do something that had not been available to the past generation and, as such, it was often perceived as a new route to self-fulfilment.

However, there was an undercurrent of uncertainty in the media about what the impact of the 'affluent society' might be. Optimists argued that Britain was entering a new era of prosperity that would destroy the old class divisions and bring a new harmony. Pessimists believed a more materialistic outlook would encourage selfishness, destroying traditional family and community relationships, and widening the gulf between the affluent majority and the less socially privileged. There were certainly some left behind, either through lack of employment or through discrimination on the grounds of sex or race.

People were able to gain access to an unprecedented range of products – phones, white goods, televisions, cameras, cleaning products, packaged foods, cheap colourful clothing, cars and their accessories. This was prosperity and consumption as a way of life and this way of life stood for the opposite of the past; it was large, open, prosperous and youthful.

*Tony Judt, **Post-war: A History of Europe Since 1945**, 2007*

So far as anything in the sixties can be blamed for the fragmentation of society, it was the natural desire of the 'masses' to lead easier, pleasanter lives, own their own homes, follow their own fancies. Indeed, the very labour-saving domestic appliances launched onto the market by the sixties consumer boom speeded the meltdown of communality by allowing people to function in a private world, segregated from each other by TVs, telephones, record players, washing machines and home cookers.

*I. MacDonald, **Revolution in the Head: The Beatles, Records and the Sixties**, 1995*

Some of the possible effects of affluence can be seen in the story of Viv Nicholson, whose particular circumstances were quite unique but whose attitude and behaviour were very much of the time in which she lived.

Activity

Source analysis

Explain how far the views in Source 2 differ from those in Source 1 in relation to the impact of the growth in affluence.

Activity

Challenge your thinking

Do you agree that modern technology has destroyed 'communality' and encouraged people to retreat into a 'private world'?

Fig. 3 *Vivian Nicholson, the Football Pools winner, with her new Chevrolet car in 1961*

■ A closer look

Viv Nicholson and the 'Spend, spend, spend' mentality

When Viv Nicholson won £152,000 on the Littlewoods Football Pools in 1961, all she wanted to do with it was 'Spend, spend, spend.'

The week before we won, we desperately needed some money. My husband Keith was working on a night shift for £7 a week and I was earning £7 a week in a cake factory. After paying the bills it was hard to make ends meet. We found out on Saturday evening that we'd won the pools. It's unbelievable that I remember the exact amount we won so clearly – it was £152,300, 18 shillings and eight pence. Back then, even the eight pence meant something. When we went by train to London to collect our winnings we were met by hordes of reporters, and they all asked, 'What are you going to do now?' And there I was, wearing a pair of tights I had to borrow from my sister, and I said I was going to 'Spend, spend, spend!'

She bought a new home and filled it with the latest gadgets. She enjoyed expensive fashions, holidays and cars. She was able, for a short while at least, to fulfil many of the aspirations of the consumer society in which she lived, although in her case, it all went tragically wrong.

We bought a big bungalow and I used to have a new car every six months. I used them to learn to drive. I was awful at reversing and I would always reverse into somebody's plant pot or door. Keith died in a car accident in 1965. We'd already spent most of the money by then, and it all went to the taxman after that. Who would have thought your husband would be dead at 27?

3

Adapted from an article quoting Viv Nicholson in
The Observer, 6 July 2003

■ Key profile

Vivian Nicholson

Vivian Nicholson (born 1936), like many members of ordinary working-class families, enjoyed completing the football pools. This involved guessing the numbers of wins and draws that football clubs would have. However, her big win cut her off from her family and community. In four years, the money was spent and her husband was dead. She married three more times, recorded a pop song 'Spend, Spend, Spend', appeared in a strip club singing 'Big Spender', got into trouble with the police, was briefly admitted to a mental home and attempted to commit suicide. In her biography *Spend, Spend, Spend* (1977), she admitted that the days before her pools win were 'the best times I ever had'.

Scientific developments

The scientific revolution cannot become a reality unless we are prepared to make far-reaching changes in the economic and social attitudes which permeate our whole system of society. The Britain that is going to be forged in the white heat of this revolution will be no place for restrictive practices or for outdated methods on either side of industry. In our cabinet room and the boardroom alike, those charged with the control of our affairs must be ready to think and to speak in the language of our scientific age.

4 *From a speech at the Labour Party Conference by Harold Wilson, 1 October 1963*

Cross-reference

Read page 96 to discover more about **Anthony Wedgwood Benn**.

In the 1960s, the pace of change got faster and the 'white heat' of scientific progress, as Wilson referred to it, manifested itself in a number of different ways. Technological developments were seen as the way of the future, scientists were called upon to take executive positions in companies and the competition between businesses to satisfy consumer demand by developing new technologies became intense. Unilever, for example, ran four separate research establishments in the 1960s and the areas of investigation ranged from the production of synthetic fats to recipes for ice cream and ways of controlling foam in detergents. Wilson's decision to set up a separate Ministry of Technology under Frank Cousins after his election win in 1964 was recognition of the fact that scientists were deemed important to the future prosperity of the country. This was yet another blast against the Establishment, which had for so long relied on arts graduates and classically trained civil servants. In 1966, Anthony Wedgwood Benn who, despite his public school/Oxford background had chosen to renounce his peerage in order to sit in the House of Commons as Tony Benn, took over the post of Minister of Technology (which he held to 1970). His excitement about this new appointment can be determined in the extracts from his diary.

Fig. 4 *A woman feeds paper into an IBM machine, one of the first computers, which was installed in the Rowntree factory in York, 1962*

Thursday 30 June 1966

I am in the cabinet with a chance to create a new department that can really change the face of Britain and its prospects for survival.

Thursday 25 August 1966

The whole family went to the Bradwell Nuclear Power Station this morning. They laid on a superb tour for us and we saw the station which cost £58 million to build. We saw the gantry that moves the nuclear fuel, the heat exchanger and the turbines. It was altogether an enjoyable day. I had to drive out of my mind all my primitive knowledge of how power stations worked burning coal, heating water and using steam and try to think of the implications of atomic energy.

5   *Adapted from Tony Benn, **The Benn Diaries 1940–1990**, 1995*

Bernard Levin, *The Times* critic, had this to say of Benn's tenure of office:

Benn was one of the most characteristic figures of the decade; the ministering priest to the great god of technology whose worship, by the time the sixties ended, had, for many, become the State religion. Benn flung himself into the sixties technology with the enthusiasm of a newly enrolled boy scout demonstrating knot-tying to his indulgent parents. Presently the entire land echoed to his pronouncements, and many shuddered at his vision of a hygienic, remote-controlled, automated future.

6   *Bernard Levin, **The Pendulum Years: Britain in the Sixties**, 2003*

Activity

Source analysis

Explain how far the views in Source 6 differ from those in Source 4 about the importance of science in the State.

The scientific and technological developments of the post-war world had a profound effect on people's lives. Few of these developments were exclusively British and some were the culmination of the discoveries and inventions of earlier years, yet 1960s Britain was characterised by a new faith in, and optimism about, the power of scientific progress. It was the time of the 'space age' and science was portrayed as exciting and dynamic and popularised through TV programmes such as *Doctor Who* and children's comics and toys.

New consumer goods

Many of the consumer goods that found their way into the homes of the 1960s were the products of continuing scientific and technological development. Kitchen items such as refrigerators and washing machines (found in 69 per cent and 64 per cent of homes respectively by 1971) became smaller and more efficient, while TVs (found in 91 per cent of homes by the same date) grew bigger and more advanced. Spin driers, vacuum cleaners, phones, cheap record players and transistor radios all marked the advance of science, while ready-made furniture units, 'synthetic' furnishings and a variety of electrical equipment indicated how new technologies were being applied for domestic purposes.

There was something of a 'food revolution' as advances in processes such as freezing and drying created a new convenience food industry. The rise of the supermarket, made possible by the development of domestic refrigerators and family cars, in turn encouraged food technologists to devise new methods for the mass production of foodstuffs such as yoghurt, breakfast cereals, ice creams, crisps, easy-spread margarines, sliced bread, fish fingers and canned soft drinks. Lifestyles were changed. The amount spent on pre-packaged goods rose from around a fifth of all expenditure on food in 1960 to a quarter by 1970.

The supermarket shelves carried an extensive range of new cleaning and other household products. Fairy Liquid made its appearance in 1960 and other products of the decade included J Cloths, Pledge, aerosols, sprays, disinfectants and ever-changing detergents, which by 1965 could be broken down biologically.

Clothes too were influenced by the scientific revolution as new synthetic fabrics were more widely used. Nylon, Terylene, Dacron and Lycra offered new possibilities, while PVC became the 'must have' fabric for rainwear. The cosmetics industry boomed as scientific research permitted the development of new face creams and make-up.

Other everyday items that first made their appearance in the 1960s ranged from polythene and bubblewrap to Teflon-coated non-stick pans and the ring-pull can.

Communications and the colour television

The 1960s saw a huge expansion in mass communications, including television and artificial satellites, beginning with Telstar which relayed the first TV pictures in 1962, transistor radios and computers. The Post Office Tower in London was opened in 1965 as the centrepiece of Britain's new telecommunications network, while in boardrooms the first 'small' computers (about the size of a two-drawer filing cabinet) began to make their mark. These permitted engineers and medical researchers to undertake new projects previously inconceivable or endlessly time consuming, and by 1970 information could be transferred by floppy disk.

Colour television broadcasts arrived in Britain in July 1967 and marked a decisive break with the old world of black and white. Of course, colour in film and photography was already in existence but the impact of colour beamed straight into the living room opened up new vistas. The green grass of Wimbledon was seen on screen for the first time that year and even the new 'test card', which filled the screen when there were no programmes to be broadcast, was provided in colour.

The colour service was, however, limited to London, southern England, the Midlands and the north initially. It was also only found on BBC2 and, until the conversion of television centres, only used for outside broadcasts and films. By the end of 1967, the service had been extended into the south west and south Wales, south-east and eastern England, and colour transmissions from ITV and BBC1 followed in November 1969. Two months later, British audiences could see colour television pictures from the *Apollo 11* spacecraft on its way to the moon and increasing numbers

Fig. 5 *An advertisement for the new colour television*

Exploring the detail

Colour television

John Logie Baird had demonstrated colour television in 1928 using rotating discs and a colour wheel. However, developments were slow and were suspended during the war. In 1955, the BBC began testing colour transmission using the American NTSC system. However, the distortion was such that the television engineers nicknamed NTSC as 'Never Twice the Same Colour'. Eventually, a German system, known as PAL ('Perfection At Last') was tested in May 1965 and this was what the BBC finally adopted.

Fig. 6 *The growth of car ownership transformed outlooks – in all senses of the word!*

hurried out to buy the latest sets, so as not to miss out. By the end of 1969, the number of domestic colour sets had reached 200,000 and within five years colour sets were outselling black and white.

Transport

Although space travel and the 1969 moon landing fired the imagination, the more immediate impact of scientific development for most British people in the 1960s was the availability of new and cheaper means of transport. Car ownership had reached 8 million by 1964 and 11.5 million by the end of the 1960s, making cars the greatest single measure of 1960s prosperity. The possibility of mass car ownership was the result of developments in mass production, copied from America. The Morris Minor and Austin A30 were developed as two-door cars, cheap to buy, cheap to run and easy to fix, while the Mini car, designed for the British Motor Corporation (BMC) in 1959, became a motoring icon – small, efficient, fashionable and affordable. The aircraft industry also expanded. The big advances included the development of turboprop airliners and Concorde, the first passenger plane to fly faster than sound. However, it was the expansion of passenger air travel that made huge differences to leisure time and holidays. The British could also claim one scientific breakthrough in transport as their own. In 1959, Christopher Cockerell demonstrated the hovercraft, or 'flying boat', to great acclaim. From 1963, this was used for fast passenger services to France.

Medical developments and the oral contraceptive pill

Some medical advances were the product of wartime demands and by the 1960s a new generation was reaping the benefits of polio immunisation, penicillin and a greater understanding of vitamins. Computers enabled scientists to map human genes and advances in photography permitted the development of more sophisticated X-ray equipment. Chemical engineering led to the development of analgesics and sulphonamides, while the research that produced the transistor radio was transferred to a new type of hearing aid. The National Health Service (NHS) helped ensure that advances were rapidly spread to the general population and advances in kidney and liver operations, blood transfusions and complicated heart surgery permitted the improvement and preservation of life. By the end of the decade, people were living longer and more healthily than ever before and experiments were well under way that would open the door to transplant surgery and genetic engineering.

Fig. 7 *By the later 1960s, the oral contraceptive pill was a popular form of birth control*

Of all the scientific developments, the one most associated with the 1960s must be the development of the oral contraceptive pill. For the first time in history, 'the pill' allowed women to control their own fertility. It affected attitudes, lifestyles, marriage, the family and female employment.

The pill was licensed for use in Britain in 1961, but its launch before this in the USA led to a flurry of media interest, previously unknown. The radio programme, *Woman's Hour*, advertised a broadcast on 19 September 1960, which carried the following warning:

We think we should say that today's talk is intended for adults; and there may be listeners who would prefer to rejoin us after it is over. They may like to know that the talk lasts just over five minutes. The subject is contraception and the controversy over birth control by pills.

7   *Woman's Hour, 'In my opinion' broadcast, 1960*

The talk which followed was given by Ethel Dukes, Honorary Secretary of the Marriage Guidance Council Medical Advisory Board.

As a woman doctor who has been interested for many years in the problems of marriage, I think the less one interferes with the course of nature the better. I fear the pill may be harmful if taken in its present form during the long reproductive years stretching ahead of many women. After all we are talking about something that is a very powerful chemical. Its whole purpose as a contraceptive is to interfere with a process that is not only natural but basic to women. I hope that something less harmful for long-term use will be found soon.

8   *Woman's Hour, 'In my opinion' broadcast, 1960*

Despite such concerns, following trials with hundreds of married women volunteers in Birmingham and Slough, the pill became available from January 1961 and, by the end of the year, could be prescribed on the National Health Service, although only for married women. Within Europe, Britain was exceptional in approving the contraceptive pill for use at this time. In many parts of western and eastern Europe, it was still forbidden even to give information on contraception.

The debate about the pill's safety continued, as did arguments over its cost (at just over £1 per woman per month) and its effects. The media was dominated by 'pill' stories. In late 1961 and early 1962, a survey found that the press carried over 400 items on teenage sexual behaviour in just four months. However, its immediate impact should not be exaggerated. Although its usage was increased after the Family Planning Act 1967 allowed local authorities to provide contraceptives and planning advice to all and the pill became available to single women, by 1970 only 19 per cent of married couples under 45 were using the pill and 9 per cent of single women.

Summary questions

1. Explain why people became so excited about scientific developments in the 1960s.

2. 'The development of the oral contraceptive pill was the most important scientific advance of the 1960s.' Explain why you agree or disagree with this statement.

Did you know?

The 'combined oral contraceptive pill' (COC) contains a combination of two artificially produced female hormones that mimic pregnancy and suppress ovulation, thereby preventing conception. The first COCs contained quite large doses of synthetic hormones. Carl Djerassi had discovered how to synthesise hormones from the Mexican yam in 1951. His discoveries were publicised after the Tokyo Medical Conference of 1955 but, partly because of medical uncertainty and partly because of moral concerns, it was some time before 'the pill' became widely used.

Cross-reference

For more information on the **permissive society**, read pages 88–92.

Activity

Thinking point

What differences do you suppose scientific developments made to the world of work; leisure; daily life?

4   The expansion of the mass media

Fig. 1 *An advertisment for Bird's Eye fish fingers, a typical example of the 'convenience foods' that began to flood the shops in the early to mid-1960s*

In the 1960s, people's visual and aural senses were bombarded with a huge range of new stimuli as the mass media grew in size and type. The message was to, 'go out and buy' and a profusion of channels of communication in the form of television, the transistor radio, newspapers, magazines and advertising billboards served the dual purpose of feeding off new attitudes and spreading them far and wide.

Until the 1950s, everything had been far more provincial and bland. Black and white newspapers or a reader on the 'wireless' had kept people up to date with national news, while for entertainment there had been family or local pleasures – the countryside or a park, and for those near enough to a major town – dance halls, cinemas and football stadiums.

Compared with this, the pervasive influence of TV in the 1950s and colour TV in the 1960s transformed life beyond all recognition. TV became available everywhere, creating a uniformity of culture which ended the isolation of distant communities and helped impose a national standard of taste and behaviour. The news was no longer relayed by a disembodied voice or lifeless newspaper and world leaders and politicians had to adapt to their presence in the home. Families could no longer just hear, but also see, what was going on in the world around them, making 'news' far more immediate and important to them. TV also rapidly supplanted the cinema as a means of entertainment and no one needed to leave the home any more to escape from boredom. TV took on a life of its own and the fortunes of fictional TV families soon became the substance of everyday conversation. Football and other sports could be viewed from the comfort of the living room and with channels competing to broadcast what the public wanted, the status and income of professional sportsmen, celebrities and pop stars was raised to a new iconic level.

Radio survived, helped by the development of the transistor and the spread of car radios. It broadcast a mixture of serious radio journalism, often at times when the TV channels were closed, and light 'background' entertainment from pop music to easy-listening comedy and quiz shows. Live theatre, on the other hand, shrank rapidly, especially outside major cities, while attendance at football matches and other 'live' events also suffered. The press was forced to adapt as TV took on the function of the main provider of news and entertainment and did so with a switch of emphasis from news to comment – be it academic or sensationalist. The tabloids operated a policy of 'if you can't beat 'em, join 'em' and exploited the potential of TV, relying on celebrities to provide sensationalist material. Advertising too, although already ubiquitous by the 1960s, expanded still further with the spread of the TV. With the help of the TV screen, advertisers could get straight into the family sitting room and tempt customers with attractive models that extolled consumption and reinforced the brand names of goods.

The growth of television ownership

Table 1 *Television licences*

1950	1955	1960	1965	1975
344,000	4,504,000	10,470,000	13,253,000	17,701,000

Clearly, the figures in Table 1 show the huge expansion in TV ownership that took place after 1950. By 1961, 75 per cent of the population had a TV in their home and by 1971 it was 91 per cent. Homes actually contained more TVs than bathtubs by the end of the 1960s! TV was regarded as exciting because it was new. It had only been in 1958 that the amount spent by the BBC on TV had outstripped that which it spent on radio, and that more television licences had been issued than radio licences. By 1969, TV accounted for 23 per cent of leisure time, its popularity being both a cause and consequence of the social changes that took place in the 1960s.

Activity

Thinking point

In pairs, make a list of the effects that might have resulted from increased TV ownership.

Exploring the detail

The birth of TV

Although there had been some TV broadcasts before the war, they were suspended in wartime. Television was only reintroduced in 1946. Initially, the BBC had a monopoly as it was said to provide a 'public service', but the Television Act 1954 changed this. While the BBC remained the 'official' channel, funded from licence fees, from 1955 ITV was allowed to run a commercial network, dependent on advertising revenue. By 1957, ITV had 76 per cent of the market share. Its light-hearted entertainment was popular and the top 10 'most watched programmes' on British television in 1960 were shown here.

Fig. 2 *The Radio Times became essential household reading*

Television's rise to become a near universal presence in people's homes was the most important cultural transformation of the sixties. This omnipresence changed social life and habits. It was the era when the British television found its feet, adopting new technologies, programme formats and production values. Here was a medium that was still young enough to invent itself. The pioneers of the sixties were free to enjoy this form as an adventure playground.

Mark Donnelly,
***Sixties Britain**, 2005*

The spread of broadcasting

The aim of the BBC must be to conserve and strengthen serious listening. While satisfying the legitimate public demand for recreation and entertainment, the BBC must never lose sight of its cultural mission. The BBC is a single instrument and must see that the nation derives the best advantage from this fact.

Sir William Haley,
Director-General of the BBC
(1942–52), Policy statement, 1949

I believe we have a duty to take account of the changes in society, to be ahead of public opinion, rather than always to wait upon it. I believe that great broadcasting organisations, with their immense powers of patronage for writers and artists, should not neglect to cultivate young writers who may, by many, be considered 'too advanced' or 'shocking'.

Hugh Greene,
Director-General of the BBC
(1960–9), 'The Conscience of the
Programme Director', 1965

Activity

Source analysis

Explain how far the views in Source 3 differ from those in Source 2 in relation to the responsibilities of the BBC to its audience.

Activity

Research exercise

Choose two or more of the programmes listed in Figure 3 and find out more about them using the internet. You may even be able to see a recording of a programme or talk to older people who remember viewing some of them. Prepare an illustrated presentation to give to your class, in which you tell them about your chosen programmes. Explain why you feel they were so popular and what they have taught you about the 1960s.

When Hugh Greene became Director-General of the BBC in 1960, he set out to transform it. Money was diverted from radio to television, a new TV centre was established in Shepherd's Bush, guidelines on nudity and swearing were revised, a new style of news presentation and more popular programmes were commissioned. The Pilkington Enquiry examined the state of TV between 1960 and 1962 and concluded that, while ITV programming was 'trivial', the BBC had achieved a good blend.

Key profile

Hugh Greene

Hugh Greene 1910–87 was a decisive influence on British broadcasting. He was Director-General from 1960 to 1969 and, under his leadership, subjects previously avoided were tackled on the air. He introduced satire with *That Was The Week That Was* (1962–3) and encouraged the realistic police drama *Z Cars* (1962–78), the unconventional sitcoms *Steptoe and Son* (1962–74) and *Till Death Us Do Part* (1966–75), and the often controversial *The Wednesday Play* (1964–70), which included the screening of 'Cathy Come Home', drawing attention to the plight of the homeless and dealing with issues like mental breakdown and alcoholism. Some plays also contained nudity and 'offensive' language.

Pilkington's report established new benchmarks of 'good' television. On Pilkington's recommendations, the Independent Television Authority (ITA) was required to ensure that all ITV franchises broadcast a certain amount of serious listening – by the later 1960s this meant one weekday and one weekend play, two weekly current affairs programmes and the *News at Ten*. Its praise for the BBC, which had begun to produce quality programmes with mass appeal, meant that it won the competition to run a new third TV channel and that its charter was extended. BBC2 was launched in April 1964, largely as a channel for the arts but with a more open-minded approach to 'public service' broadcasting. BBC2 also used a new 625-line UHF transmission system that provided clearer definition.

A closer look

The launch of BBC2

The opening of BBC2 on the evening of 20 April 1964 was ruined by a major power failure following a fire at Battersea power station. A glittering start had been planned, billed as a night of music, comedy and celebratory fireworks.

Denis Tuohy, who was to be the first presenter on the new channel explains what happened:

> The sense of occasion had us fired up and I was feeling very nervous. We had been rehearsing all day and we went up to the BBC bar for a drink to settle our nerves. When I went back down to the gallery with about half an hour to go, I noticed all the television screens were blank and there were a lot of people shouting something about Battersea.

Robert Longman, who was in charge of engineering that night, spent the evening running around with a candle stuck in a paper cup, as he desperately tried to find a way to get the new channel on air. He continues the story:

> It got to about 6.30pm when I noticed that the power frequency was falling slightly, then we lost power completely. I went around telling everyone that we would be able to sort it out and not to panic, when we found out the whole of west London had gone. I just froze and thought 'oh dear', because it was an engineering problem – my problem – and the place was packed with people. In the end we just sent everyone up to the BBC Club, where there was emergency lighting, for a drink.

Consequently, the new channel began with a short news bulletin from Alexandra Palace, which had been unaffected by the power cut. The newsreader, Gerald Priestland, explained what had happened but this broadcast began without sound for the first two and a half minutes! The rest of the launch evening consisted of a series of test cards reading 'BBC will follow shortly' and music interspersed with characteristic BBC-style apologies.

As a result of the disastrous launch, BBC2's first scheduled programme to go ahead was *Play School* at 11am the following day and that evening the channel showed the items planned for the opening night. They were opened by the announcer Denis Tuohy who symbolically blew out a candle in a darkened studio and apologised for the previous night's problems:

> We knew we had to make some reference to the blackout so there I was with my mod haircut, blowing out a candle. That image is run again and again every time there is a reference to the BBC2 launch, but it was so long ago that most people these days don't have a clue what it's all about.

4   *Adapted from articles on the BBC website*

 Activity

Source analysis

Using Sources 1 to 4, Figure 3 and your own knowledge, explain how far television broadcasting changed between 1959 and 1969.

▪ Cross-reference

Look ahead to pages 80–1 for further discussion on the impact of **TV**.

Other technological developments brought further change. Live transatlantic television was made possible by Telstar, the satellite launched in 1962; from 1966, the transistor revolution allowed sets to become smaller; and in July 1967 BBC2 became the first channel

SERIAL DRAMA AND SOAPS

Coronation Street (ITV 1960 onwards) – attracted 20 million viewers (over a third of the population)

Crossroads (ITV 1964–88)

Dr Finlay's Casebook (BBC 1962–71)

Z Cars (BBC 1962–78) – attracted 15 million viewers

ACTION ADVENTURE AND SPIES

The Avengers (ITV 1961–9)

Danger Man (ITV 1960–1 & 1964–7)

Doctor Who (BBC 1963–89)

The Man from UNCLE (BBC 1965–8)

The Saint (ITV 1962–9)

COMEDY, SATIRE AND VARIETY SHOWS

The Billy Cotton Band Show (BBC 1956–65)

The Black and White Minstrel Show (BBC 1958–78)

Dad's Army (BBC 1968–78)

Harry Worth (1960–74)

The Ken Dodd Show (BBC 1959–63)

The Likely Lads (BBC 1964–76)

Monty Python's Flying Circus (BBC 1969–70 & 1972–4)

The Morecambe and Wise Show (ITV 1961–4 & BBC 1966–8)

Steptoe and Son (BBC 1962–5)

Sunday Night at the London Palladium (ITV 1955–67)

That Was The Week That Was (BBC 1962–3)

Till Death Us Do Part (BBC 1966–8, 1972 & 1974–5)

CHILDREN, YOUTH AND POP MUSIC PROGRAMMES

Camberwick Green (BBC 1966)

Captain Scarlet (1967)

Juke Box Jury (BBC 1959–67)

The Magic Roundabout (1965–77)

Play School (BBC 1964–88)

Ready Steady Go! (ITV 1963–6)

Stingray (1964)

Thunderbirds (1965)

Top of the Pops (BBC 1964–2006)

Trumpton (BBC 1967)

Watch with Mother (BBC 1952–73)

Fig. 3 *'On the box' in the 1960s*

NEWS AND SPORT

Grandstand (BBC 1958 onwards)

Match of the Day (1964 onwards)

Tonight (BBC 1957–65)

World in Action (ITV 1963–93)

World of Sport (ITV 1965–85)

GAME SHOWS, QUIZZES AND TALENT COMPETITIONS

Double Your Money (ITV 1955–68)

Opportunity Knocks (ITV 1956, 1961–78)

University Challenge (ITV 1962–87 & BBC 1994 onwards)

MORE SERIOUS TV (MAINLY BBC2)

The Forsyte Saga (BBC 1967) – adapted from John Galsworthy's novels

The Great War (BBC 1964) – a 26-part documentary

Horizon (BBC 1964 onwards)

The Wednesday Play (BBC 1964–70)

to broadcast regular colour programmes. The launch of BBC2 allowed BBC1 to grow more popularist. More sport was shown, for example the Football World Cup in 1966, and by the time of the Mexico Olympics in 1968 over a fifth of BBC1's output was sports coverage. News and current affairs broadcasting continued and were supplemented by a diet of serials, soaps, comedy and action–adventure programmes, as well as American programmes, Westerns, quiz shows and old films.

Radio

There were few households that did not have a radio by 1960. A large valve-driven wireless took pride of place in many 1950s homes and in the evening the family would gather round to listen. All this changed when new technology in 1954 made cheap, light and portable transistor radios possible. These became the radios of the 1960s and, together with the long-life battery and earphones, they opened the way for a new type of radio suited to an age of increased mobility. They could be taken to the beach or a park or carried upstairs to the privacy of the bedroom. Teenagers no longer had to listen to what their parents wanted to hear and personal radios meant that programmes could be targeted at different audiences.

At the beginning of the 1960s, the BBC was the only organisation licensed to run radio stations in the UK and there were just three BBC radio stations – the Home Service (now Radio Four) for news, talks, drama, comedy and discussion shows; the Light Programme (now Radio Two) for entertainment; and the third programme (now Radio Three), which provided more intellectual fare. There was no station for popular recorded music and the BBC Light Programme played only a few hours of records a week, while using live musicians to perform their own versions of popular 'hits' in the gaps between programmes.

Fig. 4 *The 'pop pirates' of the ship Radio Caroline photographed at Walton police station after they had been rescued during the 1966 storms. Their smiles were not to last long, however: Radio Caroline's days were numbered*

Commercial enterprise seized on this gap in the market. Young people who could obtain the signal listened to the nightly broadcasts of pop music from Radio Luxembourg and in 1964 a 'pirate station' – Radio Caroline – started broadcasting to London and the south east from a ship moored outside territorial waters off the Essex coast. It was an immediate success and a sister station was opened off the Isle of Man to cater for listeners in Liverpool, Manchester, Dublin and Belfast.

Radio Caroline was, in turn, joined by Radio London – broadcast from another ship anchored off the Essex coast. Both stations served up a diet of pop music introduced by DJs such as Johnnie Walker and Tony Blackburn. Other 'pirate' stations followed, including Radio 390, which broadcast classical and jazz music from a former Second World War gun tower in the Thames estuary and Radio Scotland, which mixed pop with ceilidh music from a former lightship anchored in the Firth of Clyde. Radio Britain and Radio England tried to follow suit, broadcasting from ships off the Essex coast from May 1966, but both collapsed in less than a year – the latter quite literally when the ship's antenna was broken off in a storm.

Although the pirate stations acquired a very loyal following and were supported by musicians, the BBC and politicians claimed that they interfered with legitimate broadcasting, played music they had not paid for and endangered shipping.

Exploring the detail

Radio Luxembourg

Radio Luxembourg had begun broadcasting English language radio programmes in the 1930s. Broadcasts had been suspended in the war years, but they resumed after this, although only at night. Since the radio station relied on record companies for sponsorship, by the early 1960s its programmes consisted almost entirely of records. In order to give maximum publicity to as many new releases as possible, it would squeeze as many records as it could into each show, often playing only 20–30 seconds of each one.

■ Key chronology

The changing press

1959
24 August

Manchester Guardian changes its title to the *Guardian*, based in London.

1961

Second (Shawcross) Royal Commission on the Press.

1961
5 February

Sunday Telegraph launched.

1962
4 February

Launch of *Sunday Times* magazine as *Sunday Times Colour Section*.

1964

Press Council replaces the General Council of the Press.

1964
9 June

Death of Lord Beaverbrook.

1964
6 September

Observer colour supplement launched.

1964
15 September

Daily Herald becomes the *Sun*.

1964
25 September

Daily Telegraph magazine launched.

1966

Times is bought by Roy Thomson, owner of the *Sunday Times*.

1966
3 May

Times begins printing news on the front page.

1969

News of the World is bought by Rupert Murdoch.

1969
17 November

Sun is relaunched as a tabloid by Rupert Murdoch.

1974–7

Third (McGregor) Royal Commission on the Press.

■ Cross-reference

To recap on the **Profumo affair**, return to pages 23–5.

Wednesday 15 December 1965

The pirate radio letters are continuing to flood in and there must now be 2,000 or more. I decided to make it clear that there would be a gap between the warning and the prosecution of the pirates and I think the prosecutions cannot begin until after the white paper on broadcasting.

5   *Tony Benn, **The Benn Diaries 1940–1990**, 1995*

Despite a fierce campaign to 'save the pirates', the UK government introduced the Marine Broadcasting Act in August 1967, designed to make offshore radio illegal. In compensation, a BBC pop music channel was promised and a month later Radio One was born. The station made use of former pirate DJs and soon won many converts.

The four separate BBC channels thus established separate identities, matching the predominant cultural groupings of the 1960s. This situation remained unchallenged until 1973, when government legislation permitted the advent of the first commercial local radio station, starting with London's Capital Radio.

■ Changes in the press and print

Some predicted that the arrival of the TV would mark the end of the print media. Sales of newspapers fell from their peak in the 1950s, and five national newspapers (including the *News Chronicle*) had to close between 1960 and 1962, as well as some provincial papers. Advertising revenue fell along with readership, but those newspapers and magazines that survived changed and grew stronger. The *Sun*, for example, launched in 1964, replaced the serious working-class newspaper, the *Daily Herald*, and set out to be 'the only newspaper born of the age we live in'. Its new values were made clear in the first edition.

We welcome the age of automation, electronics, computers. We will campaign for the rapid modernisation of Britain, regardless of the vested interests of the management or workers. The *Sun* is a newspaper with a social conscience, championing progressive ideas.

6   *The **Sun**, 15 September 1964*

In 1969, the *Sun* was bought by the Australian newspaper tycoon Rupert Murdoch. He associated it with the more permissive attitudes of the age and its popularity grew enormously. Copying TV tactics, the tabloids exploited celebrity stories, exposed the famous 'in the public interest' and sought out individuals with a tale to sell. They had learnt how papers could be sold through sensational tales about members of the Establishment during the Profumo affair of 1963 and, thereafter, politicians were reluctant to interfere with press freedom lest they became the subject of its investigations.

The 'quality' press retained its distance, but even these papers were happy to report a certain amount of celebrity gossip and to broaden their views as to what was acceptable in terms of both the language used and the topics under discussion. Whilst 'quality' newspapers represented only a fraction of total sales, their readership expanded and the *Guardian* emerged (from the *Manchester Guardian*) in 1959 to take its place alongside the *Daily Telegraph*, *The Times*, the *Observer* and the *Sunday*

Times. British Sunday papers, beginning with the *Sunday Times* in 1961 and followed by the *Sunday Telegraph* and the *Observer* in 1964, added colour supplements carrying investigative stories and a strong pictoral element. Such magazines won back some of the advertising contracts and proved a great success.

New magazines also sprang up covering 'hot' topics like music, records, teenage interests and satire. *Private Eye* edited by Christopher Booker was launched in October 1961. Aimed at a youthful audience, it set out to expose pompous behaviour and make fun of politicians and the Establishment. Richard Ingrams, Willie Rushton, Dudley Moore, Jonathan Miller and Alan Bennett were contributors and, although the tone was distinctly 'public school' (which was hardly surprising given its Oxbridge-educated writers), a receptive audience enjoyed its wit and sarcasm.

Glossy lifestyle, youth and women's magazines targeted their particular audiences with plentiful colour and photography. They used new photo-litho printing techniques to produce layouts that were strongly visual. Teenage magazines featured comic strips conveying romantic fantasies together with pictures of pop stars, while older women were treated to technicolour fashion photography. In 1966–7, the 'underground' press led the way in visual experimentation. *Oz*, first published in 1967, was printed in small coloured type over pictures and used 'psychedelic' colours like pink on orange, encouraging readers to 'experience' rather than read its print. Book covers were also revamped as the world of print learned from the world of advertising.

■ The spread of advertising

The consumer society and the growth of the mass media meant a huge growth in advertising. Expenditure on retail advertising rose from £102 million a year in 1951 to £2.5 billion by 1978. From 1955, advertisers sought slots on commercial television and, by 1959, ITV's advertising revenue was greater than that of all the Fleet Street newspapers combined. The television's share of advertising rose from 3.4 per cent in 1956 to 17.5 per cent in 1960 and 24.4 per cent in 1975. Colour supplements and magazines became popular with advertisers, as did billboards along the fast-growing road network. The percentage of advertising revenue going to the cinema, however, steadily declined.

Advertising paid, and the sales figures of heavily advertised products regularly outstripped their less well promoted competitors. In 1955, the writer J. B. Priestley described the world he saw emerging around him as 'admass':

> Admass is my name for the whole system of increasing productivity, plus inflation, plus a rising standard of living, plus high pressure advertising and salesmanship, plus mass communications, plus cultural democracy and the creation of the mass mind, the mass man.

7

The historian Arthur Marwick in his book *The Sixties* provided a rather different view.

Fig. 5 *There was a growing market for glossy and colourful women's magazines*

> Advertising may well be thought the very soul of deceit, the sworn enemy of frankness and openness. But the new advertising of the sixties was also bold, uninhibited, witty, naturalistic, and rather in the manner of some of the sixties novels, explicit, and, of course, fully exploitative of the appeal of a beautiful face and figure, whether female or male. The new advertising was involving, rather than distant and authoritarian; it advertised the artefacts of the consumer society rather than the quack medicines of the past.

8   *Arthur Marwick, The Sixties, 1998*

Activity

Source analysis

Explain how far the views in Source 8 differ from those in Source 7 in relation to advertising.

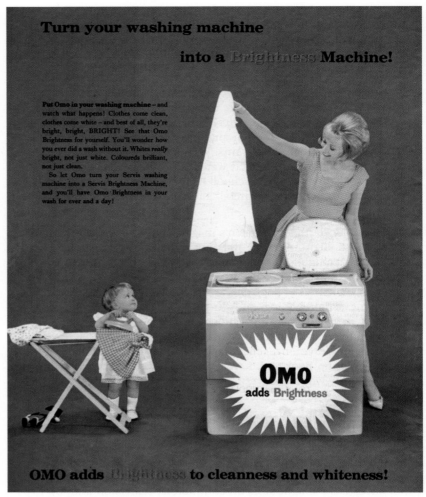

Fig. 6 *A striking slogan and snappy image helped to sell products in the 1960s. Who could resist this advertisement for the washing powder Omo?*

Activity

Thinking point

A Guide to Modern Manners was published in 1969, updating a similar book first written in 1956. Consider the views given in the extract from it below.

> *It seems inconceivable that when we first wrote this book the use of the word 'bloody' on television caused a public furore. One of the significant changes in manners over the last few years has been the liberalisation of attitudes towards what can be said in mixed company. Candour, frankness and honesty in conversation have become admired attributes. Television, film, certain newspapers and weekly magazines, novels and plays and autobiographies have for many people broken down the taboos on what can be discussed in public. This particularly this relates to the old inadmissibles, intimate sexual experiences, detailed descriptions of violence and every kind of physical expression and emotion.*

*Quoted in A. Marwick, **The Sixties**, 1998*

Summary question

How far did developments in the mass media in the 1960s promote cultural change?

5   The growth in leisure

In this chapter you will learn about:

- why and how leisure time increased and what leisure activities were popular

- the impact of scientific and technological developments, which helped increase car ownership and permitted more opportunities for travel, particularly overseas.

We certainly began to travel around more. We got our first car in 1958 and we began to venture further afield. We holidayed in Dorset, Somerset and Devon to start with and then we became more ambitious and went to Cornwall and Wales. We preferred self-catering, because that was easier with a young family. We stayed in a caravan once, I recall, but I don't know how we managed when I think back on that – it was so cramped! I think it was in 1970 that we first went abroad. That was really something. We took the car on the ferry and drove down to the Loire valley in France. Of course, we had friends who tried package holidays, but that didn't appeal to me. I've never been on an aeroplane to this day!

By Mollie Golding (aged 85 years) recalling holidays in the 1960s when she lived in Essex

Fig. 1 *At leisure in the home*

Like Mollie in Source 1, many individuals and families broadened their horizons in the 1960s. This was because the period not only saw more individuals with money to spare, it also brought an expansion to leisure time and to the range of activities and holidays that they might enjoy.

Key factors behind the growth of leisure time and leisure activities included:

- Shorter working hours, which allowed more time for leisure. The average working week for a manual-labour job before the Second World War had been 48 hours, but in the 1950s this fell to 40 hours. By the 1960s, fewer people were expected to work on Saturday mornings and weekends could be given over to leisure activities.

- 99 out of 100 industrial companies had increased their workers' paid leave to two weeks per annum, while professionals often received more.

- Rising incomes and improved living standards.

- Mass ownership of cars, which permitted travel.

- Mass ownership of televisions, which opened minds to new and different experiences as well as advertising leisure possibilities.

- The spread of education and increased social mobility, which increased expectations and aspirations.

- The growth of tourist companies, passenger aircraft and the falling costs of overseas travel, particularly through the 'package holiday'.

Activity

Thinking point

Which of the given key factors do you consider to have been the most important in encouraging the growth of leisure activities in the 1960s? Explain your answer.

Fig. 2 *DIY became a new leisure activity and sales of related magazines boomed*

The expansion of leisure activities

Within the home

The family home remained the centre of many leisure activities, and these expanded to include TV viewing, listening to music, including tapes, and enjoying the proliferation of magazines and cheap paperbacks that flooded the market at this time. There was also a vogue for 'do-it-yourself' (DIY) house repairs and gardening, encouraged by TV programmes featuring personalities such as Barry Bucknell (*Bucknell's House*) and Percy Thrower (*Gardeners' World*). Decorating, installing central heating and adding extensions became popular hobbies. Sales of wallpaper, tools and specialist magazines like *Man About the House* and *Practical Householder* boomed, making DIY a multi-million pound industry.

Four out of every five homes possessed a garden that provided a private escape from urban life. Even new suburban estates provided householders with a small garden, and to support the gardener's activities, a multitude of chemical weedkillers, composts, plastic garden tools and other paraphernalia appeared on sale at local garden centres. Manufacturers invested in horticultural research and, in 1969, the world's first electric hover-mower, the Flymo (based on the hovercraft principle) was launched.

Women were often keen gardeners too, but cookery, needlework and knitting still had a place in the 1960s home, and were also encouraged by both new gadgetry and the ease with which tasks such as knitting could be combined with TV viewing. Kitchen gadgets helped make cooking a pleasure and since so many household tasks had become less time consuming, women had more time to devote to the creative activities. Women's magazines reflected such interests, whether via specialist publications such as *Stitchcraft* or more general magazines with a regular recipe, knitting pattern or embroidery feature.

Key profiles

Barry Bucknell

Barry Bucknell (1912–2003) became the BBC's own DIY expert and helped transform DIY from the solitary 'garden shed' image into a fun, fashionable and profitable pastime. His 1950s series *Do It Yourself* attracted 7 million viewers and made him a household name. In 1962, the BBC bought a derelict house in Ealing and set Barry Bucknell to renovate it. *Bucknell's House* became a 39-week series that millions watched and tried to emulate.

Percy Thrower

Percy Thrower (1913–88) was working as a park superintendant in Shrewsbury when, in 1947, Godfrey Baseley, presenter of a radio programme called *Beyond the Back Door* visited and asked Percy to join him on the programme. From 1955, Percy Thrower presented the *Gardening Club* and became a household name. He made the transition from radio to television in 1962 and took over *Gardeners' World* in 1969, in which he demonstrated his expertise and passed on his advice and tips.

Fig. 3 *Dining out was a popular way to spend an evening, as seen here in 1962*

Outside the home

Although pubs and working men's clubs remained popular, some of the older activities, such as playing and watching outdoor games or attending the cinema, experienced a relative decline. It was the spread of cars and foreign travel experiences, as well as rising living standards, that encouraged new activities such as eating out, which had never been a major part of the British leisure scene before. To cater for those who wished to spend an evening in a restaurant or wine bar, a proliferation of eating establishments appeared, catering for all tastes. Shopping also became a leisure activity in its own right as mass production, fuelled by advertising, crammed high streets with tempting goods. Cars permitted travel to alternative shopping centres and leisure facilities and activities from caravanning to golf and sailing all built up a devoted following. For the providers of equipment and facilities, leisure had become a profitable business.

Cross-reference

The rise of **television** is covered in more detail on pages 38–43.

■ Increased car ownership

Car ownership had increased in the 1950s but it accelerated far more rapidly in the 1960s. Passenger bus, coach and train travel declined as the use of the car grew to account for 77 per cent of journeys by 1974 (up from 39 per cent in 1954). Figures 4 and 5 give further measures of the expansion of car travel.

Cars were bought for a variety of reasons. First and foremost, they provided an easy means of travelling around. They catered for personal needs and provided a relatively comfortable ride, whilst also offering a means of transporting the whole family, goods and luggage. What is more, thanks to technological improvements and designers' endeavours, they had become affordable. The Mini car of 1959, designed by Alec Issigonis, was priced at under £500 and set the trend towards small, basic cars that, at least as second hand, fell within the price range of the reasonably paid worker. The Hornet and Riley Elf became popular for their fuel economy, while the Austin 1100 and Morris 1100 launched in 1962 had hydrolastic fluid suspension to give a smoother ride. The Renault 4 with its innovative hatchback also arrived from France in 1961, while other popular cars of the 1960s included the Ford Capri (1962), the Ford Cortina (1962), which at £639 was the choice of affluent professionals, and the Ford Escort (1968).

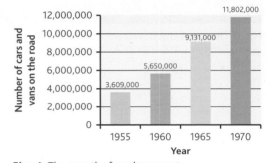

Fig. 4 *The growth of road transport*

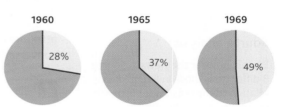

Fig. 5 *Percentage of households that owned a car*

Key profile

Alec Issigonis

Alec Issigonis (1906–88) was commissioned to develop a cheap economical British car to rival imported 'bubble' cars. He produced a revolutionary design that placed the engine over the wheels to provide more passenger space, and the Mini was born. When Issigonis presented Princess Margaret's husband, Lord Snowdon, with a Mini as a birthday present, its popularity boomed. The 'cheap, no frills' car became the car of the decade.

However, cars were not simply bought as an efficient means of transport. They were also a status symbol. Even a small car showed that a family had risen up the ladder of affluence. Advertising and celebrity endorsement sold cars in their hundreds. The easy-to-park Mini became

Fig. 6 *The Mini had definitely arrived when Prince Charles used one to reach Trinity College, Cambridge in October 1967*

the symbol of 'Swinging London'. Lord Snowdon, Peter Sellers and Twiggy all drove one and others rushed to copy them. For those with more cash to spare, the E-type Jaguar (launched in 1961 at £2,200) encapsulated the ideal of many a male driver. It had a streamlined body and the fastest speed of any car on the market at 150 mph.

The thrill of speed and power was often in itself enough to encourage car purchase, particularly among young males. Petrol companies used this as an advertising ploy, most famously seen in Esso's 'I've got a tiger in my tank' advertising campaign, which ran from 1963 and allowed purchasers to obtain a mini 'tiger's tail', which could be attached to a radio aerial or petrol cap.

Activity

Source analysis

Explain how far the views in Source 3 differ from those in Source 2 in relation to the reasons for increased car ownership in the 1960s.

This individualistic means of transport was regarded as either a temple, a toy or a murder weapon. It was essential to purchase the kind of car which said something about one's personality. What it usually said was that the owner was incapable of expressing personal attributes in the old ways, such as conversation.

2 Mark Garnett and Richard Weight, ***Modern British History***, 2004

Once I acquired a car, out came the map and we were able to go places that we'd only dreamed of before. It was possible to go to the Lake District and Scotland. It was like going to a foreign land. You were seeing things that you'd only read about in a book. It opened up new horizons and what a lot we learned.

3 *A Cornishman's recollections of the sixties*

Increased car ownership brought environmental changes. Britain was increasingly criss-crossed by a network of bypasses, ring roads, trunk roads and dual carriageways. In December 1958, the opening of the 13 km (8 mile) Preston bypass, the first major road to be built for 20 years, reflected the new desire for speed and in 1959 the first long stretch of the modern M1 motorway, 108 km (67 miles) from London to Yorkshire, heralded the arrival of fast road travel. It was built in 19 months, had three lanes in either direction and contained the first motorway service station – Watford Gap. Between 1960 and 1963, parts of the M60 and M6 were built. The A1(M) was opened in 1961 and the M5 in 1962. Scotland's first motorway, the M8, opened in 1967 and the early 1970s saw even more dramatic expansion that was to continue to the mid-1980s. In terms of usage, the motorways were a great success.

Changes in road patterns led to changes in patterns of settlement. Farms and estates were broken up and some residential districts were sacrificed as road builders sought straight routes that ignored the landscape and existing land use. Whilst new roads could take traffic away from old town centres, they sometimes led to the demolition of historic buildings and encouraged sprawling development. New estates, built in a modernist, utilitarian style that subsequent decades have deemed ugly, tower blocks of flats (made possible by advances in building techniques), square box homes, fly-overs and concrete are the legacy of the car culture of the 1960s.

The growth of cars and road travel had the same effect on the railways as the growth of television had on the cinema. British Rail had still been making a profit at the beginning of the 1950s but by 1960 it faced a £68 million loss and by 1962 this had increased to £104 million. In 1961, Dr Richard Beeching (one of the new type of 'scientific-industrialists') was appointed as Chairman of the British Transport Commission and, faced with this grim reality, he made a series of drastic proposals.

Fig. 7 *The camper van was marketed as an opportunity for families to enjoy a flexible and individual style of holiday*

> Neither modernisation nor more economical working can make the railways viable in their existing form. A reshaping of the whole pattern of business is necessary as well. Now, after the post-war growth of competition from road transport, it is no longer socially necessary for the railways to provide such a major part of the total variety of internal transport services as they did in the past, and it is certainly not possible for them to operate profitably if they do so.

4   *From the foreword to the Beeching Report*

Activity

Thinking point

'Beeching's Axe' roused fierce controversy at the time and has done so ever since. Were Beeching's proposals justified? Are our judgements coloured by our present-day views on travel and the environment?

Beeching's recommendations were for:

- the closure of all branch lines
- the closure of 2,359 local stations
- the dismantling of 8,000 km (5,000 miles) of track to reduce the network from 21,000 km (13,000 miles) to 13,000 km (8,000 miles)
- the loss of 160,000 jobs over seven years.

The scheme went ahead in 1963 despite fierce public opposition, although the reduction in track stopped at 18,000 km.

There were other effects too. The car was a very personal means of travel. Like the television, it encouraged individuals and families to shun communal activities and transport by bus and train in favour of private trips and family outings. Cars were not only used for day trips but also for touring holidays (incidentally opening up formerly quiet and exclusive areas like Devon and Cornwall). Caravaning became a popular spin-off and the Caravan Club's membership figures doubled over the decade. They acquired 200 designated sites, mainly along Britain's coasts, and by 1970 caravans represented around a fifth of all holiday accommodation.

■ **Exploring the detail**

Car safety

There were neither speed limits on country roads before 1967 nor seat belts, so escalating traffic led to some frightening accidents. Double white lines had been introduced to limit overtaking in dangerous places but, when Barbara Castle became Minister of Transport in 1965, 8000 people a year were being killed on the roads. Despite outcries against infringement of personal liberty, the Road Safety Act 1967 introduced:

■ a penalty of a year's disqualification for motorists found guilty of drunken driving through breathalyser tests

■ a maximum speed limit of 70 mph

■ compulsory seat belts in all new cars.

■ **Exploring the detail**

Butlins holiday camps

Billy Butlin opened his first holiday camp at Skegness in 1936. He offered a week's holiday, at between 35 shillings to £3 a week according to the time of year, with three meals a day and free entertainment. The camps were an immediate success. People flocked to enjoy an inclusive holiday with activities for young and old organised by the Redcoats who amused campers with their variety acts and silly competitions.

Weekly trips to an out-of-town supermarket, with its discounts, own brands and plentiful parking increasingly became a way of life. There had been only about 300 supermarkets in Britain in 1958, but by 1972 there were about 5,000, while 60,000 smaller grocers had been forced to close. Supermarket shopping was not ubiquitous in the 1960s – a survey found that over half of all households still shopped on four days a week and some of the major supermarkets closed on Mondays (as well as Sundays) – but, thanks to the car, shopping styles were beginning to change.

Suburban living and commuting also received a boost. Work and home became more distinct and, for example, only 42 per cent of those who worked in Newcastle in 1971 lived in the city; most of the remainder commuted by car. Even education was affected as it became possible to transport children beyond the local area to a 'better' school. Indeed, there were few walks of life in which the possession of a car did not make a difference. A lack of personal mobility increasingly became a symbol of the 'underclass'.

So, whilst increased car ownership brought traffic jams, accidents and personal isolation, it also opened up new social and career possibilities, widened horizons and allowed people to escape the claustrophobic confines of their own community.

■ Mass tourism

The 1960s saw leisure travel turn into mass tourism as the number of holidays (stays of more than three days at a tourist destination) increased.

Table 1 *Holidays, 1951–73*

	1951	1961	1971	1973
Holidays in total	27 million	34 million	41 million	49 million
Holidays abroad	2 million	4 million	7 million	8 million

Many holidaymakers still opted for traditional British seaside resorts or holiday camps with built-in entertainment, such as those run by Butlins. British resorts could be reached by car, but their image suffered a blow when reports of contaminated water and beaches appeared in the press. At Blackpool, for example, it was reported that millions of tonnes of raw sewage were being pumped into the harbour and swept back on to the beach by the tide.

Holiday providers were forced to adapt to retain custom in the face of change. Landladies renamed their 'boarding houses' (which were often run according to house rules) 'guest houses' in an attempt to appear more welcoming. Butlins tried advertising for the growing teenage market, only to find the camps branded as dens of vice and vandalism, which drove families away. Butlins had to ban single teenagers in 1968, but the damage had been done and the aspiring adult market found alternatives elsewhere.

Coach companies blossomed, particularly those offering tours for the older holidaymaker, and the luxury cruise had not yet quite had its day. The world's largest passenger ship, Cunard's *Queen Elizabeth II*, made its maiden voyage to New York in 1969. However, it was passenger air travel overseas and the arrival of the cheap package trip at the end of the decade that really brought about a breakthrough in the concept of the British holiday. In 1960, British Overseas Airways Corporation

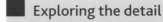

(BOAC) inaugurated its first regular Boeing 707 service between London and New York, while Britannia Airways was founded in 1964 to serve holidaymakers wishing to fly to Spain, the Canary Islands, Malta, Bulgaria and North Africa. Competition that would help lower the price of flights and permit mass travel was, however, restricted until 1971 by the International Air Transport Association. Charter flights could operate at a discount, but only if passengers had six months' membership of a group whose main purpose was not travel. This encouraged bogus societies, but it did not prevent entrepreneurs like Freddie Laker from exploiting the potential holiday market.

General Franco, the Spanish leader, was as eager to encourage overseas tourists as they were to travel. He sought foreign currency, while they sought sea and sun and he encouraged the development of the Balearic Islands as well as the south and eastern coasts of Spain (the Costa Brava and the Costa del Sol) as tourist resorts. Benidorm, a tiny village in Valencia with fewer than 3,000 inhabitants in 1957, for example, was transformed by new buildings, hotels and cinemas in the late 1960s to become a Mecca for British and German travellers. With two weeks in Spain costing as little as £20, it is not surprising that 30 per cent of all overseas package holidays were taken there.

Exploring the detail

Entrepreneurship – Freddie Laker

Freddie Laker is a striking example of 1960s entrepreneurship. He was the son of a scrap dealer and had once been bottom of his class at school. Nevertheless, with just £240 capital, he founded a business dealing in aircraft spare parts and in 1948 at the age of 26 persuaded a Scottish banker to help him buy 12 converted Halifax bombers, which he used to aid the Berlin airlift. He continued to deal in army surplus planes and had made enough money by 1965 to found Laker Airways. At first he operated charter flights but, once the ruling on air fare competition was overturned, his business expanded enormously.

Fig. 8 *The package holiday brought a chance to escape to the sun – but was it all gain?*

Figures for the issue of new passports (580,000 in 1956, 980,000 in 1966) are another measure of the growing popularity of overseas travel, but for most of the 1960s holidays abroad were still largely the preserve of the middle classes. The costs of air travel and government restrictions on the amount of money that could be taken abroad from 1966 (then £50) no doubt hindered developments. The package deals were still in their infancy by the end of the 1960s, although they had grown from under 4 per cent of total holidays in 1966 to 8.4 per cent in 1971. Certainly by the early 1970s a cheap trip to the sun was a possibility for the affluent worker.

Activity

Talking point

Talk to older friends and family who lived through the 1960s about the types of holiday they enjoyed at that time. To what extent were their experiences different from your own holidays?

The impact of mass tourism

Travel abroad did not make the average Briton immediately 'European' in outlook. Indeed, many travel writers have noted with some derision that many a British holidaymaker liked either to take his own provisions with him or to go to a destination where 'fish and chips' were sold. However, mass tourism did begin to inject some continental flavour into British tastes, even if it was only among the better-off middle classes. Wine became more popular and annual wine consumption doubled between 1960 and 1970. Coffee, too, began to make inroads on the traditional British tea-drinking and Nescafé enjoyed good sales. Lager, which had accounted for only 3 per cent of beer sales at the beginning of the 1960s, grew in popularity, while some continental foods such as pasta, aubergines, green peppers, courgettes, avocados, herbs and garlic appeared in shops. Cookbooks like Elizabeth David's *French Provincial Cooking* (1960) were widely bought and read and quiche lorraine and coq au vin enjoyed a vogue. In 1964, the first of Terence Conran's Habitat shops opened, offering a new continental style of furnishing and household accessories, while on high streets, French, Italian and Greek restaurants appeared.

Foreign travel was eventually to have wider cultural implications, but many of these still lay in the future. For those who chose to let it, travel opened horizons and broadened the mind. Yet for those whose ambitions were limited to a week around a pool in Benidorm, overseas travel had no more of an impact than the simple joy of doing nothing!

■ Key profile

Elizabeth David

Elizabeth David (1913–92) developed a taste for 'foreign' cuisine while living in France. She believed that food and cooking were a way of life and good, simple, natural ingredients were always best. She wrote *Mediterranean Food* in 1950 (when rationing was still in force), *French Country Cooking* in 1951, *Italian Food* in 1954 and *Summer Cooking* in 1955. *French Provincial Cooking* followed in 1960 and by 1964 all five books were available as Penguin paperbacks. By then, the ingredients were more widely available. A combination of her own enthusiasm and style of writing and the growing experience of foreign travel ensured the books' success.

Learning outcomes

In this section you have examined some of the ingredients that helped create the social and cultural changes of the 1960s. You have seen how a mixture of greater affluence and the wider availability of goods and services, brought about by scientific and technological change, combined to offer new opportunities and to widen the world in which people lived. The expansion of mass communications and changes in patterns of leisure and leisure activities provided those living through the 1960s with a host of new experiences, which encouraged a questioning of much that had long been regarded as 'established' in Britain. In the next section, you will see how that questioning attitude brought changes in culture and society.

AQA Examination-style questions

(a) Explain why the number of holidays taken
abroad increased during the 1960s. *(12 marks)*

AQA Examiner's tip — Start by making a list of ideas. You will probably want to include money, technology, leisure time and advertising, as well as others. Before you start to write, think about which you consider the main reason to emphasise. Try to show your factors interlink and provide a relevant and supported conclusion.

(b) 'During the 1960s, leisure activities became
more private and individualistic.' Explain why
you agree or disagree with this statement. *(24 marks)*

AQA Examiner's tip — First, list the activities that support the quotation, e.g. you might compare 1960s TV with 1950s cinema or 1960s cars with trains. Then list those that disagree, e.g. communal caravanning/Butlins or a package holiday. Decide your position and argue throughout your answer. Don't forget to mention the points on the other side though – just show how they are less convincing than your own view.

In this chapter you will learn about:

■ why the 1960s are referred to as the 'decade of youth'

■ what is meant by the 'youth culture' of the 1960s and its impact

■ what new fashion trends developed and what these changes meant

■ how popular music changed and its relevance.

On 30 October 1965, Jean Shrimpton, the young British supermodel, appeared on Derby Day, during Melbourne Cup week in Australia, in a tiny white shift dress that ended high above her knees. She wore her hair loose with no hat, no stockings and no gloves. The conservative Australian racegoers were shocked but the British press loved the image and 'the Shrimp' appeared on the front page of almost every British newspaper the next day. Young, liberated and scornful of convention, Shrimpton epitomised the 1960s as the 'decade of youth'.

Fig. 1 _Jean Shrimpton, 1965_

■ The emergence of youth culture

By the end of the 1950s, the generation born in the baby boom that followed the end of the Second World War was reaching its teenage years. These youngsters were too young to remember the depression of the 1930s or the shortages and deprivations of the war years through which their parents had lived. Instead, they had been brought up in a seemingly prosperous and stable country. The post-war improvements in medical care, welfare, food and housing meant that most young people were healthier than ever before. Family sizes had fallen and the increase in real wages meant that many could enjoy an upbringing that was far removed from that of just a generation earlier.

Those born into homes that had benefited from the 1950s affluence could expect a life of reasonable comfort and, thanks to new domestic labour-saving devices, parents were less inclined to require their children to help with family chores in their spare time. It was not difficult for young people to supplement their pocket money with Saturday or part-time jobs and, for the majority that left school at 15 years, there were plentiful job opportunities. Unskilled and semi-skilled labour was in demand and the hourly pay rates for young workers had grown faster than those for adults.

■ Cross-reference

The new **labour-saving devices** are discussed in Chapter 3.

Whereas in past generations, working-class youngsters continuing to live at home had been expected to hand over their earnings to their parents and so shoulder their share of the family expenditure, the rising affluence of the late 1950s had helped change attitudes. More young wage-earners were continuing to live with their parents and enjoy a life with no fixed financial commitments. Young men did not even need to leave to perform their National Service after November 1960.

> Every week I'd buy at least two or three singles [pop records]. I had so much money to spend, it's unbelievable looking back. There were so many well-paid jobs for teenagers connected with the car industry. I'd spend £10 every weekend on myself, on clothes, on going out and most of all on music.

1   *From a report by a young man living in Coventry in the early 1960s*

Middle-class youngsters usually stayed at school until they were 16 and increasing numbers continued their education at universities or in other further education institutes after this. These young people often got the best of both worlds; home comforts and parental support followed by student independence with fees paid for by the State and generous maintenance grants. Between 1961 and 1969, the number of students in full-time further education in the UK almost doubled from 200,000 to 390,000.

For the first time in history, therefore, young people, who accounted for a larger proportion of the population than ever before, had spare cash to spend on themselves. With fewer commitments, they might even be comparatively better off than their parents. The new name 'teenagers' was an acknowledgement of the position of youth as a potent new force in society.

> Vernon was one of the generations that grew up before teenagers existed. In poor Vernon's era there just weren't any. Can you believe it? In those days, it seems, you were just an overgrown boy, or an undergrown man. Life didn't seem to cater for anything else in between.

2   *From a novel by Colin MacInnes, **Absolute Beginners**, 1959*

The existence of a new type of 'affluent teenager' was confirmed by the research of Mark Abrams who looked at young people's spending patterns in 1959 and 1961. He showed how teenagers had prospered relative to adults and calculated that in 1959 young people had around £830 million to spend. This amounted to an average of £8 a week. According to his surveys, teenagers spent just under half their total income on entertainment. They were responsible for a third of all cinema admissions and provided 40 per cent of the market for records and record players. Other popular youth purchases included a third of all bicycles and motorbikes and nearly a third of all cosmetics.

> Teenagers were a class in themselves whose vibrant, leisure-orientated lifestyle seemed to offer a foretaste of the kind of prosperity that would soon be within everyone's grasp. The newly affluent young consumers patronised a leisure market of unprecedented scale. The range of products geared to this growing market was literally boundless; consumer industries interacting with and reinforcing one another as they sought to cash in on youth spending.

3   *Bill Osgerby, 'The Teenage Revolution', 1998*

Exploring the detail

National Service

This was introduced under the National Service Act 1947. All 18-year-old men were required to spend 18 months – and from 1950 two years – in the armed forces followed by four years in the reserves. Although it was abolished in the defence cuts of 1960, the last National Service conscripts were not discharged until 1963.

Cross-reference

Mark Abrams's research is also discussed on pages 16–17 and 30.

Activity

Revision exercise

The youth 'leisure market' was not only the product of the increased affluence of the young, it also reflected the changes in technology and the growth of leisure time noted in Chapters 3, 4 and 5.

a   Copy Figure 2 to show the various influences that created the 'decade of youth'. Add a few bullet points below each label to explain the influences on young people.

b   Look at your diagram. Write a paragraph to explain which influence on young people you believe to have been of greatest importance in creating a new type of 'youth'.

Fig. 2 *Factors influencing the 'decade of youth'*

Labels: Changes in upbringing · Earning potential · Greater leisure time · Technological change · Influence of education · Influence of the media

The new youth culture

Fig. 3 *Jackie was a favourite girls' magazine during the 1960s and was still popular in 1975*

A gap between the 1960s youth and their parents was marked by the development of new values, styles and ways of behaviour among young people. These contributed to a distinctive 'youth culture' that revolved around the popular music that young people liked to listen to and the pop idols whose image they liked to imitate. Linked to this was a preoccupation with 'style'. Certain types of clothing, hair and fashion accessories became essential (for both sexes) and fashion models achieved new cult status. Youth culture was also about sex – at least to the extent that the fashion and music of the young suggested a liberated sexual style – but it was only towards the end of the decade that it came to embrace drugs and politics, and these were never more than minority interests. Essentially, youth culture was about being different, rebelling against the past and appearing 'swinging' and 'with it'.

This new youth culture was spread by the media. Newspapers included articles on pop music and teen fashions, published chart lists and interviewed 'celebrities'. New female teen magazines sprang up, such as *Honey* (1960), *Jackie* and *Fabulous* (1964), and radio and TV adapted to and extolled youthful themes. Although youth culture was more about shared generational values than wealth and status, it was helpful to have money. Money gave young people a greater degree of independence, a means of asserting themselves and, in turn, a greater degree of confidence in challenging the world around them.

Kids discovered that for the first time since centuries of kingdom-come, they'd money, which had always been denied to us at the best times in life to use it, namely, when you're young and strong. We found no one could sit on our faces anymore because we'd loot to spend at last, and the world was to be 'our world'.

| **4** | *Colin MacInnes*, **Absolute Beginners**, 1959 |

Cross-reference

Examples of the **radicalisation of youth** are found in Chapter 7.

The coincidence of increased living standards, the spread of education and the growth of leisure time helped to create a youth generation that was more inclined to question and more ready to assert its right to choose. Mods and rockers fought on the beaches, hippies 'dropped out' and university students showed their collective strength through marches, sit-ins and demonstrations about political issues. However, such actions were not the typical behaviour of British youth in the 1960s. Far more comon were clashes over fashion, musical tastes and moral standards with parents whose patterns of behaviour had been moulded by the wartime years of austerity. Teenage boys, for example, might show their rebellious tendencies by growing their hair long (no National Service meant no need for a military crew cut), while the girls horrified their mothers by walking out in ever shorter mini-skirts. The degree of daring might vary but, in a society bombarded by images of youthful exuberance, it was hard for young people not to get caught up in the trends.

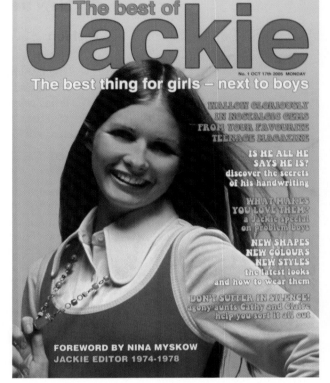

It was such a defining decade. Youngsters in the Sixties were embracing new freedoms – the right to enjoy oneself, the right to an independent mind, the right to promiscuity and the right to 'alter your mind' with illegal substances.

| **5** | *S. Hattenstone*, **The Best of Times**, 2006 |

Fig. 4 *Nostalgia Jackie magazine. What can we learn from Figures 3 and 4 about the interests of teenage girls in the 1960s?*

Religious teachings and 'unwritten' rules, such as that which taught that sex before marriage was wrong, were also being questioned. With earlier physical maturation as a result of healthier lifestyles and better methods of contraception available, the 'right to enjoy oneself' meant a more liberal attitude to sexual relations. The media and consumer industry tried to appeal to youth through an emphasis on sex, while changes in the law, for example permitting abortion and homosexuality, encouraged (and reflected) a further questioning of norms. For some youngsters there were other new experiences. Cannabis was popularised by cult groups like the Beatles and the Rolling Stones, and smoking 'dope' enjoyed a vogue particularly among students in the later 1960s.

Such behaviour caused a good deal of concern among the older generation and there was much discussion of the nation's moral decline. Nevertheless, the extent of teenage promiscuity and drug-taking must be kept in proportion. The picture portrayed in the media represented the extremes

Cross-reference

You will find further details on the development of **contraception** on pages 36–7 and 88–90 and the laws on **abortion** and **homosexuality** and the extent of the **'permissive society'** on pages 88–92.

Activity

Source analysis

Use Sources 1, 3, 4 and 5 and your own knowledge. How important was the growth of affluence in the emergence of a distinctive 1960s youth culture?

more often than the mainstream. Alcohol, tobacco and caffeine were more usual stimulants than LSD and, according to a survey in 1969, young people spent more time listening to music in their bedrooms than at youth clubs or rock festivals. Michael Schofield's study of over 2,000 teenagers in 1965 found that most were still virgins at 19, while Pearl Jephott's survey of Glaswegian youth in 1964–6 reported on boys who liked to play football and girls who spent their time visiting friends. Such activities are hardly indicative of a massive degeneration in the moral standards of the young.

New trends in fashion and popular music

Fashion

> The fashion revolution has been the most significant influence on the mood and ways of the younger generation in Britain in the last decade. It has seized the threads of all contemporary cults and has woven them together in a strand that binds all the younger generation with a new sense of identity and vitality.

6 *Jonathan Aitken, journalist, writing in the 1970s*

Clothing designers, manufacturers and retailers in the 1960s were quick to exploit the lucrative 'teenage' market. By 1967, 50 per cent of women's clothes manufactured in Britain were sold to people in the 15–19 years age group. The fashion trends often began with celebrities, models and pop stars and new styles were disseminated at a speed previously unknown. By the mid-1960s, the fashion industry employed 30,000 people and there were *around* 2,000 boutiques in London alone. The rapidity with which looks changed was in itself a challenge to convention. There was no longer any point in buying (or making) clothes designed to last. Fashion in the 1960s was literally 'up to the minute'; to be enjoyed then disposed of.

So, for a short while in the 1960s, London was the capital of the fashion world. It produced able, young designers who responded to demand and produced fashions that rejected formality and ignored class status. Traditional rules were abandoned. It became acceptable to wear the same outfit to work and for the evening. Women might equally well appear in trousers, as a skirt, and for men velvets, satins and brightly-coloured fabrics could be sported in a way undreamed of by the past generation. As the decade progressed, these trends became more extreme and the distinction traditionally made between clothing made specifically for men and that for women became less obvious. Changing fashions, in their

Fig. 5 *1960s fashion*

own way, thus helped override, or at least mask, some of the old social divisions, both between sexes and between classes.

Key profile

Mary Quant

Mary Quant (born 1934) and her husband Alexander Plunkett Greene opened a boutique called Bazaar in King's Road, Chelsea in 1955, selling innovative handmade clothes. The shop was an immediate success and took five times its expected earnings in its first week. A second boutique, designed by Terence Conran, opened in Knightsbridge in 1957 and by 1961 the business had become a limited company. By 1966, Quant was producing over 500 designs a year and her companies had an income of more than £6 million.

Barbara Hulanicki

In 1964, Barbara Hulanicki (born 1936) opened a boutique called Biba in Kensington. She offered glamorous clothes at cheap prices, with a throw-away-and-buy-another philosophy. The clothes were made in London's East End and designs changed every week. Celebrities jostled with schoolgirls to snap up the latest offerings and Biba became a tourist attraction in its own right. In 1969, it moved to larger premises but it overstretched itself and was forced to close in 1975.

Laura Ashley

In the late 1960s the Welsh designer Laura Ashley (1925–85) won a following with her 'new-style' traditional clothes, which emphasised Victoriana, Edwardian Lady and 'Englishness'. She became known for her long-skirted milkmaid dresses in flower-print calico and her pinafores worn with frilly blouses. In the next decade, the Ashleys expanded into home furnishing and by 1980 they had 5,000 retail outlets throughout the world.

The changes in fashion were the product of a variety of factors, but they certainly reflected some of the wider changes of the 1960s that are explored elsewhere in this book:

- The development of the affluent society.
- The growth of a consumer culture.
- The increasing assertiveness of teenagers.
- The changing role of women.
- The growing frankness about sex and lack of sexual inhibition.
- The development of technology and science.

Figure 6 on pages 62–3 gives some idea of these changing fashions.

Key profile

Twiggy

Twiggy (born 1949) was born   as Lesley Hornby. She was an ordinary fashion-conscious teenage girl from a working-class background in Neasden when, in 1965, she started dating Justin de Villeneuve. One of Justin's friends – a fashion photographer – suggested she tried some modelling. She was small and skinny, but she had distinctive looks, and once given a new haircut at an exclusive Mayfair salon, her big eyes and slender neck were shown off to advantage. With her waif-like figure, boyish hair cut and striking eye lashes, Lesley, now renamed 'Twiggy', was propelled to supermodel fame and created an image that came to epitomise the era.

Cross-reference

Mods and **rockers** are discussed on page 69.

Fig. 6 *1960s fashion*

End of the 1950s/early 1960s

The American teddy boy/beatnik look gave way in the early 1960s to a new 'British' style – divided between the 'mod' look – the scooter owners – (short jackets and drainpipe trousers; polo shirts or turtle neck sweaters; suede shoes or boots) based on a fairly conservative suit and the motorcycle-owning rockers (studded leather jackets; jeans; winkle-picker shoes). These were primarily masculine fashions. Mod girls aimed for a neat 'Italian' look and hemlines began to creep up while Rocker girls adopted the 'leathers' (skirts and tight trousers) to look like their boyfriends.

Mid 1960s

Girls: the mini skirt appeared and rose from just above the knee to mid thigh by 1967. Girls wore childlike pared down garments (particularly pinafores) with short/mini skirts, lacey tights or knee-high socks, T-bar shoes, mid-calf boots (later to reach the knees or even thighs) – some in white waterproof plastic. They copied geometric haircuts of Vidal Sassoon (1966) with deep symmetric or asymmetric fringes or had long straight hair hung below the shoulders. Pale-faced make-up with big eyes (eye liner; mascara; false eyelashes) and pale lips were the fashion.

Boys: the rocker style continued and some (e.g. the Rolling Stones) deliberately cultivated unconventional scruffy clothing. However, a more important development was the refinement of the Mod style with tighter fitting suits and Chelsea boots. From 1963 'Beatle jackets' worn with tight-fitting trousers became popular. Coloured suits started to appear and men adopted a far more individualistic style of dress.

Late 1960s

Boys: 'anything goes' with psychedelic imagery (gleaned from the use of hallucinogenic drugs), effeminate military-style jackets worn in a 'thrown together' style. Frilled dress shirts, rainbow coloured velvet jeans, hip-hugging trousers and unisex kaftans.

Girls: a variety of skirt lengths from the very skimpy mini to the calf length 'midi' and full length 'maxi'. Biba (which had opened in 1964) and Laura Ashley encouraged a return to a more romantic past with flowing skirts that went to the ground. Hair became more elaborately styled and the frizzy 'Afro' was encouraged by the 'Black is beautiful' movement.

Bovver boys or skinheads, successors to the rockers, had shaven heads, braces and skinny jeans and thick soled boots.

The hippy movement from America also began to infiltrate the British scene from 1967 with clothes that reflected the culture of India or Afghanistan – coloured cottons, shawls, ponchos, kaftans, Afghan coats and second-hand and Indian accessories. Long hair, beads, bare feet (or sandals) and bell bottoms were popular for both sexes, while men sported eastern style tunics with embroidered waistcoats and denims or velvet trousers.

> ■ **Activity**
>
> ### Divide into groups
>
> Each should choose a Sixties designer, model or fashion style to research. Prepare a colourful side presentation for the rest of the class and create a poster for a classroom display on 'Sixties fashion'.

Early 1970s

Girls: full length skirts, shawls and capes coexisted with a more scruffy 'trouser' image. A minuscule 'hot pants' fashion, higher heels and platform soles come into vogue.

I was in the salon for about seven hours and they were cutting and colouring my hair. It was all extremely exciting for me … I went from this mouse-like brown to the colour which I have kept now.

I got on the bus and went to meet this really sweet, lovely man who was to take my photos. I mean I'd never been in front of a camera before! [The hairdresser] hung them up in his salon and Deidre McSharry of the *Daily Express* saw them and said 'Who is this girl?' Anyway she phoned us up and we went along to her office and she wrote this big article on me which appeared in the *Daily Express* declaring me the new 'Face Of' 66 and it all happened from there really!

7 *From Twiggy Laws on, on how her image was created*

Fig. 7 The 'little girl look' with Twiggy, the top 1960s model, on the right

Questions

1 In Source 8, Quant suggests her clothes permitted physical freedom. Did they express any other types of freedom too?

2 Can you explain why Quant's clothes were such a success?

Exploring the detail

The technology behind the fashions of the 1960s

New synthetic fabrics made cheap and colourful clothes possible. Nylon (first branded in 1938), Terylene and Crimplene were tough, hard wearing and easy to dye. Fine and patterned nylon (e.g. with Mary Quant's daisy logo) was used for tights. Clothes made from polyester and acrylic (branded as Dacron, Orlon, Lycra and Antron) held their shape, were crease-resistant and easy to dry. There were experiments with nylon-reinforced paper underwear, but this never really caught on. PVC (polyvinyl chloride) dyed well and was a popular alternative to leather, while supple Corfam was used for boots.

Did you know?

Swinging London

'Swinging London' was the name given to the city in the American *Time* magazine in 1966. Thanks to its status as the home of many new trends – clothing, music, photography, modelling, advertising and even mass-market magazines– London changed its image. At its heart was Carnaby Street where the 'Swinging London' style was for sale. Popular shops included 'Mr Fish', 'I was Lord Kitchener's Valet' and 'Granny Takes a Trip'.

The first generation of 1960s fashion designers, led by Quant, helped create the 'minimalist' look – clothes that were childlike and easy to wear, yet daring, rebellious and provocative. Quant's designs were worn by models like Twiggy, with pale faces and big staring eyes, suggesting childish innocence.

Fashion and science were entwined in the use of white plastic for boots and brightly-coloured PVC for raincoats and skirts (from 1965). Strong geometric shapes were popular, and this included the Mary Quant 'bob', popularised by Vidal Sassoon; a hairstyle that was short at the back and long at the sides – with no fuss or ornamentation.

> I wanted clothes that were for life, for real people, for being young and alive in. Clothes to move and run and dance in. Clothes that could be put on first thing in the morning and still feel right at midnight; clothes that go happily to the office and equally happily out to dinner. I just happened to start when that something in the air was coming to the boil. The clothes I made happened to fit in exactly with the teenage trend, with pop records and expresso bars and jazz clubs.

8   *Mary Quant reminisces*

The second wave of designers included John Bates (who designed the tight-fitting leather trousers worn by Diana Rigg in the TV series, *The Avengers*), Ossie Clark of Quorum, Barbara Hulanicki of Biba and Marion Foale and Sally Tuffin who founded a studio in London's Carnaby Street. They created a range of bright, fun dresses, skirts and tops, and were among the first to experiment with making women's trousers into flattering, sexy garments. Their patronage of what was already developing as the epicentre of fashion for the young, helped create the Carnaby Street image as the heart of 'Swinging London'.

John Stephen was the original 'King of Carnaby Street'. He designed cheap but flamboyant clothes for men, and was famous for his cravats, tight red corduroy trousers and fitted black shirts. The cheap and disposable Carnaby Street fashion soon became more coveted than expensive wear bought in traditional department stores.

> On any twilight evening when the day's work is done, Carnaby Street pulses with slender young men in black tight pants that fit on the hips like ski-pants, their tulip-like girlfriends on their arms, peering into the garishly lit windows at the burgundy coloured suede jackets with slanted, pleated pockets – very hot stuff with the mods right now. The impact of Carnaby Street is becoming world wide. Tony Curtis wears Carnaby Street clothes. So do Peter Sellers and the Beatles. This is Swinging London.

9   *From an article 'London, the Most Exciting City in the World',*
*by John Crosby in **Weekend Telegraph**, 16 April 1965*

Of course the impact of 'Swinging London' and the new fashion trends emanating from the capital were not universal, as Source 10 suggests:

> During the mid-sixties I was working as a filleter's labourer in a fish factory in Grimsby. When I came down to London in 1968, it might have been swinging, but living in cheap bedsits with building workers and kitchen porters for neighbours, I hardly noticed.

10   *From Robert Murphy (historian)*

Studying changes in fashion may appear frivolous, but it can teach a good deal because it reflected some of the changing attitudes and values of the decade. It has even been suggested that women's hemlines were a barometer of contemporary feeling – when optimism was at its highest, so were the hemlines, when it subsided amidst concern for the future towards the end of the decade, the hemlines descended.

Activity

Source analysis

1. Explain how far the views in Source 10 differ from those in Source 9 in relation to contemporary attitudes to Swinging London.

2. Re-read the sources in this section. Using these sources and your own knowledge, how far did changing fashions reflect a new 'youth culture'?

Popular music

Popular music was another means by which the young forged a separate identity. Recently developed transistor radios offered a cheap and portable means of keeping up to date with the latest releases. Young people could enjoy almost continuous 'pop' by tuning into one of the offshore radio stations or, from 1967, BBC Radio One. Television responded to demand with programmes like *Ready Steady Go!* (ITV 1963) and *Top of the Pops* (BBC 1964), which helped spread the latest trends in music, dance, jargon, attitude and dress. Cheap plastic record players, records and record shops, and, for some, discotheques, live concerts and festivals, made music accessible to all and any aspiring teenage boutique ensured a background diet of popular hits made shopping go with a 'swing'.

It was really the American Elvis Presley who heralded the arrival of a new type of youth music in the mid-1950s. With his tight trousers and gyrating pelvis, the link he established between music, fashion and sex shocked the older generation as much as it delighted the younger one. Britain's first direct encounter with this new style of music came in 1956 when Bill Hayley's film *Rock Around the Clock* was first shown in British cinemas. It caused an outcry and some towns even banned it for its incitement to rowdy behaviour.

It did not take long before British **skiffle groups** began exploring this new rock style and from these emerged the British pop groups of the 1960s. The major exponents of the new style were often art college students – men like John Lennon (Liverpool – the Beatles); Ray Davies (Hornsey – the Kinks); Peter Townshend (Ealing – the Who); Keith Richards (Sidcup – the Rolling Stones). Since art colleges were places where reasonably bright and creative individuals went in the days before the expansion of university education, the connection is not too surprising.

The advance of 1960s pop was also dependent on technological change, including improvements in the production of 45 rpm 7 inch 'singles', which lowered prices and the advent of cheap record players and radios. Loud electric guitars (first invented in 1948) and more sophisticated microphones, stereo sound from 1966, and developments in recording and playback techniques all encouraged experimentation.

Money and management were needed too. Recording companies, concert promoters and group managers, like Brian Epstein who managed the

Activity

'Fashions changed in the 1960s simply because young people had more money to spend.' Explain why you agree or disagree with this view.

Key term

Skiffle groups: groups that used homemade instruments like a washboard and tea-chest bass to accompany performances of hybrid music – folk, country, jazz and pop. They flourished in coffee bars and jazz clubs in the 1950s and some, such as the Quarrymen (which became the Beatles) and the Railroaders (which became the Shadows) evolved into 1960s pop groups.

Fig. 8 *A discotheque in the 1960s*

Cross-reference

Offshore radio stations and their replacement by Radio One are discussed on pages 43–4.

Beatles, realised there was money to be made from the 1960s youth. Television, films and magazines also played a part and they helped turn pop into a cult. Sometimes there was conflict between the marketeers and the performers, whose music could lose authenticity in the drive for sales, but it was the sales that made the stars. According to Andrew Marr (Source 11):

> It was classic, capitalist, market-driven competition, with profits and status dependent on beating the rest, and measured by sales week after week. Yet pop music was from below or it was nothing. A band's success was based on its members' skills but also on their claim to be kids from the streets whose anger, enthusiasm, boredom and wit reflected the actual Britain all round them; the lives of the people who would save up and buy their songs.

11   *Andrew Marr, **A History of Modern Britain**, 2007*

Fig. 9 *The 'mop-topped' Beatles in the early 1960s. From left to right: John Lennon, George Harrison, Paul McCartney and Ringo Starr*

However, the dominance of British pop in the 1960s would never have been possible without talented stars. The songwriters Lennon/McCartney and the Beatles were the biggest success story. The only group to rival them in fame was the Rolling Stones, whose 'bad boy' rocker image distinguished them from the mod-style suited, clean-cut and 'mop-topped' Beatles of the earlier 1960s. The Jagger/Richards partnership was equally, if not more, innovative, and their aggressive anti-establishment stance ensured a world market for their songs. British hits dominated the charts on both sides of the Atlantic. In May 1965, British recordings held 9 of the top 10 places in the US singles chart, while the British charts almost exclusively featured home-grown groups and singers.

■ A closer look

1960s pop icons

The early 1960s were dominated by singers like Tommy Steele, Cliff Richards, Billy Fury, the Shadows and the Tornadoes. However, it was the emergence of the new-scene guitar groups, the 'Merseybeat pop' epitomised by the Beatles (first record release October 1962) and the 'blues-rock' of the Rolling Stones (first release December 1963), which epitomised the new pop scene. The pioneers of the new-style music included groups such as Gerry and the Pacemakers, Freddie and the Dreamers, Brian Poole and the Tremeloes, the Dave Clark Five, the Who, the Kinks and the Small Faces. Famous female artists included Cilla Black, Helen Shapiro, Dusty Springfield, Sandie Shaw and Lulu.

The Beatles

The Beatles – John Lennon, Paul McCartney, George Harrison and, from 1962, Ringo Starr – grew out of Lennon's skiffle group, the Quarrymen, formed 1956. In 1962, they recorded *Love Me Do*, which reached the top 20, and more than 40 different singles, albums and EPs subsequently reached number one. Harold Wilson presented them with Variety Club awards in 1964 and they received OBEs in 1965. Their visit to the USA in 1964 established them as artists of world renown, and by 1985 they had sold over 1 billion discs and tapes worldwide. They explored a variety of different musical styles. Although their early lyrics were of the boy/girl type (e.g. *I wanna hold your hand*), they went on to record the more perplexing *Penny Lane* and *Lucy in the Sky with Diamonds* – with its explicit link to LSD. In the late 1960s they adopted psychedelic clothing, took drugs and deliberately set about challenging the world around them, as evidenced in the *Sergeant Pepper* album. Their association with alternative culture and the Indian guru, the Maharishi, eventually led to the break-up of the group.

The Rolling Stones

The Rolling Stones were formed in London in 1962, when schoolmates Mick Jagger, formerly a student at the London School of Economics (LSE), and art-college educated Keith Richards met Brian Jones. Bill Wyman and Charlie Watts joined later. They soon gained a reputation for frantic, highly energetic songs and a charged stage presence. By being deliberately unkempt and surly in appearance, swearing on stage, taking drugs and, at least by reputation, behaving in a promiscuous way, they became synonymous with the rebellious spirit of the 1960s. The *News of the World* targeted them and, in 1967, Richards was given a year's sentence for possessing cannabis and Jagger four months for amphetamine tablets. Towards the later 1960s, the Stones' musical style changed and disputes between members and the death of Brian Jones, found dead at the bottom of his swimming pool in 1968, ended one era of the band's history.

Activity

Thinking point

Try to get hold of some of the records by the pop stars that have been mentioned and listen carefully to the lyrics. What can this type of music tell us about the 1960s?

Of course, not everyone listened to pop. Despite the fame of *the* pop groups and the vitality of the singing, the most popular album in 1960 was *The Sound of Music* soundtrack and in 1963 it was 'The Black and White Minstrel Show' (mainly traditional ballads). In 1965, at the height of the 1960s pop scene, the bestsellers of the year were *Tears,* a ballad sung by Ken Dodd, and *The Carnival is Over* by the Australian folk group the Seekers. Even in 1967, the 'summer of love', Engelbert Humperdinck's traditional *Release me* beat the Beatles' *Strawberry Fields/Penny Lane* to the top of the hit parade. Obviously, some of these sales can be accounted for by older record buyers, but the size of sales suggests thay were also purchased by teenagers who still enjoyed something fairly conventional.

Summary questions

1   Explain why a new style of popular music emerged in Britain in the 1960s.

2   'The changes in fashion and popular music in the 1960s only affected a minority of the population.' Explain why you agree or disagree with this statement.

7   The radicalism of youth

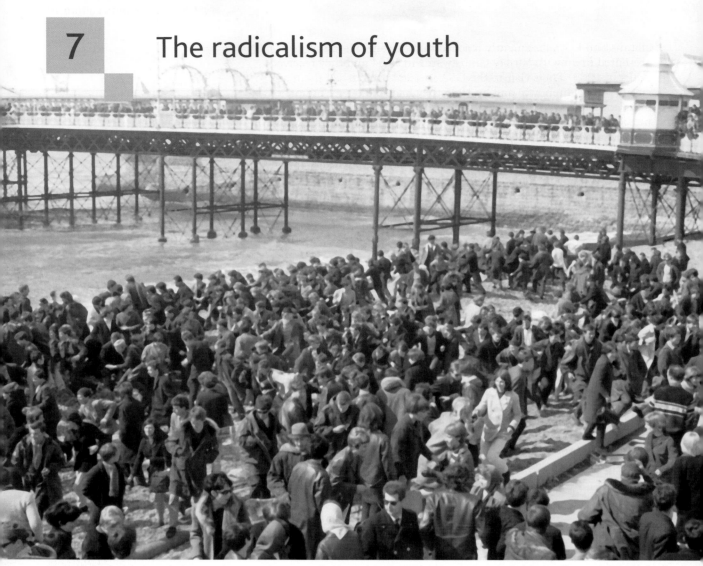

Fig. 1 *Mods and rockers clash on Brighton Beach*

In this chapter you will learn about:

- the spread of rebellious and radical behaviour among young people of differing backgrounds

- the connection between rebellious behaviour and other developments in the 1960s

- the impact and extent of such activity

- the activities and impact of the CND movement and the anti-Vietnam demonstrations.

Teenagers of the late fifties and early sixties did not aspire to change the world. They had grown up in security and a modest affluence. Most of them just wanted to look different, travel more, play pop music and buy stuff. In this they reflected the behaviour and tastes of their favourite singers and the disc-jockeys they listened to on their transistors. But all the same they were the thin end of a revolutionary wedge.

1   *Tony Judt, **Post-war: A History of Europe Since 1945**, 2007*

Rebellion and radicalism

The 'Teddy Boys' who had emerged as a distinctive working-class youth subculture in the 1950s were the first of a new breed of youth gang, defined by its dress, behaviour and rebellious attitude. Their direct descendants at the beginning of the 1960s were the motorbike fraternity, the rockers, who were rapidly damned by the press as symptomatic of the depravity and delinquency of youth at the time. In contrast to them came the mods. They were more warmly received (not least for their 'respectable' dress) until a series of mod/rocker clashes at seaside resorts in 1964 placed them too on the media blacklist.

There were skirmishes and fights at a number of seaside resorts in 1964. The best known of these took place on the Brighton beaches over the bank holiday weekend of Whitsun 1964. The events were given exceptional prominence on the front pages of the national press.

Table 1 *Characteristics of mods and rockers*

Mods	Rockers
Wore: suits – clean and respectable 　　　short jackets or Parkas 　　　narrow (drainpipe) trousers 　　　poloshirts or turtleneck sweaters 　　　pork-pie hats 　　　suede shoes or boots	Wore: deliberately scruffy clothes 　　　leather jackets with studs 　　　dirty jeans or leathers 　　　T-shirts or vests 　　　motorbike helmets 　　　Winkle Picker shoes
Well-groomed hair	Straggly hair
Rode scooters, especially Italian Lambrettas or Vespas	Rode motorbikes, especially Nortons
Liked Ska, the Who and 'cool jazz'	Liked rock 'n' roll, Elvis, Eddie Cochran and John Lee Hooker
Some took amphetamines	Some took cocaine

Fighting teenagers hurled milk bottles, deckchairs and stones. Brighton looked more like a Middle East trouble spot than an English seaside resort. I asked several teenagers why they were in Brighton. A 15-year-old girl told me 'I don't know. Just looking for something to happen, I suppose.' When a rocker and his girl were sighted, a great jeer went up. The couple were roughly jostled and kicked and one youth knocked the boy in the ear and pulled him over onto his back. During the night thousands of deckchairs had been scattered far and wide, many broken and ripped, some burned to light bonfires on the beaches. Just before noon a strong force of police began ushering a crowd of about 600 mods eastwards out of the centre of the town.

2　　　　　　　　*David Loshak writing in the **Daily Telegraph**, May 1964*

It is unlikely that the air of this town has ever been polluted by hordes of hooligans, male and female, so intent on violence, such as we have seen this weekend and of whom you are an example.

3　　　*Dr George Simpson, Chairman of the Margate Bench, prosecuting youths charged with disturbances, in Brighton 1964*

Fig. 2 *Mods and rockers*

Activity

Source analysis

Explain how far the views in Source 3 differ from those in Source 2 in relation to the intentions of the mods and rockers in the beach clashes of 1964.

In reality, the mod–rocker violence was nothing like as extensive or dangerous as the media made out. Many incidents were little more than petty vandalism by bored youths and were only made worse by suspicious landladies and heavy-handed policing. It was actually the media stigmatisation and negative stereotyping that helped define and popularise these groups, frightening the older generation and adding to their appeal for the young. In the course of the decade, they gave way to other youth subcultures. Football hooligans became a constant press concern from about 1966, while the skinheads took centre stage towards the end of the 1960s. Characterised by their shaven heads, braces and Dr Marten boots, they were the heirs of the rockers, while the descendants of the mods – the hippies – rejected social convention and establishment attitudes in

■ Exploring the detail

The skinhead movement

The skinhead movement evolved in Britain in the later 1960s. It was a hard, working-class youth cult and skinheads became involved in football hooliganism and drunken brawls. In the 1970s the movement developed a racial motivation, as discussed in Chapter 12.

■ Activity

Revision exercise

In pairs, list as many reasons as you can to explain youth rebellion and radicalism in the early 1960s. You may like to refer back to Chapter 6 to help you with this.

favour of peace and love. They embraced 'flower power', which emanated from America, and favoured alternative lifestyles with an emphasis on environmentalism, alternative therapies and free love.

Fig. 3 *'Flower power' in the 1960s at an outdoor pop festival*

The hippy movement primarily attracted middle-class teenagers who were keen to be seen to be different. Yet, it was the very affluence that they claimed to despise that allowed them time for other priorities – 'opting out' (usually only for a short spell) from the society that had made them what they were and seeking a new identity. Middle-class youth protest was sometimes channelled into political pressure groups too, but while purporting to harbour radical opinions and favour the erosion of class boundaries, most youths were often conservative and conformist at heart. Only at the London School of Economics, in the cosmopolitan capital and in touch with continental influences, did student agitation take on a truly revolutionary character.

In politics there is little that is new in present day youth. They lean towards the politics of the moderate centre. Disapproval of class distinctions is very widespread but they do not demand the abolition of the class system, only the loosening and widening of it to allow for the full emergence of talent and merit. Greater social mobility and the abolition of educational privileges are demanded, that is all. The image of America is not very favourable. Its excessive influence on Britain is rather resented and many are afraid that what America is today, Britain may become tomorrow.

4   *Ferdinand Zweig, who conducted a survey of students at Oxford and Manchester in 1962 – The Student in an Age of Anxiety, 1963*

The rise of CND

Among the middle-class youth, there were young idealists whose sensibilities were alarmed by the testing of nuclear weapons. Britain had first tested an atomic weapon in 1952, but it was in May 1957, when Britain successfully tested a hydrogen bomb and the Labour Party Conference rejected unilateral disarmament, that an anti-nuclear protest faction began to form. Popular writers like J. B. Priestley and the philosopher Bertrand Russell wrote of the need to ban such weapons and a disparate group of Quakers, pacifists and journalists met at the house of Canon John Collins of St Paul's Cathedral in January 1958 to found the Campaign for Nuclear Disarmament (CND).

Priestley made a patriotic appeal in the *New Statesman*, 2 November 1957.

> The British often seem to be waiting for something better than party squabbles and appeals to their narrowest self-interest, something great and noble in its intention that would make them feel good again. This might well be a declaration to the world that one power able to engage in nuclear warfare will reject the evil thing for ever.

5
*David Childs, **Britain Since 1945**, Routledge, 1997*

Exploring the detail

Disarmament and the hydrogen bomb

The Labour Party was traditionally associated with pacifism (anti-war) but in 1955 the party had divided over whether Britain should manufacture a hydrogen (H-) bomb – a nuclear weapon that could be delivered by a missile. Bevan opposed but the Prime Minister, Attlee, wanted the weapon to act as a deterrent to other countries. Production went ahead and Bevan abandoned his campaign for Britain to disarm independently – a procedure known as unilateral disarmament. This upset some Labour supporters who were consequently attracted by the CND movement.

The movement held a particular appeal for many young middle-class people who were unexcited by conventional party politics that seemed remote and out of touch. Perhaps it was because they had the most to lose, or because working-class youngsters were too preoccupied with earning a living and more prepared to accept the argument that nuclear weapons were necessary as a deterrent. These young middle-class idealists saw the campaign against the bomb as a moral crusade. They wore its badge, an upturned Y, based on semaphore, with pride, and when, at Easter 1958, CND organised a march from central London to the

Fig. 4 *The CND march from London to Aldermaston, Easter 1958*

Atomic Weapons Research Establishment at Aldermaston in Berkshire, 90 per cent of the marchers were under 25. The four-day, 80 km walk was completed by around 4,000 people, showing the attraction of the cause.

A closer look

The CND movement

CND was a political protest movement committed to the adoption of unilateral nuclear disarmament. It had a left-wing image but it was also supported by independently minded Conservatives and cut across party boundaries. Among its intellectual supporters were Bertrand Russell, the philosopher; writers such as Doris Lessing and Iris Murdoch; actress Vanessa Redgrave; film directors Anthony Asquith and Basil Wright, and historian A. J. P. Taylor.

Annual marches followed, although in subsequent years the number of young people declined in proportion to the older stalwarts. During the first two years of the 1960s, the campaign attracted 50,000 to 150,000 supporters and the Aldermaston marches between Trafalgar Square and the research base gained massive press coverage. The issues promoted by CND became a matter for widespread discussion and its organisation and methods provided a training that was to be copied by other protest groups such as Women's Liberation.

However, the arguments became more academic when, in 1960, the government chose to cancel the British Blue Streak missile that would have provided a means of delivering the bomb, so leaving Britain reliant on America and its missiles. Although, to the delight of CND, the Labour Party Conference that year adopted a resolution in favour of Britain's unilateral nuclear disarmament, the rejection of a similar resolution in 1961 led the movement to lose its impetus and it went on to split amid disagreements over tactics.

Activity

Source analysis

1 What do you think A. J. P. Taylor meant by the words quoted in Source 7?

2 Using Sources 5, 6 and 7 and your own knowledge, explain why the CND movement was so attractive to middle-class youth.

Exploring the detail

The Vietnam War

The Vietnam War was an American war in which American troops fought for the South Vietnamese Republic against the communist North. The British Prime Minister, Wilson, would not commit Britain militarily in support of its ally, but he dared not condemn the USA because Britain was dependent on American financial support. His offer to mediate and give words of support for the US President Johnson did him little good, however. They simply infuriated the Americans, who wanted direct action, while at the same time antagonising a section of the British public that was anti-war and anti-America.

I was born in 1944 so my memories of the sixties are those of a twenty year old. Although I wouldn't really describe my family as particularly political in the traditional sense, we all ate together in the evenings and often debated the issues of the day. Sometimes the discussion got quite heated and I particularly remember how passionately everyone felt about CND. There was something special about it. We were going to change the world – or so we thought. I remember my mother and two elder sisters, wrapped up in their duffel coats, going on the first Aldermaston marches. They really thought they were part of an exceptional movement and I was desperately excited and proud of them.

6 *Sally Carewe, a young CND supporter, offers her personal reminiscences*

We thought that Great Britain was still a great power whose example would affect the rest of the world. Ironically, we were the last imperialists.

7 *A. J. P. Taylor, **Personal History**, 1983*

From the outset, there had been disagreements about how the campaign should work: whether to focus on persuading politicians by reasoned argument or to indulge in civil disobedience – non-violent direct action that broke the law, or 'sit-down' protests in public places. These internal disputes were never resolved and in 1962 a breakaway group favouring direct action, known as the Committee of 100, was formed. The peaceful resolution of the Cuban Missile Crisis of 1962, and an international agreement banning nuclear tests in the atmosphere in 1963, added to the CND's rapid decline. Membership shrank to a few thousand and the young people who had been CND's most active supporters turned their attention elsewhere – to the student movements and protests against the Vietnam War in particular.

■ Anti-war protest

Political activism by students was given a new lease of life when some CND leaders took a key role in planning the first anti-Vietnam War demonstration in 1965. CND was completely eclipsed by the Vietnam Solidarity Campaign or VSC, which gained considerable support among university students. In the summer of 1965, there were teach-ins on Vietnam at Oxford and the London School of Economics (LSE) and, once again, Bertrand Russell was a prominent campaigner.

The anti-war protest coincided with, and encouraged, the first stirrings of wider student unrest in the universities. Such unrest was already making itself felt elsewhere in Europe, particularly in France and Italy, and was connected with matters immediately affecting students' interests such as a demand for more student control over the curriculum, teaching methods and organisation. There were complaints about lack of amenities, for example at Essex University, and cramped facilities, particularly at the LSE. The Radical Students' Alliance was founded in 1966 to campaign on both student and anti-war issues. However, until 1968, its activities remained limited and its membership small.

Fig. 5 *The anti-Vietnam War demonstration in Grosvenor Square, London in March 1968*

The LSE became the centre of radical activity. The decision, in 1966, to appoint Dr Adams, formerly Principal of University College, Rhodesia and someone who, in the students' minds, was associated with **white supremacist** ideas, sparked a series of sit-ins and a 'Daffodil March' through London in March 1967. This march was supported by students from other universities and London colleges. However, it was the VSC that harnessed some of the ill-feeling in an outburst of radical activity including demonstrations in 1967 and again in 1968. On 17 March, there were violent scenes at an anti-Vietnam demonstration in London, near the American Embassy in Grosvenor Square.

■ Key term

White supremacist: a form of apartheid that discriminated against the majority black population and was practised in Rhodesia (part of the Old British Empire). Public opinion in Britian was strongly hostile to such behaviour.

An independent TV news reporter's account was accompanied by vivid television pictures.

> It's going, it's going. The police are being pushed backwards. The police are just holding, but they can't hold any more. The column, I gather, is about a mile long. There are about three lines of policemen three or four deep here and they're just managing to hold it. There are several smoke bombs.
>
> Now they're through – yes, the first are through now, the first are through. The horses are moving in – they're screaming now, absolute hysteria and the horses are moving them back. Now the fire crackers are being thrown at the police horses. There's a horse I see down there with stain all up its legs. Yes, there goes another one right in front of the police horses, but they're standing their ground. Now you can see the banners being used as clubs and flags hurled at the police and the horses and the police are being hit with the banners.

8   *Independent TV report, March 1968*

Tariq Ali (a leading figure in the VSC) launched a new Marxist journal, *The Black Dwarf,* and wrote:

> The movement was on the increase and in subsequent demonstrations our numbers doubled and trebled as did the violence. Our violence was defensive – a response to the repressive violence of the State machine. Moreover we were not going to be told how to demonstrate. We would occupy the streets, march with lined arms and not let our comrades be arrested.

9   *Tariq Ali, The Black Dwarf*

Activity

Source analysis

Explain how far the views in Source 9 differ from those in Source 8 in relation to the anti-war protests of 1968.

The same month, CND held a more peaceful anti-war demonstration and six demonstrators were allowed to hand in a petition at the front door of No. 10, but on 28 March a third, and still more violent, protest organised by the VSC took place that was to become known as the Battle of Grosvenor Square. The final demonstration in October 1968 in which 30,000 took part was, however, relatively peaceful.

The year 1968 also saw a number of other anti-war protests, often combined with demands for more student power, in a variety of different universities. At Sussex, a speaker on the Vietnam War, from the American Embassy, was covered in red paint, while at Essex, two Conservative MPs (including Enoch Powell) were physically attacked. Patrick Gordon-Walker, the Labour Secretary of State for Education and Science, was shouted down in Manchester and Denis Healey, the Labour Defence Secretary, almost had his car overturned by Cambridge students.

It is hard to pinpoint the precise reasons for the burst of student activity in 1968. Certainly, the Vietnam War was one but many of the complaints were more specific to British university life and it is interesting to note that it was at the most cramped (LSE) or isolated (Essex) sites that some of the most extreme activity occurred. The expansion of higher education and the activities of students abroad must also have played a part. Rebellious student activity has also been linked to the spread of new freedoms, the dominant youth culture and the 'generation gap', soft drugs and provocative pop music.

Cross-reference

The new **freedoms of youth** are examined in Chapter 6.

A closer look

1968

The year 1968 was a defining year for students everywhere. There was a wave of upheavals, mainly in the form of street protests, in the USA, France, Italy and in communist eastern Europe. Some focused on local grievances, while others had a marked political element. Some embraced opposition to the Vietnam War and reflected political disillusionment, which was particularly strong in the West after the assassinations of Robert Kennedy, the US President, and the freedom fighter, Martin Luther King. The most extreme riots, in Paris in May, involved students from the Sorbonne who set up barricades in the streets and provoked a crisis of public order. Over a million students and workers fought street battles with the police, and tanks were brought to the Parisian outskirts, bringing the country close to political revolution. In the summer of 1968, the focus of student radicalism shifted to America, where students expressed their disillusionment with capitalist democracy and Czechoslovakia, where they sought to embrace it. In August, young people assembled in the streets of Prague to protest against the crushing of the Velvet Revolution (an attempt to introduce some democracy in this communist country) by the USSR. There was trouble as far afield as Sweden, Mexico City (where 25 students were killed), Pakistan, Japan, Greece and Spain. In many instances, troubles were quite localised though and by the end of the year the excitement had faded. However, the place of youth in European society was never quite the same again.

Activity

Thinking point

1. How would you explain the attraction of the anti-war movement for young people?

2. What was special about 1968 in the context of youth radicalism?

3. Try to research a little more into the student activities of 1968, both in Britain and elsewhere.

In Britain, student radicalism never reached the heights it did elsewhere in Europe. Several factors help account for this. The British university population was small and many of the specific issues over which the students protested were of little interest to the general public. Indeed, students tended to be regarded unfavourably as a pampered elite who were wasting taxpayers' money. For example, following troubles at Hornsea Art College in London in 1968, the following appeared in the local press.

> A bunch of crackpots, here in Haringey, or in Grosvenor Square, or Paris, or Berlin, or Mexico, can never overthrow an established system. They may dislike having to conform to a system in which they are required to study and follow set programmes and take examinations or their equivalents; and acknowledge that in doing so they are, through the indulgence of others, preparing themselves for a lifetime of earning. The system is ours. We are the ordinary people, the nine-to-five, Monday-to-Friday semi-detached, suburban wage-earners, who are the system. We are not victims of it. We are not slaves to it. We are it, and we like it. Does any bunch of twopenny-halfpenny kids think they can turn us upside down? They'll learn.

10   *Editorial in the **Wood Green, Southgate and Palmers Green Weekly Herald***

There may have been a growth in awareness among students that they had the potential to exercise a political voice but, for the most part, common sense prevailed. There was none of the horrifying violence seen in Europe and, after the long summer holiday, the storm died down.

Fig. 6 *The Beatle John Lennon and wife Yoko Ono staged a seven-day 'love-in' as a protest against war from their bedroom in the Hilton Hotel, Amsterdam, 25 March 1969*

Summary question

'The youth protests of the 1960s demonstrated that a new spirit of confrontation and violence had entered society.' Explain why you agree or disagree with this view.

8   The liberal society

There is the need for the State to do less to restrict personal freedom. There is the need for the State to create a climate of opinion which is favourable to gaiety, tolerance and beauty, and unfavourable to restriction, to petty-minded disapproval, to hypocrisy and to a dreary, ugly pattern of life.

1   *Adapted from Roy Jenkins, **The Labour Case**, Penguin, 1959*

When Roy Jenkins became the Labour Home Secretary in December 1965 and was finally in a position to act on his own advice, the tide of liberalism was already well underway. The quest for greater personal 'freedom' was already being seen in the development of youth culture and mirrored by the content of films, the theatre and TV. Nevertheless, changes in the law were needed if further advances were to be made.

Key profile

Roy Jenkins

Roy Jenkins (1920–2003) was the son of a Welsh miner who had entered parliament as a Labour MP in 1950. Under the premiership of Harold Wilson, he was made Home Secretary (1965–7) and Chancellor of the Exchequer (1967–70). In 1981, he went on to found and lead the SDP, a new centre-left political party, which subsequently merged with the Liberal Party to create the Liberal Democrats in 1988.

Key term

Censorship: refers to the attempt to limit what people can read, see, hear and do through state controls and regulation. It is used to prevent inappropriate political messages or offensive or corrupting material reaching the public. However, there is a fine line between protecting the public and manipulating it. Censorship provides a form of social control. It prevents controversial issues being openly discussed and shields the existing social and political orders from criticism, so helping to preserve them.

Cross-reference

Licensing rules and the development of **commercial television** are covered on pages 38–43.

Activity

Talking point

In groups, consider Jenkins's views as expressed in Source 1. Do you agree with his view of the State's duties? Which group of voters do you think Jenkins was trying to appeal to when he wrote this in 1959? Which type of people might agree/disagree with him?

The reduction of censorship and the liberalisation of laws

Censorship

Until the 1960s, the State had tried to maintain a firm control over the opinions and morals of the people. Citizens were not allowed to read or see anything judged 'obscene' or of a politically sensitive nature. Government agencies (under the Lord Chamberlain) were responsible for the **censorship** of theatre, cinema and literature, while radio and TV also operated under strict licensing rules. Even commercial television was strictly regulated and obliged to provide 'enlightenment and information'.

Fig. 1 *As soon as Penguin had been acquitted in the Lady Chatterley trial, people rushed out to buy D. H. Lawrence's book. Here, a window cleaner, Stan Buckle, takes a break to catch up on some classical reading*

Fig. 2 *Film censorship 'to preserve an acceptable standard of screen entertainment' was carried out by the British Board of Film Censors*

Exploring the detail

'New wave' films

New wave films (1959–64) were highminded but 'earthy' films that tackled social issues and challenged conventions. They included:

■ *Room at the Top* (1959), based on John Braine's novel

■ Alan Sillitoe's *Saturday Night and Sunday Morning* (1960) and *The Loneliness of the Long Distance Runner* (1962)

■ *A Taste of Honey* (1961), which dealt with a preganant schoolgirl and a homosexual

■ *This Sporting Life* (1963), which brought an inarticulate rugby league footballer to the screen.

Literature

This stringent state control was partly challenged by the Obscene Publications Act 1959, which said that adult literature that was 'in the interests of science, literature, art or learning' should be exempt from censorship. In October 1960, this law was put to the test when Penguin was taken to court for publishing the first, uncut, edition in Britain of *Lady Chatterley's Lover*, a novel by D. H. Lawrence. Its explicitly sexual content, its four-letter words and its challenge to traditional class attitudes ensured the case was well covered by the media.

When Penguin was acquitted, a path was opened for the further erosion of literary censorship. *Fanny Hill*, a pornographic 18th-century novel by John Cleland, was published in 1963 and *Last Exit to Brooklyn*, which featured scenes of gang rape, in 1966.

There were still some boundaries. In January 1970, three directors of the 'underground' newspaper, the *International Times*, were imprisoned for allowing gay contact adverts in the publication and the editors of the magazine *Oz* were convicted in 1971 for their 1970 'School Kids Issue', although this was quashed on appeal. Nevertheless, what had once been deemed shocking became more acceptable as the decade progressed and traditional 'Victorian' morality lost its hold.

Cinema

Censorship lasted longer on the screen and films remained subject to strict categorisation by the British Board of Film Censors. Nevertheless, the 1960s saw a gradual broadening of what was considered acceptable. The 'new wave' cinema of the early 1960s explored issues relating to youth culture, sex and class but even these were tame by the standards of a generation later. The pop-group movies of the mid-1960s grew more daring, with films like *Darling* (1965), *Alfie* (1966) and *Here We Go Round the Mulberry Bush* (1967), while in 1966 Michelangelo Antonioni produced *Blow-Up* and François Truffaut *Fahrenheit 451* in England. By the end of the decade, screen violence and sex had become acceptable and their depiction more explicit, as seen in the 1971 film *A Clockwork Orange* based on Anthony Burgess's novel.

Theatre

Following the pattern set by John Osborne, Arnold Wesker and Harold Pinter, writers and producers began experimenting with new styles of plays, often addressing social issues. The Royal Court Theatre in London was at the centre of innovation but this led to clashes with the Lord Chamberlain. After *Early Morning*, a controversial play by Edward Bond was banned, the backbench MP, George Strauss, introduced a bill to abolish theatrical censorship. With Roy Jenkins's support and the testimony of the famous actor Lawrence Olivier, this was passed in 1968.

A closer look

Lady Chatterley's Lover

D. H. Lawrence had written *Lady Chatterley's Lover* in 1927. It concerns a love affair between Lady Chatterley and George Mellors, her husband's gamekeeper and contains 13 descriptions of the couple enjoying sex! Although previously censored, Penguin believed that its literary merit permitted the book to be published under the terms of the new Obscenity Act but in October 1960 the State took Penguin to court. The jury was asked to decide whether the novel would 'deprave and corrupt persons' or was 'justified as being for the public good'.

Mr Mervyn Griffiths-Jones, for the prosecution, asked: 'Would the jury approve of their young sons and daughters reading the novel? Is it a book you would wish even your wife or your servants to read? He explained: 'The curtain is never drawn. One follows [the lovers] not only into the bedroom but into bed and one remains with them there.' He also referred to the use of 'old Anglo-Saxon four-letter words', one of which appeared 30 times. In Penguin's defence, Mr Gerald Gardiner called 35 expert witnesses to testify to the novel's worth.

The following statements were heard.

By Dr John Robinson, Bishop of Woolwich, in reply to the question 'Is this a book which, in your view, Christians ought to read?':

> 'Yes I think it is. What Lawrence is trying to do, I think, is to portray the sex relation as something sacred.'

By Richard Hoggart, lecturer in English Literature at Leicester University:

> 'The novel is one of the 20 best we have had written in Britain in the last 30 years.'

By Norman St John-Stevas, Roman Catholic barrister and academic:

> 'I have no hesitation in saying that every Catholic priest and every Catholic moralist would profit by reading this book.'

By Miss Bernadine Wall, aged 21, convent schoolgirl and 'typical' young reader, in reply to the question 'Did you know the four-letter words?':

> 'Yes.'

The jury of nine men and three women were sent to a special room to read the 317-page book and their verdict was in favour of Penguin who celebrated by putting 200,000 books on sale. A *Daily Telegraph* reporter wrote:

> 'I searched from Fleet Street to Charing Cross Road and called at more than 20 shops before I could obtain a copy. They were being sold at the rate of one every two or three seconds. In queues, men far outnumbered women.'

*Extracts from Christopher Howse (ed.), **How We Saw It: 150 Years of the Daily Telegraph 1855-2005**, 2004*

The removal of theatrical censorship permitted nudity on stage and the new act was celebrated when 13 members of the cast of *Hair*, an American tribal musical in production at the Shaftesbury Theatre in London, stood up and faced the audience naked for 30 seconds.

The *Daily Telegraph* reported on 28 September 1968:

> We had been told that, as in America, the scene would take place in very dim lighting and would pass almost unnoticed. Even in row N, the 12th row from the front of the stalls, there was nothing dim about the lighting, which last night illuminated nine women and four men. The scene went off without apparent embarrassment either to the performers or the audience. Advance bookings stand at £40,000.

2 *From the Daily Telegraph, September 28, 1968*

Activity

Watch some 1960s 'new wave' films. Try to identify what makes them belong to the new wave genre and why some might have found them shocking at the time they were produced.

Exploring the detail

The plays of Edward Bond

Edward Bond (born 1934) became a member of the writers' group at the Royal Court where the English Stage Company was dedicated to nurturing new talent. His play *Saved* was refused a public performance licence in 1965 and *Early Morning* was closed by censorship after two performances. His plays were judged to be too violent, shocking and immoral. In *Saved*, for example, Len pursues a promiscuous young woman with a dysfunctional family. It has since been described as a masterpiece of social drama.

Activity

Thinking point

How far was the decision to acquit Penguin, in the Lady Chatterley case, the result of the prosecution's out-dated attitudes?

W. A. Darlington, a drama critic, wrote a review just before retiring, after 48 years.

> I have seldom been more out of anything as I was of this production. Obviously I am the wrong age for it and possibly the wrong nationality. To me the evening was a bore. It was noisy, it was ugly and quite desperately unfunny. As for the much discussed nudes, there were some bare looking skins at one point in the shadows at the back of the stage, but if that's all it amounts to, some people are going to be disappointed. The company have enormous vitality and a great sense of rhythm. This, added to their infantile desire to flout established standards, may earn them a success. But I doubt it.

3

*W. A. Darlington, **Daily Telegraph**, 28 September 1968*

The Theatre Act did not pass without criticism. Shows like *Oh Calcutta!*, an avant-garde theatrical revue created by British drama critic Kenneth Tynan and described by him as 'an evening of elegant erotica', provoked a good deal of media disapproval. Nevertheless, the reduction of censorship did not create an immediate wave of depravity and it largely legitimised changes that had already taken place.

TV

TV was both affected by and helped to develop more liberal attitudes. As the 1960s progressed, issues of sex, violence, politics and religion, which had previously been banned or considered unsuitable for public broadcasting, were tackled. *The Wednesday Play* (BBC 1964–70) featured issues like abortion, while even the populist *Coronation Street* (launched in 1960 by ITV) shocked older audiences with its realistic portrayal of failed marriages and illicit affairs. Satires, most notably *That Was The Week That Was*, lampooned political figures and broached previously taboo subjects. Kenneth Tynan was the first to use a four-letter word on TV in 1965, but once the barrier was broken the floodgates opened. The popular series, *Steptoe and Son* (BBC 1962–5) and the still more infamous *Till Death Us Do Part* (BBC 1966–8 and 1972) contained language that would have been considered inadmissible 10 years earlier.

A closer look

That Was The Week That Was

That Was The Week That Was, nicknamed TW3, grew out of the satire boom of the early 1960s. Satire had established itself as a successful genre with the revue *Beyond the Fringe*, which had popularised the Oxbridge undergraduate humour of Alan Bennett, Dudley Moore, Peter Cook and Jonathan Miller. The satirical magazine *Private Eye*, produced by Richard Ingrams, Christopher Booker and Willie Rushton had also proved a success and, in 1962, Sir Hugh Greene, Director-General of the BBC, decided to introduce some satirical fun to television. Produced by Ned Sherrin, TW3 began with Millicent Martin's song 'That was the week that was, It's over, let it go' and included calypsos composed by Lance Percival on topics suggested by the studio audience and on-stage cartoons from Timothy Birdsall. The programme was technically innovative. It was the first to show the full studio, including the cameras. David Frost tore a studio guest to shreds each week, while hastily rehearsed sketches had fun with the previously taboo topics of politics, religion, royalty and sex. Willie Rushton was a star as a bumbling Macmillan and a merciless sketch in October 1963 satirising Sir Alec Douglas-Home provoked 600 phone calls and 300 letters of complaint. One critic called Sherrin and Frost 'pedlars of filth and smut and destroyers of all that Britain holds dear' and questions were asked in the House of Commons. Despite a weekly audience of 12 million, the programme was closed after little over a year.

Question

'The reduction in censorship in the 1960s was a necessary step forward in the creation of a more civilised society.' Explain why you agree or disagree with this view.

Further liberalisation

Activity

Revision exercise

Further liberalisation of society was brought about through four important pieces of legislation:

- The Murder (Abolition of the Death Penalty) Act 1965
- The Divorce Reform Act 1969
- The Abortion Act 1967
- The Sexual Offences Act 1967

As you read about each one on the following pages, complete the table below.

Act and date	Background/support and promoter	Details of Act	Impact and success

The abolition of the death penalty

Arguments against the death penalty had been advanced in the 1950s and, although public opinion remained sharply divided, the anti-hanging campaign had received a particular boost from the public sympathy shown in the case of Ruth Ellis, a young mother who had murdered her unfaithful lover in 1955. In 1957, the Tories had reduced the number of cases carrying the death penalty but Sydney Silverman, a Jewish Labour backbencher, campaigned tirelessly to win support for a total abolition. In 1965, on a **free vote**, hanging was abolished for a trial period of five years, and in 1969 this was made permanent.

AQA Examiner's tip

Remember you will need to define what you understand by the term 'civilised society' in order to answer this question. You may like to discuss this before you attempt to write.

Key term

Free vote: although the vast majority of bills passing through parliament are public bills, sponsored by the government, there is also provision for backbench MPs who do not hold a government office to introduce and promote bills. When a 'free vote' is agreed, individual MPs are invited to vote according to their own conscience rather than following an official party line. Neverthless, bills need the sympathetic support of prominent government figures to become law.

Roy Jenkins refused to authorise the beating of prisoners, which ceased after 1967, and he brought in 'majority' verdicts for English juries rather than demanding unanimity. This helped convict many dangerous and professional criminals but the abolition of hanging did not significantly reduce the number of murders or violent crimes, as its supporters had hoped.

Fig. 3 *The campaign against hanging was already under way in 1959, as seen here in this small demonstration outside Wandsworth Prison on the occasion of a hanging that year*

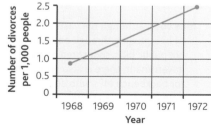

Fig. 4 *Divorce rates, 1968–72*

New liberalising laws

Divorce

Until the 1960s, divorce law demanded evidence that one party had committed adultery. To gain this, the well-to-do had resorted to private detectives and cameras but, for the less well off, evidence was difficult to obtain and divorce often impossible as a result. Jenkins believed the laws were outmoded and the Divorce Reform Act was passed in 1969. This allowed for 'no-fault divorce' following the 'irretrievable breakdown' of a marriage. Couples could divorce if:

- they had lived apart for two years and both wanted it
- they had lived apart for five years and one partner wanted it.

Following the reform there was a huge increase in the number of divorces. In 1950, there had been fewer than two divorce decrees per

1,000 married couples in England and Wales, but by the mid-1970s nearly one in every two marriages ended this way. This could, of course, be partly explained by growing female independence, but it is very likely the Act played a major role.

Abortion

Until 1967, abortion (except on strictly medical grounds) was illegal. The only way of terminating a pregnancy was to find a private clinic, if the fees were affordable, or to search out a 'backstreet' abortionist if they were not. Between 100,000 and 200,000 illegal abortions were performed each year and about 35,000 women were admitted to hospitals with complications as a result. Worse still, between 1958 and 1960, 82 women died after backstreet abortions and many others were left permanently damaged.

The Society for the Protection of the Unborn Child and the Abortion Law Reform Association had campaigned for a reform in the law since 1945, but the thalidomide disaster of 1959–62 did more

Fig. 5 *Even after the Abortion Act 1967, campaigns like this continued, in order to try to persuade the government to broaden the terms of the act*

to sway public opinion than any of their arguments. David Steel led the reform campaign in parliament, while Roy Jenkins ensured an all-night Commons sitting in order to pass the bill.

The Abortion Act 1967 permitted the legal termination of a pregnancy within the first 28 weeks, under medical supervision and with the written consent of two doctors. Importantly, the only justification needed was the 'mental suffering' of the pregnant woman, not her medical condition. Pro-abortionists celebrated, but hopes that demands for abortions would fall because of the availability of more effective contraception and better education proved false. The number of abortions increased from 4 per 100 live births in 1968 (35,000) to 17.6 in 1975 (141,000). An article in the *Express* in the mid-1960s pointed to the irony of parliament abolishing the death penalty for murderers because it was deemed unacceptable in 'civilised society', yet at the same time sanctioning the destruction of unborn life, also in the name of civilised society. Opponents, including the Catholic Church, pressurised for the amendment or abolition of the act.

Homosexuality

In the post-war era, amidst fears about spies and security, homosexuals were perceived to be potential security risks and, like John Vassall, easily blackmailed and morally weak. Consequently, governments tried to crack down on homosexuality, enforcing a law that carried a penalty of two years' imprisonment for homosexual relations between men. (Female sexual relations had never been subject to law and lesbianism was therefore legal.)

However, the 1950s purges actually helped turn public opinion in favour of a reform in the law and in 1957 a committee under John Wolfenden reported in favour of decriminalisation. When the Conservative government rejected its recommendations, the Homosexual Law Reform Society was founded and its first meeting in London in May 1958 attracted 1,000 people.

▪ **Exploring the detail**

Thalidomide

During the 1960s, the drug thalidomide, which was prescribed for pregnant women with morning sickness, was found to produce congenital deformities in children when taken in early pregnancy. Children were commonly born without the long bones of the arms and the legs and feet could also be affected. In reaction to this, opinion polls showed a majority in favour of abortions when an abnormality had been detected in a foetus.

▪ Cross-reference

Details on **John Vassall** can be found on page 25.

Activity

Talking point

In groups, discuss which of the new laws or changes was likely to have the most effect:

- The reduction of censorship.
- The abolition of the death penalty.
- The liberalisation of divorce.
- The legalisation of abortion.
- The legalisation of homosexuality.

Take each of these measures in turn and debate its importance with the rest of the class.

The Labour government of 1964 was divided on the issue. Tony Crosland and Roy Jenkins were in favour, while Harold Wilson was privately hostile and it was left to Leo Abse (like Silverman, a Jewish Labour backbencher) to take up the cause. Thanks to Jenkins's support, he was able to get enough parliamentary time for his Private Members' Bill to become law as the Sexual Offences Act 1967.

The act allowed homosexual relations by consenting males over the age of 21, provided they took place 'in private'. Obviously, the act was welcomed by men who had previously been afraid to declare their sexuality and, in some cases, been forced to lead double lives. However, the act was quite narrowly interpreted and it did not mean the complete end of prosecutions for homosexual practices.

Question

'The legal changes of the 1960s were an essential ingredient of the social revolution in Britain in the 1960s.' Explain why you agree or disagree with this statement.

Challenges to traditional ideas of women's role in society

The 1960s was not only the era of youth, it was also a time when the position of women underwent a gradual change even though some of the new trends actually served, in the short term, to reinforce the conventional female role as seen in the propositions below.

Activity

Challenge your thinking

Consider the following contradictions:

1. Labour-saving devices in the home freed women from the drudgery of the kitchen, but also, through advertising, reinforced the female role as a housewife.

2. Increased education and access to higher education encouraged women to develop higher expectations, but often made slow and difficult progress along career paths all the more frustrating.

3. The increased availability of jobs gave women greater independence but also added to their sense of guilt at leaving their homes, husbands and children in order to work.

4. Changes in fashion, hair and make-up appeared liberating but in many cases merely reinforced female stereotypes.

5. Greater control over family planning liberated women from the 'burden' of pregnancy but also reinforced their position as 'sex objects'.

6. Changes in attitudes to marriage, for example easier divorce, combined freedom with a greater sense of insecurity.

Before reading on, debate each of these propositions in pairs and try to decide which of the two contradictory sentiments was likely to affect women is the 1960s more. Were women likely to feel more or less valued and fulfilled as a result of the changes that took place?

Women as housewives

The belief that the duty of a woman was to be a good wife and mother, keeping a clean home and feeding children and husband, remained strong for most of the 1960s, particularly among the working classes. Women were encouraged to give up their job and personal independence when they married or on the arrival of the first child and, whilst new electrical household appliances and convenience foods might make their life easier, they did not change society's perception of their role.

> The female kitchen is the temple of those twin symbols of the new life – the refrigerator and the washing machine. It is the heart of the feminine dream, full of gadgetry, whirring and wires.

4   *Harry Hopkins in 'The New Look', 1964*

The plight of 'desperate housewives' who found life in the kitchen no 'feminine dream' was picked up by the more liberal newspapers of the early 1960s. This led to the foundation of the National Housewives' Register, which acted as a mutual support network for bored housewives, organising talks and coffee mornings in order to inject a little more stimulating conversation into the housewife's daily routine.

Fig. 6 *The image of women as primarily housewives remained strong for most of the 1960s*

Education and work

Frustration with the housewife's lot was partly the result of the growth in female education. At the lower end of the social scale, girls' education still carried a domestic slant and females frequently left school at the minimum age and married young. However, better educated middle-class girls were not always content to settle for a life of domesticity. The attraction of extra 'pocket money' and the chance to meet others encouraged increasing numbers to seek employment outside the home.

There was no shortage of jobs for women (not least because, before 1970, employers could pay them less than men) but many of these were in the clerical and service sector with no prospects and poor pay. Some women were pleased to accept any work – perhaps on a part-time basis – even when they had children, but working mothers were often portrayed as unnatural and selfish by the media. Childminders were rare in the 1960s and private nurseries only available for the well-to-do. Even Margaret Thatcher struggled:

Exploring the detail

National Housewives' Register

In 1960, Maureen Nicol, a Wirral housewife, wrote in response to an article in the *Guardian*: 'perhaps housebound wives with liberal interests and a desire to remain individuals could form a national register so that whenever one moves one can contact like-minded friends'. This led to the setting up of the Housebound Wives' Register and Nicol was the first national organiser. A national newsletter was published giving news of the activities of local groups and providing profiles of members. In 1966, the organisation became known as the National Housewives' Register. By 1970, there were 15,000 members.

■ Cross-reference

Details on the spread of **female education**, the fight for **equal pay for women** and legislation relating to **married women's property** and **divorce** are found in chapter 10.

The reform of the **divorce law** was also discussed earlier on pages 82–3.

■ Exploring the detail

More open discussion

Books like, *Human Sexual Response* (1966) by Masters and Johnson and *The Myth of the Vaginal Orgasm* (1970) by Anne Koedt made both men and women more aware of female sexuality. Such literature eventually helped lead to better understanding within relationships, but the initial impact was to leave many women feeling frustrated and unfulfilled.

■ Question

How far did changes in the position of women in the 1960s increase their independence?

■ Exploring the detail

Feminism

Feminist movements have emerged and fought for female rights at various times in history. During the late 19th and early 20th centuries, Suffragists and Suffragettes fought to establish women's rights in education and the professions and to obtain the vote, which was granted in 1918. In the inter-war years, there was a further feminist wave to establish women's rights with regard to contraception and the family. The 'new' feminism of the 1960s grew out of the student protests of 1968 but it embraced women of all ages and demanded a radical shift in male–female relations.

■ Cross-reference

The **student protests of 1968** are discussed on pages 73–5.

I didn't become an MP until after my children had started to go to school because I think that when they are very young they need mum. Mum certainly needs to be with them. Women who do their own job outside the home just have to keep going, in the evenings and at weekends.

> **5** *Margaret Thatcher interviewed by* **Woman's Hour** *in 1976*

Few made it to the top professions. Women accounted for only 28 per cent of students in higher education in 1970 and only 5 per cent of women ever reached managerial posts. Times were changing, but the 1960s were a period of evolution, not revolution, for women.

Female insecurity

In some respects, women became less, rather than more, secure. Whilst new fashions like the mini-skirt were heralded as a sign of female liberation, they also reinforced the stereotype of women as 'sex objects' whose role in life was to attract men. The advent of better methods of contraception that took away the inevitability of pregnancy and childbirth was certainly liberating, but this was as much true for men as for women and it could leave women uncertain about relationships. The 'sexual revolution' brought about by more open discussion also had the effect of making women more aware of what was often a lack of personal satisfaction in their sex lives.

The realities of marriage could certainly be far from the idyllic picture created in the teen and women's magazines, and by the end of the 1960s marriage was becoming less important. The number of illegitimate births rose from 5.8 per cent in 1960 to 8.2 per cent in 1970, and the number of marriages ending in divorce also rose. New legislation helped women escape difficult relationships, yet it was often the women who were left struggling to support themselves and perhaps to bring up children on their own.

Feminism

Frustration with the slow pace of change led to the emergence of a new-style feminist movement in the later 1960s. The movement was encouraged by the publication of articles and books exploring the position of women such as *Women: The Longest Revolution* (1966) by Juliet Mitchell and *The Female Eunuch* by the Australian feminist Germaine Greer, published in October 1970. A number of 'women's lib' groups sprang up around the UK, of which the Peckham Rye Group was the most influential. Women like Vanessa Redgrave, the actress, and Barbara Castle, the politician, gave support. These groups established support networks, analysed women's roles and relationships in society, and campaigned for social and economic equality for women.

■ Key profile

Vanessa Redgrave

Vanessa Redgrave was born into a famous theatrical family in 1937. She enjoyed a distinguished acting career but also sought to use her high social profile for political causes. In the 1960s, she supported a range of human and social rights movements including opposition to the Vietnam War, the Campaign for Nuclear Disarmament (CND), anti-racism and feminism. She has always held strong left-wing, socialist-communist views.

The feminist movement drew inspiration from the USA where, in 1966, Betty Friedan had set up the National Organisation of Women to campaign for 'a truly equal partnership between the sexes'. Members had symbolically dumped their bras in rubbish bins after the Miss America contest of 1968. A rally in Britain in 1969 led to the establishment of the Women's National Co-ordination Committee, which brought the various strands of the feminist movement together. At the first National Women's Liberation Conference held at Ruskin College, Oxford in February 1970, four demands were put forward:

- equal pay
- free contraception and abortion on request
- equal educational and job opportunities
- free 24-hour childcare.

The feminist movement did not really make much headway until the 1970s, although scenes at the Miss World Contest, held at the Albert Hall in November 1970, when the compère, Bob Hope, was pelted with flour and smoke bombs, helped give the campaign the publicity it sought. The movement's demands were printed on banners and their slogan was 'We're not beautiful, we're not ugly, we're angry'. A petition was handed to the prime minister on 6 March 1971 after 4,000 marched through London on the movement's first International Women's Day.

Nevertheless, for most women, the feminist movement was regarded as a minority obsession and a movement of affluent middle-class 'lefties', whose antics provoked amusement and curiosity. Their general emphasis on 'self-fulfilment' was too abstract to win widespread support.

Kate Millett, an American feminist and member of the National Organsation for Women, was interviewed on *Woman's Hour* in 1971, when her book *Sexual Politics* was published in the UK.

> **Interviewer:** How do you feel the press handle 'women's lib'?
>
> **Answer:** I think they handle it with the kind of contempt that is general in our society; the contempt that is reserved for women. They feel really deeply threatened by the idea of women's liberation.
>
> **Interviewer:** Why has it taken women so long to rebel and do something about it?
>
> **Answer:** There is very careful indoctrination into a sort of cooperation with one's oppression. Women have been carefully trained to put up with it and also have very few options.

6   *Kate Millett, interviewed for Woman's Hour, 1971*

	Question

Explain Kate Millett's comments in Source 6 in relation to 'women's lib' and:

a the attitude of the press

b the attitude of women.

By the end of the 1960s, inequalities and discrimination still existed and the traditional stereotyping of roles remained strong. However, certain breakthroughs had occurred. Girls were more likely to obtain a reasonable education and they had many more choices, not least to choose whether and when to have children and whether to work or stay at home. Bearing an illegitimate child was no longer regarded as the sin it had once been and living together outside marriage was becoming increasingly

■ Exploring the detail

The Samaritans

The Samaritans began in London in 1953 when a young vicar, Chad Varah, wanted to help people in distress with no one to turn to. One example was a girl aged 14 whom he had buried after she had taken her own life. She had started her periods but, having no one to talk to, had believed that she had a sexually transmitted disease. Varah launched a confidential emergency phoneline for the suicidal, with volunteers manning the lines. By 1963, there were 41 branches across the UK and the Samaritans became a limited company. By 1973, this had grown to 143 branches with 17,209 volunteers.

■ Activity

Revision exercise

Make a spider diagram to show what you believe to have been the main influences that worked together to create a permissive society in the 1960s. As you read through the rest of this section you can add to your diagram.

■ Cross-reference

Information on the advent of the **contraceptive pill** can be found on pages 36–7.

acceptable. It could be said that all this amounted to a 'social revolution'. Yet, as far as women were concerned, it was certainly not all gain. There was the loss of courtesies paid by men to women, the loss of permanence in marriage and changes in traditional family relationships to adjust to. For some women, the 1960s brought new anxieties and frustrations and these became a factor in the growth of mental health problems. It is no coincidence that the 1960s saw a boom in the sale of tranquillisers and that charitable organisations and helplines like the one operated by the Samaritans grew.

Question

Explain why a feminist movement developed in Britain at the end of the 1960s.

■ The permissive society

A poem by the former poet laureate Philip Larkin, written later in the decade, claims:

> Sexual intercourse began
> In nineteen sixty-three
> (Which was rather late for me) –
> Between the end of the Chatterley ban
> And the Beatles' first LP.

 7

*Philip Larkin, **Collected Poems**, 2003*

In this poem, Larkin links the 1960s to the birth of the 'permissive society'. This refers to a time of general sexual liberation, with changes in public and private morals and a new frankness, openness and, in some respects, honesty in personal relationships and in modes of expression. Critics used the term in a negative way, railing against uninhibited theatrical performances, displays of nudity in magazines, fashions that stressed sex appeal and inappropriate sexual behaviour. They believed that the 1960s witnened a decline in conventional moral standards, which was encouraged by changes ranging from, from the advent of the contraceptive pill to the spread of the mass media and the enactment of liberal legislation.

The influence of the contraceptive pill

With the availability of the contraceptive pill from 1961, changes in the law relating to abortion and homosexuality, and the reduction in censorship, some of the old restraints and fears about sex disappeared and a more liberal attitude emerged. However, old moral attitudes took time to change and theologians and many members of the older generation, brought up to accept a religious teaching that was hostile to 'permissive' behaviour, viewed developments with concern.

Malcolm Muggeridge, who became Rector of Edinburgh University in 1967, was one outspoken critic. He was appalled to find a request from the student body asking that contraceptive pills be made available from the university's health centre. He promptly resigned his post and made an announcement from the pulpit of St Giles Cathedral, Edinburgh.

Fig. 7 *A new openness about issues of family planning and birth control helped change the outlook of the younger generation*

The students in this university are the ultimate beneficiaries in our welfare system. They are supposed to be the spearhead of progress, flattered and paid for by their admiring seniors. How sad it is that all they put forward should be a demand for 'the pill'. It is the most tenth rate form of indulgence ever known. It is the resort of any old slobbering debauchee anywhere in the world at any time. The feeling raised in me is not so much disapproval as contempt. This, as you may imagine, makes it difficult, indeed impossible, for me, as Rector, to fulfil my function.

 8

*Quoted in Bernard Levin, **The Pendulum Years: Britain in the Sixties**, 2003*

The Catholic Church was also hostile. Pope Paul VI issued the **encyclical Humanae Vitae**, which upheld the view that contraception was contrary to God's law and therefore sinful. Not all prominent Catholics were happy with such a pronouncement and the Catholic MP Norman St John-Stevas wrote a critical essay entitled 'The Pope, the Pill and the People' in 1968. Nevertheless, despite some attempt to allow for 'private disagreement', the use of the pill among Roman Catholics was officially forbidden.

The pill opens up a wide and easy road toward marital infidelity and the general lowering of morality. Man, growing used to contraceptive practices, may lose respect for the woman and come to the point of considering her as a mere instrument of selfish enjoyment, and no longer as his respected and beloved companion.

 9

From the Encyclical Humanae Vitae, 25 July 1968

In 1960, *Woman's Hour* devoted a programme to 'casual relationships', asking what the correct relationship between a teenage boy and girl should be. By 1964, the same programme was warning of the dangers of promiscuous sex and, in 1966, a talk on 'self-control' insisted that all young people should say a firm 'no' before marriage.

 Key term

Encyclical Humanae Vitae: an encyclical is a papal pronouncement that should be obeyed by loyal Catholics. This particular encylical concerned human life.

Activity

Source analysis

List the arguments put forward by the opponents of the pill in Sources 8 and 9. Are these arguments convincing?

By the end of the 1960s some were even beginning to wonder whether the Pope had been proved right when, following warnings from scientists, a huge reaction against the pill, on medical grounds, occurred. Many brands were withdrawn from sale and new research undertaken into the potential side-effects. Science ultimately proved more powerful than theology in curbing the use of the pill, although it was only a temporary setback, soon counteracted by a new, safer pill.

The influence of the media

Permissive ideas were spread by the media, from 'teen' magazines with their agony aunt columns, which helped to establish new norms and expectations through to all types of adult literature, including a growing number of racy, uncensored novels. Previously taboo subjects were discussed in books, on the radio and on television. By 1970, *The Joy of Sex* might be found sitting on family bookshelves, providing details for the ordinary couple of sexual practices formerly only associated with prostitutes.

Theatre and the cinema took advantage of the decline in censorship to reflect the permissive society on stage and screen, while in cities, particularly in London, striptease clubs flourished.

Mary Whitehouse, a school teacher from Shropshire, became famous for her campaigns to clean up television and to reverse some of the new legislation that she believed had contributed to the 'permissive 1960s'. However, despite her campaigning, nothing changed. She attracted a good deal of sympathy but she also incurred gibes that she was a 'prig' who could not face up to changing times.

A closer look

Mary Whitehouse

Mary Whitehouse (1910–2001) was a senior mistress at Madeley Secondary School in Shropshire, when she became concerned that television was affecting her pupils' sexual and moral standards. She believed that television was undermining family life, social cohesion and attacking the Christian values she believed in. She launched the Clean Up TV Campaign and organised a nationwide petition, which attracted nearly half a million signatures.

On 5 May 1964, she addressed a meeting attended by over 3,000 people in Birmingham Town Hall.

Activity

Source analysis

Use Sources 10 to 12 and your own knowledge.

1. Explain how far the views in Sources 11 and 12 differ from those in Source 10 in relation to the work and views of Mary Whitehouse.

2. Look back to Chapter 4 and the list of popular TV programmes on page 42. In groups, try to work out which programmes Mary Whitehouse might have criticised and why.

The immediate object of this campaign is to restore the BBC to its position of respect and leadership in this country. The BBC says that it should show the work of playwrights which write of the world in which they live. If that is the world in which they live then I am truly sorry for them. But it is not our world and it is not the world of the vast majority of the people in this country and we don't want it in our homes. If violence is constantly portrayed as normal on the television screen it will help to create a violent society. I am not narrow-minded or old-fashioned. But I am square, and proud of it, if that means having a sense of values.

10　　　　　*Adapted from a speech by Mary Whitehouse, 5 May 1964*

The publicity and support that Mrs Whitehouse received led to the setting up of the National Viewers' and Listeners' Association in 1965, and this soon had 100,000 members. However, despite her lobbying, Whitehouse failed to have any impact on the programmes shown. On her death in 2001, the following comments were made (Sources 11 and 12):

> She was very witty, she was a great debater, she was very courageous and she had a very sincere view, but it was out of touch entirely with the real world. She really wanted television to be propaganda for a very moral view of the world, not the imperfect world we live in.

11 *Michael Grade, Director-General of the BBC (2001), from 'Whitehouse Kept TV on its Toes', BBC Obituary, 23 November 2001*

> She was in some obvious senses narrow-minded. She believed with passion that she was promoting virtue and righteousness; but her overriding puritanism determined that her main focus was on sex, followed by bad language and violence. She was the authentic voice of middle England, fearful of the costs and challenges of change, oblivious of its opportunities.

12 *Richard Hoggart, journalist (2001), from 'Valid Arguments Lost in an Obsession over Sex', article in the **Guardian**, 24 November 2001*

The development of the drug culture and other depravity

Another challenge to established behaviour came in the spread of the drug culture. Cocaine and heroine addiction rose 10 times in the first half of the 1960s and use of soft drugs was more commonplace by the end of the decade. The 'hippy lifestyle', with its emphasis on 'free love' and 'flower power', promoted the drug culture and even the Beatles turned to LSD. Not only did drug abuse grow during the 1960s, there were also other signs of 'permissive' behaviour and depravity. By the end of the decade, rates of sexually transmitted infections and drug abuse were on the rise, especially among the young. Rape and sexual offences had also increased. Whereas there had been 300 rape cases in 1950, by the mid-1970s there were 1,500. In 1966, there was an outcry when the Moors murder case was made public – showing the depths to which Ian Brady and Myra Hindley had fallen.

There followed something of a backlash against the permissiveness of the decade. The Dangerous Drugs Act 1967 made it unlawful to possess drugs such as cannabis and cocaine, and pop stars such as the Rolling Stones were made examples of in court in an attempt to reimpose moral standards. Although the Wootton Report of 1968 suggested legalising soft drugs like cannabis, the recommendation was rejected on the grounds that it was time, as the Home Secretary James Callaghan put it, 'to call a halt to the rising tide of permissiveness'. In 1970 the maximum sentence for drug pushers was increased to 14 years' imprisonment. By 1970, the tide seemed to have turned against cultural experiment, even for the majority of young people, and permissiveness appeared to be under greater control.

Conclusions

The degree to which liberal permissiveness actually influenced attitudes and behaviour in the 1960s can be exaggerated. What appeared in magazines or films was probably never a true reflection of the actual

Activity

Thinking point

 1 Since television remained unchanged, are Mary Whitehouse's views worth studying?

2 Do you agree with Mary Whitehouse's views about the influence of the media on society?

 Exploring the detail

The Moors murders

Myra Hindley met Ian Brady when she was a teenager in Manchester. Within 18 months of becoming lovers, Hindley helped Brady in the first of a chilling series of child murders. In July 1963, a neighbour, 16-year-old Pauline Reade, helped Hindley search for a glove on nearby Saddleworth Moor. Her body was found two decades later; her throat had been cut. Hindley and Brady went on to kill five children aged from 10 to 17 in a series of horrific murders. For example, Hindley taped the last, terrified cries of 10-year-old Lesley Anne Downey as she begged for help. In May 1966, Hindley and Brady were both sentenced to life imprisonment.

Exploring the detail

The Rolling Stones and drugs

In February 1967, the police raided Redlands, Keith Richards's manor house in Sussex. Both Richards and Mick Jagger were arrested on charges of possessing amphetamines and dope. They were given hefty fines and sentenced to imprisonment, although they were released on appeal after two days. This set off a national debate. *The Times* produced an editorial, 'Who Breaks a Butterfly Upon a Wheel' and the editor, William Rees-Mogg questioned the severity of the sentence for a mild drug case. A month later, *The Times* produced a full-page advert that declared the law against marijuana immoral and unworkable. This was signed by 65 medical experts, Nobel prize winners, politicians, the novelist Graham Greene and the Beatles.

Cross-reference

To recap on the **Rolling Stones**, see page 67.

1960s lifestyle and the extent of the permissive society is open to question. In practice, many people remained completely untouched by the so-called revolution of the 1960s. A poll published by the *Sunday Times* in the summer of 1966 suggested that a large proportion of the population were bored with hearing about 'mini-skirts, pop music and bingo' and wanted the media to spend more time on serious issues like 'the state of the economy'.

Surveys by Michael Schofield on the sexual behaviour of young people (1965) and Geoffrey Gorer on *Sex and Marriage in England Today* (1969, published 1971) found that promiscuity was not common teenage behaviour and most young people were either virgins on marriage or married their first and only sexual partner. A mixture of ignorance and social constraints served to keep promiscuity in check and, while liberal legislation opened the way to change, it represented only an inroad into the old religious and moral restraints and fears that had governed society for so many years.

All we can say with certainty is that from around 1959 a conjunction of circumstances meant that some of these restraints were beginning to crumble. A secular and pragmatic morality was gradually replacing one grounded in Christian ethical principles. Roy Jenkins argued that this made the country 'more civilised'.

Learning outcomes

In this section you have examined the main changes that are said to have constituted the 'social and cultural revolution' of the 1960s. These include the development of youth culture, the growth of rebellion and radicalism, and the liberalisation of society through legal change and broader changes in attitude. You have considered how the position of women altered and the final section on the 'permissive society' should have helped you to put some of these changes into perspective by questioning their extent and impact. Of course, change did not stop at the end of the 1960s and some of the themes examined in this section will be continued in Chapter 10.

 Examination-style questions

Roy Jenkins, during a speech in Abingdon in July 1969, commented on how the government had made more money available for the arts and how the laws on abortion, homosexuality and divorce, and theatre and literary censorship, had been radically reformed. He then continued:

> Despite the successes, the forces of liberalism and human freedom are now to some extent on the defensive. The 'permissive society' – always a misleading description – has been allowed to become a dirty phrase. A better phrase is the 'civilised society', a society based on the belief that different individuals will wish to make different decisions about their patterns of behaviour, and that, provided these do not restrict the freedom of others, they should be allowed to do so, within a framework of understanding and tolerance.

A   *Speech by Roy Jenkins, quoted in the **Sunday Times**, 20 July 1969*

Sir, I believe, and I'm by no means the only one who does, that Mr Roy Jenkins's Obscene Publications Act introduced in 1959 was an unmitigated disaster. He was, throughout his time as an MP and particularly as Home Secretary, a 'permissive' and his personal philosophy and social disasters littered the 'permissive' years. In 1969, he tried to claim that Britain had become a better place in which to live over the last 10 years. I say that it was in this period that the moral state of our nation was weakened, and the outlook for our children made uncertain.

B

From a letter by Mary Whitehouse published in the **Glasgow Herald**, *22 August 1982*

A permissive state is not necessarily the same as a permissive society. People may have had more freedom to all kinds of things in the sixties (and indeed they may have welcomed it) but they did not necessarily exercise that freedom. Individuals often expressed liberal attitudes on issues of personal morality but behaved in ways that were little different from their more morally buttoned up predecessors. Surveys consistently highlighted the continued power of moral conservatism across age ranges and class divisions throughout the decade.

C

From Mark Donnelly, **Sixties Britain**, *2005*

(a) Explain how far the views in Source B differ from those in Source A in relation to Roy Jenkins' attempt to bring about liberal change in the sixties. *(12 marks)*

Start by identifying several differences between the views of Sources A and B and try to pick out a short phrase from each to use as a quotation in support of your claims. For example, the 'forces of liberalism and human freedom' (Source A) could be contrasted with the comment about the weakening moral state of the nation (Source B) and Jenkins's claims about creating a 'civilised society' set against the 'unmitigated disaster' which the writer of Source B attributes to Jenkins's 'permissive' attitudes. It would also be helpful to explain the different interpretations of 'permissive' given in these two sources.

Finally, look for some similarity between the two sources to show the limitations to their differences. Both writers accept there have been changes but in your conclusion you might point out that they disagree over whether these had made Britain better or worse.

(b) Use Sources A, B and C and your own knowledge. How far did the changes of the 1960s in Britain create a 'permissive society'? *(24 marks)*

You will need to decide whether you think the changes did create a permissive soicety, only did so to a certain extent, or not at all. Plan your paragraphs to reflect a range of different changes that support your case. You will need a good deal of your own knowledge for this but don't forget that you are also required to use all three sources as evidence in support of your answer. Make sure you indicate where you will refer to them in your plan, and let your final answer lead to a conclusion that makes your judgement clear.

Exploring the detail

The Wootton Report

The recreational use of cannabis began in earnest during the 1950s when migrants from the Caribbean arrived in the UK. White jazz musicians playing in clubs in Soho in London were among the first to use it. During the 'flower power' years of the 1960s, it soared in popularity and concern was such that a home office committee was set up to investigate its use and effects. In 1968, the Wootton Report concluded: 'There is no evidence that this activity is causing violent crime or aggression, anti-social behaviour, or is producing in otherwise normal people conditions of dependence or psychosis requiring medical treatment'.

Activity

Research exercise

Try to find out more about the 'hippy' culture and experimentation with alternative lifestyles at this time. Is such behaviour evidence of a 'permissive society'?

In this chapter you will learn about:

■ the extent to which the Labour governments of 1964–70 were 'new' in style

■ the achievements of the Labour governments of 1964–70, and how the liberalism of the 1960s and the socialist ideas of the Labour governments of 1964–70 are inter-related

■ the type of Conservative government introduced by Edward Heath in 1970

■ the problem of industrial relations and the extent of Heath's success in addressing this

■ the economic and political situation in Britain by 1975.

Cross-reference

That Was The Week That Was is discussed on pages 80–1.

Further details on the **Establishment** and the political background to the **1964 election** are found on pages 20–1.

Material on the **'white heat of technology'** is given on pages 33–4.

In October 1963, when the 14th Earl of Home became the new Tory Prime Minister, the satirical British television programme *That Was The Week That Was* offered a mock address, delivered by the show's presenter, David Frost.

> My Lord, when I say that your acceptance of the Queen's commission to form an administration will prove an unmitigated catastrophe, it must not be thought that I bear you any personal ill will. You are the unwitting tool of a conspiracy of a tiny band of desperate men who have seen in you their last slippery chance of keeping the levers of power within their privileged circle. This is the choice for the electorate; on the one hand, Lord Home and on the other hand, Mr Harold Wilson. Dull Alec versus Smart Alec.

1 *David Frost, speaking on 'That Was The Week That Was', October 1963*

In the 1964 election, 'Smart Alec' won the day. 'Dull Alec' and the Establishment that he appeared to represent was forced from power and a new 'smarter' and more modern breed of politicians stepped to the front. That, at least, is what Harold Wilson's Labour supporters would have us believe. The 'Swinging 60s' were to be the 'socialist 60s' and a Labour government was a sign of the changing times.

■ New-style government

In October 1964, Labour won a narrow election victory, which the party was able to improve on in 1966.

Fig. 1 *The leaders of the Labour party cross their arms and sing the Labour anthem 'The Red Flag' at the end of their annual conference in 1968. From left to right: two unidentified party members, Mr Anthony Wedgwood Benn, W.E. Padley, Barbara Castle, Alice Bacon, Harold Wilson, Mrs White, Miss Sara Barkar, Jennie Lee, Miss Betty Lockwood, James Callaghan, George Brown, Ian Mikardo, Anthony Greenwood, A Skeffington, Bessie Braddock, and Harry Nicholas*

Table 1 *Number of seats, 1964 and 1966*

Election results by year	Labour	Conservative	Liberal	Others
1964	317	304	9	0
1966	363	253	12	2

Harold Wilson's commitment to a new-style modernist state, run by professional managers and planners, had won public support. He had promised to propel Britain into a new age moulded by the 'white heat of technology'. Investment in science, coupled with better educational provision, would, he believed, ensure the growth of the economy and bring an end to the 'stop-go' cycle of the Tory years. Science, planning, management, professionalism, public socialism: such were the bases on which Wilson's new-style government would be created.

Key profile

Harold Wilson

Harold Wilson (1922–95) was the son of an industrial chemist, educated at Wirral Grammar School and Oxford, where he read philosophy, politics and economics (PPE). Following Gaitskell's death, he was elected party leader in 1963. He took the centre ground in the divided party and tried to give it a new image, linking socialism with technological advance and avoiding being drawn into disputes over class conflict and Clause Four. He proved a charismatic leader and led Labour to victory in 1964 and 1966. He was witty, shrewd, able in debate and a superb tactician. He liked to pose as 'Huddersfield Harold', a classless leader with his Gannex raincoat and pipe. He was an excellent 'performer', especially on TV, and came across as a decent, kindly man who could identify with ordinary people and had a strong sense of social justice. Labour lost the 1970 election but won unexpectedly in 1974 – at first with only a minority administration but, in the second election of that year, with a workable majority. Wilson resigned in 1976.

Attitudes to modernisation and social change

Despite Wilson's faith in science, the new government was not helped by its own lack of expertise. Roy Jenkins, the first Minister of Aviation, later admitted that he had difficulty understanding his briefings because of his non-scientific mind, while the first Minister of Technology, Frank Cousins, was a union man who had little knowledge, and still less interest, in technological development. In 1966, when Anthony (Tony) Wedgwood Benn took over as Minister, the department performed rather better, although of the eight junior ministers who served from 1964 to 1970, only Lord Snow and Dr Jeremy Bray had any scientific or technological background. Wilson did try to encourage the cabinet to discuss technology but it met a mixed reception. Anthony Crosland recalled in his memoirs a 'dreary discussion on computers lasting an hour and a half' in June 1965.

Activity

Statistical analysis

Study Table 1. What can be learned from these results?

Activity

Preparing a presentation

Wilson's new government had a strong line-up. Choose one of the following Labour personalities and prepare a short presentation for the rest of your class. You should include reference to your politician's background and beliefs, as well as their actions and policies.

- George Brown
- James Callaghan
- Richard Crossman
- Barbara Castle
- Tony Crosland
- Denis Healey
- Roy Jenkins
- Frank Cousins
- Anthony Wedgwood Benn

Fig. 2 *Harold Wilson tried to promote a friendly, caring image*

Anthony Wedgwood Benn

Anthony Wedgwood Benn (born 1925) was educated at Westminster School and Oxford. He became a BBC producer and MP at 25. When his father, Viscount Stansgate, died, he fought to remain an MP as 'Tony Benn' and did not take the peerage. He believed in freedom of information and opposed violent intervention and nuclear weapons. He held office as Postmaster General (1964–6), Minister of Technology (1966–70), Secretary of State for Industry and Minister for Post and Telecommunications (1974–5) and Secretary of State for Energy (1975–9).

■ A closer look

Britain and science

Britain had produced many able scientists and had an impressive list of post-war Nobel prize winners. Britain had led the way in computer technology in the 1940s and Lyons Restaurants had developed the first business computer in 1951. Among Britain's 'firsts' were the TSR2 (a swing-wing plane begun in 1959), the Harrier vertical take-off jet, the hovercraft, fuel injection for car engines (1966), the Anglo-French Concorde project and the non-violent use of nuclear energy. However, research and development was costly. Britain could not compete with the USA, which spent vast government sums on research and development The Plowden Committee on the future of aviation concluded that Britain should buy American planes and, in 1964, the TRS2 project was scrapped.

In January 1965, Tony Benn lamented:

Defence, colour television, Concorde, rocket development – these are all issues raising economic considerations that reveal this country's basic inability to stay in the big league. We just can't afford it.

A more pressing and recognisable concern was the state of the economy. Labour had inherited a debt of about £800 million and some believed **devaluation** was the only way forward. However, Wilson's adamant refusal even to think about such a move led ministers to nickname devaluation, 'the unmentionable'. Wilson was convinced that problems could be solved by another of his 'modernising' ideas – careful management and planning.

George Brown was placed in charge of a new Department of Economic Affairs (DEA), where he tried to establish voluntary agreement about wages and prices in conjunction with industrialists, trades union leaders and civil servants. He set growth targets and devised a national system of 'economic planning councils', but his proposals came to nothing as the old-fashioned civil servants at the Treasury undermined his efforts, refusing to pass over papers and even tapping his phone. In 1966, Wilson moved Brown to the Ministry of Foreign Affairs and the DEA was abandoned in 1967. With it went some of Wilson's 'modernising' zeal and commitment to science, which no longer seemed the answer to Britain's problems.

■ Key term

Devaluation: lowering the value of the British pound against other countries' currencies. In 1949, the Labour Party had been forced to devalue the pound from US$4.03 to US$2.88 and memories of this humiliation lingered. Devaluation made imports expensive but encouraged the purchase of cheap British exports.

Key profile

George Brown

George Brown (1914–85) came from a working-class trade unionist background. He was Labour's shadow spokesman on Agriculture (1955–6), Supply (1955–9), Defence (1956–61) and Home Affairs (1961–4). He was defeated by Wilson in the leadership elections of 1963 and became Secretary of State for Economic Affairs in 1964 and Secretary of State for Foreign Affairs, 1966. He resigned in 1968.

The pound had grown weaker and, with an outbreak of war in the Middle East affecting oil supplies and a national dock strike in August 1967, the dreaded devaluation took place. Labour also made defence cuts and introduced hire purchase restrictions and higher interest rates; policies that looked little different from those of the previous Tory governments. Despite the 1967 devaluation, by 1969–70 inflation was running at 12 per cent.

In a TV broadcast, Harold Wilson tried to justify his decision:

> Our decision to devalue attacks our problem at the root. Tonight we must face the new situation. First what this means. From now the pound abroad is worth 14 per cent or so less in terms of other currencies. That does not mean, of course, that the pound here in Britain, in your pocket or purse or in your bank, has been devalued. What it does mean is that we shall now be able to sell more goods abroad on a competitive basis. This is a tremendous opportunity for all our exporters, and for many who have not yet started to sell their goods overseas. But it will also mean that the goods that we buy from abroad will be dearer, and so for many of these goods, it will be cheaper to buy British.

2 *Harold Wilson, TV broadcast*

Barbara Castle, the Secretary of State for Employment, dismayed that a Labour government should face trouble from the trades unions, produced a new set of proposals in a paper called 'In Place of Strife' (1969). Had her suggestions been put into effect, a radical change in industrial relations, allowing for state intervention and outlawing unofficial 'wild cat' strikes, would have occurred. However, the proposals had to be withdrawn following a unionist outcry and were replaced with a formula allowing the unions to monitor their own disputes.

Some aspects of Wilson's government were 'new style'. Its members were undoubtedly more working class and liberal in outlook than those they replaced and Wilson himself made a point of mixing with pop stars, fashion designers, footballers and photographers to give Labour an air of 'fashionability', even if the depth of his commitment to the 'Swinging 60s' can be questioned. The government's education policies including the development of comprehensive schools, the expansion of higher education and the founding of the Open University may also be seen as attempts to break down the old class barriers. Furthermore, the establishment of a Ministry of Arts under Jennie Lee provided government funding for the Arts Council and British Film Institute, showing a concern to broaden cultural opportunities for all.

Activity

Source analysis

Use Source 2 and your own knowledge.

1 How did Wilson 'sell' devaluation to the British public?

2 How convincing are his arguments?

3 Explain why the issue of devaluation caused so much trouble for Wilson and his government.

Exploring the detail

The Arts Council and British Film Institute

The Arts Council was founded in 1945 to give people full access to Britain's cultural heritage. In the 1960s, it was responsible for the distribution of grants for artistic ventures and the expansion of cultural provision on London's South Bank and in the regions.

The British Film Institute was founded in 1933 to maintain an archive library and promote British films. In 1965, its grant was increased by one third.

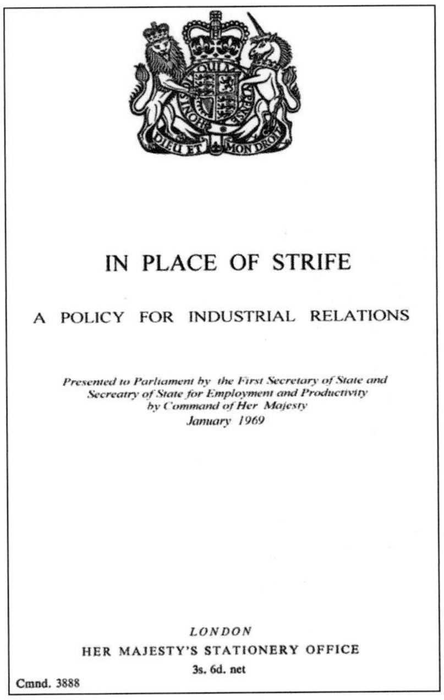

IN PLACE OF STRIFE

A POLICY FOR INDUSTRIAL RELATIONS

Presented to Parliament by the First Secretary of State and Secretary of State for Employment and Productivity by Command of Her Majesty
January 1969

LONDON
HER MAJESTY'S STATIONERY OFFICE
3s. 6d. net

Cmnd. 3888

Fig. 3 *'In Place of Strife', Barbara Castle's set of proposals to curb the power of trades unions in 1969, roused so much hostility it never became law*

Cross-reference

One example of a working-class member of Wilson's government is **Roy Jenkins**, whose work as Home Secretary is outlined on page 77.

Education policies and the work of **Jennie Lee** are discussed on pages 115–6.

To review the **anti-war movement** and **student troubles of 1966–8**, see pages 71–6.

To review the legislation on **cannabis**, refer back to page 91.

Immigration problems and the role of the **Race Relations Board** are discussed on pages 126–7.

Nevertheless, the Labour government did not set out with a 'liberalising' agenda. While Labour took the credit – or blame – for the many changes that took place while Jenkins was at the Home Office, their manifestos made no mention of moral issues. Labour leaders, like Wilson and Brown, were conservative on moral issues and many working-class Labour MPs remained suspicious of change. Nevertheless, Labour was 'new' in one respect. It favoured the use of 'expert witnesses' and a technical and rational approach to alterations in the law. The same 'measured judgement' was also seen in the government's handling of the anti-war protests and student troubles of 1966–8. It took a firm line on drugs, refusing to legalise cannabis in 1969, but it did lower the voting age to 18 in 1969. The government also tried to address problems of racial discrimination with the establishment of the Race Relations Board, although its Commonwealth Immigrants Bill of 1968 was restrictive in approach.

Wilson's 'white-hot world of technology' turned out to be a fantasy and government may have been superficially different but was fundamentally unchanged. The attempt at economic planning failed, proposed reform of the House of Lords and industrial relations fell by the wayside and an attempt to enter the EEC had to be abandoned. Wilson's political thinking was, at heart, conventional. However he might like to portray himself, he was of a previous generation and not in touch with the youth culture of his day. Wilson once said that 'A lot of politics is presentation' and some might dismiss his government as little more than that.

Activity

Revision exercise

1. Create a two-column table. In one column, list the positive changes that came about in the Wilson era and, in the other column, list the things that did not change or changed for the worst.

2. Using your table, answer the following essay question: 'Wilson's governments of 1964–70 were failures.' Explain why you agree or disagree with this view.

Heath and the growing problem of industrial relations

When Wilson called for an election in 1970, the Labour position seemed reasonably strong. Although there had been problems with the unions, the economy appeared to be improving and opinion polls were favourable. His Conservative opponent in the election was Edward Heath who, despite a different background from previous Tory leaders, was a man whom Wilson could easily trump on television. However, the publication of some economic statistics during the campaign, which suggested more problems, turned the tide of public opinion. The result was a Conservative victory.

Key profile

Edward Heath

Edward Heath (1916–2005) was the son of a carpenter and was educated at Chatham House Grammar School and Oxford. He had worked as the Chief Whip in the Conservative Party between 1955 and 1959 and, as Lord Privy Seal, had tried unsuccessfully to negotiate Britain's entry into the EEC in 1963. He became the first Tory Party leader to be elected by his fellow MPs in 1965 and, after Sir Alec Douglas-Home, his supporters hoped that a middle-class leader would help change the party's image. He was a man of great integrity, a bachelor whose interests were music and sailing. However, despite his superb lower-middle class credentials, he still appeared rather aloof and less at ease in the media spotlight than his opponent, Harold Wilson. Like Wilson, he believed in moderation, managerialism and compromise. He was a pro-business politician and, in opposition in 1970, had proposed an agenda of trades union reform, tax cuts and spending restraints. In power, he led Britain into the EEC in 1973 but for the whole of the period 1970–4 he battled to control industrial action and inflation. Two election defeats in 1974 led to his replacement by Margaret Thatcher in 1975.

Fig. 4 *Edward Heath beaming at his success in securing a Yes vote in the referendum on Britain's continuing membership of the EEC in 1975*

Edward Heath led the Conservative Party in three elections.

Table 2 *Number of seats, 1970, February 1974 and October 1974*

Election results by year	Labour	Conservative	Liberal	Others
1970	287	330	6	7
February 1974	301	297	14	23
October 1974	319	277	13	26

As seen in Table 2, Heath was only Prime Minister for three and a half years, which did not give him long to fulfil the promises he made when he first took office, namely to:

- offer the British people a new type of Conservative government
- take Britain into the EEC
- reduce taxes and allow more economic freedom
- reduce union power and cut down on 'wild cat' (unofficial) strikes
- concentrate government subsidies on those most in need of them
- rebuild Britain's economy and make the country stronger (in contrast to Labour's devaluation of sterling).

One of Heath's major achievements was to show the British people that a Conservative government could be as 'down to earth' and 'modernist' as Labour. He promoted middle-class people, like himself, to high office, among them Margaret Thatcher. He ran his cabinet in a business-like manner. He created new conglomerate ministries such as the Department of Trade and Industry and the Department of the Environment, in keeping with his belief in looking at the 'big picture', and he spent much

Activity

Thinking point

In his 1970 election campaign, Heath promised to bring an end to 'six long years of hard Labour' and 'to restore honesty to government and integrity to politics'. He argued that Labour had lost touch with the wishes of the electorate and that the conservatives would address the country's needs.

As you read through this section of the chapter, consider how far Heath succeeded in keeping these promises.

Cross-reference

Further details on **Margaret Thatcher** can be found on pages 108–9.

time setting up committees, consulting professionals, industrialists and workers to widen involvement in government. Heath is also remembered as the man who was finally able to take Britain into the EEC in 1973, an achievement of which he was justly proud.

However, his time in power was dogged by economic problems and the related problem of industrial relations. He found neither easy to address. He began by cutting public expenditure, abolishing the **National Board for Prices and Incomes (NBPI)** and reducing taxes in an attempt to increase investment. However, as inflation and unemployment accelerated and the country's growth rate slowed down, he was forced to reverse his policy and reintroduce regulation.

Fig. 5 *The dustmen's strike hits home in London in autumn 1970. This was just one of a number of industrial disputes that year*

Within months of taking office, Heath was faced with a dock strike, a large pay settlement for dustmen, a power workers' go-slow that led to power cuts, and a postal workers' strike. Ignoring the Labour experience, in December 1970 he drew up an Industrial Relations bill in an attempt to curb union power. This became law in 1971 and laid down the following:

- A system of registration for unions. Registered unions were to be given full legal status.
- A statutory right to belong to a union and be protected against unfair dismissal.
- Clear union rules stipulating which officers could instigate direct industrial action.
- The demand for a pre-strike ballot and a compulsory 'cooling off' period before a strike could be called.
- Provision for members' complaints against a union to be recorded.
- The illegality of sympathetic strikes.
- The illegality of industrial action by an unregistered union and of strikes to bring about a closed shop or change collective agreements.
- A National Industrial Relations Court to enforce these measures.

The act provoked an angry backlash and most trades unions refused to cooperate with the scheme. They refused to register and as a result 32 unions were suspended. In February 1971, 100,000 trades unionists demonstrated in London and, a month later, 1.5 million engineering workers staged a one-day strike.

In 1972, the Transport and General Workers' Union was twice fined for contempt by the National Industrial Relations Court and on 5 May some dockers – 'the Pentonville Five' – were sent to prison for breaking the terms of the act. Throughout the country, industrial action in defence of pay claims escalated with strikes by gas and power workers, engine drivers, miners, ambulance drivers, hospital staff, firemen and civil servants. In all, 1972 saw the highest number of days lost in strikes since the General Strike of 1926 – 23,909,000.

A closer look

The Pentonville Five

'The Pentonville Five' were dockers who were jailed for five days for defying the Industrial Relations Act. Employers wanted to cut costs, and jobs, by setting up inland depots to handle containers using non-dockers on low wages which threatened workers' jobs.

The dockers responded by picketing the depots, ignoring the new regulations concerning strike action. On Friday 21 July, five London dockers – Tony Merrick, Conny Clancy, Derek Watkins, Vic Turner and Bernie Steer – were taken to Pentonville prison. Within hours, dockers in all major ports in Britain were on strike and the print workers in Fleet Street shut down the national press out of sympathy. Over the next five days, 250,000 workers came out on strike at some point, and almost 100,000 on all-out unofficial strike. On Tuesday 25 July, thousands of engineering workers and transport workers in London, Sheffield and the west of Scotland held a day's sympathetic strike. They were joined by steel workers in Yorkshire, rail workers at London's Waterloo, and council workers in Tower Hamlets and Lambeth in London. The Trades Union Congress (TUC) announced that there would be a one-day general strike the following Monday but by then they knew it would not be necessary. The Law Lords set the dockers free. It was a major victory for the workers and a decisive defeat for the Tory government.

Overshadowing all these strikes was the action taken by the miners whose strike began in January 1972 and continued to dog the Conservative government for the rest of its time in power. In February 1972, a three-day week to conserve electricity had to be instituted and blackouts took place as electricity was switched off for six to nine hours a day. Heath was forced to give in and, following the recommendations of the Wilberforce Committee, the miners returned to work at the end of February with an annual increase of 21 per cent, plus 15 additional concessions.

A closer look

The miners' strike of 1972

The miners had cause to feel bitter. The coal industry was in decline and the workforce had fallen from 593,000 in 1960 to 280,000 in 1972. It had been left behind in pay negotiations and its members felt no one cared. In 1971, the Miners' Union had presented a pay demand of 43 per cent but the State-owned National Coal Board, under government pressure to keep any wage claim below 8 per cent, refused this. The miners began an overtime ban in November and, when talks broke down, called a strike in January 1972, knowing that this would hit industrialists and so put pressure on the government. Three-quarters of the electricity used in Britain came from coal-burning power stations and the strike came at a time when it would hurt – during the peak demand of the winter months.

The miners' strike began at midnight on 9 January 1972. Three months of negotiations had ended in deadlock and the mine workers laid down their tools. They used 'flying pickets' to target all power stations, steelworks, ports, coal depots and other major coal users. Arthur Scargill, a union activist working at Woolley colliery in South Yorkshire, described the first day of the picket as 'the greatest day of my life'.

Edward Heath, on the other hand, called the events: 'the most vivid, direct and terrifying challenge to the rule of law that I could ever recall emerging from within our own country'.

The strike lasted for seven weeks and all 289 British pits were closed. Schools dependent on coal-fired heating were forced to shut and by mid-February 1.2 million workers had been laid off. The strike made Arthur Scargill a national name. He was elected president of the Yorkshire National Union of Mineworkers (NUM) in 1973.

Question

Explain why Edward Heath was so alarmed by the outbreak of the miners' strike in 1972.

The tide of industrial disputes continued, despite Heath's Industry Act 1972, which established a three-way national agreement on prices and wages, investments and benefits involving the government, TUC (representing the workers) and CBI (representing the employers). Heath also increased investment in job centres to combat unemployment figures of almost a million; arranged huge grants to 'failing' companies like the Upper Clyde Shipbuilders; and devised a new scheme for regional planning committees.

Nevertheless, in October 1973, the fire service began a series of unofficial strikes and in November the electrical power engineers banned out-of-hours work, while the miners (although now among the highest paid in the working classes) banned overtime. The threat of another miners' strike was bad enough, but it came at the very moment that OPEC, the oil consortium, announced massive oil price increases following the outbreak of the Arab–Israeli war in October. Heath tried to negotiate and announced immediate emergency measures, but when the miners proved obstinate he felt the only way out was a snap general election to put the question 'Who governs Britain?' to the electorate.

There was a brief three-week election campaign in February 1974, during which the miners went ahead with their strike, supported by other unionists who refused to transport coal and oil to the power stations.

There were understandably a number of different views on this election.

Exploring the detail

Emergency measures, 1974

Plans were made for petrol rationing and coupons printed and distributed. The national speed limit was cut to 50 mph to conserve fuel. A three-day working week was announced and people were encouraged to share baths. Television was ended at 10.30pm each evening. Street lighting and flood lighting were cut to conserve electricity.

This time the strife has got to stop. Only you can stop it. It is time for you to speak with your vote.

| **3** | *Edward Heath's election speech, February 1974* |

I consider it an act of gross irresponsibility that this general election has been called in the face of the current and impending industrial action.

| **4** | *Speech by Enoch Powell (Conservative MP), February 1974* |

My own feeling is that I would prefer us to be having an election in a calm climate rather than in a position of strike action.

| **5** | *Mr Joe Gormley, leader of the NUM, February 1974* |

Activity

Source analysis

Use Sources 3, 4 and 5 and your own knowledge. How far was Edward Heath's defeat in the election of 1974 the result of the miners' strike?

Within Britain as a whole there were also mixed feelings. The union action had created a lot of hostility towards the strikers, particularly in the Tory strongholds of the south. Some even alleged a 'communist conspiracy' pointing out that the deputy leader of the mine workers, Mike McGahey, was a Communist Party member and had openly said he wanted to bring down the government. At the same time, there were those who felt that the Tories had handled affairs badly and had been responsible for the chaos of the previous two years.

Although Wilson had not expected to win, various factors played into his hands. First, he could claim that Labour had a better relationship with the unions and could deal more effectively with troubles than the Conservatives. Furthermore, he was able to substantiate this claim just before the election when he intervened to stop a series of one-day strikes by British rail drivers. Luckily for Wilson, some poor trade figures also arrived during the campaign and a mistake by the pay board was revealed that showed that the miners were relatively less well paid than formerly believed. To Labour's advantage was a surge in support for the Liberals, while Enoch Powell decided to quit the Tories and urged his supporters to vote Labour. All this helped Wilson considerably, although the results (Table 2 on page 99) gave no party an overall majority. Heath tried to cling on, trying to do a deal with the Liberals but, in the end, he had to concede defeat.

Certainly, the Heath government of 1970–4 can only be judged an abject failure. Heath was over-ideological at first and then hypnotised by the miners. The trade union reforms of these years caused more problems than they cured. He left a legacy which took years to overcome. About the only good thing that can be said for Heath is that he showed a degree of sensitivity when it came to unemployment.

| **6** | *Adapted from Nick Tiratsoo (ed.),* ***From Blitz to Blair****, 1998* |

Cross-reference

Enoch Powell is discussed in more detail on pages 128–30.

Activity

Source analysis

Read Sources 6 and 7. Explain how far the views in Source 7 differ from those in Source 6 in relation to Heath's premiership.

Heath is a political leader whose reputation deserves to be revisited. He was the first outsider to break through the class barriers of the old Tory party. His European vision came first hand. He was a genuinely compassionate and unusually brave politician. His struggle with trade union power, conducted at the worst possible time, was relentless, but he was up against forces too big to conquer quickly. Mostly Edward Heath was plain unlucky.

7
*Adapted from Andrew Marr, **A History of Modern Britain**, 2007*

To provide a balanced assessment of Heath's time in power, some context is necessary. Britain's fortunes were bound up with what was happening in the world economy, where the steady growth experienced since 1945 was suddenly brought to a halt by the wars in the Middle East that affected oil prices. Although the British unions elicited much public sympathy in their struggle to maintain wage levels, the most vociferous represented groups, like dockers and miners, whose place in the modern world had to change. Although it is easy to criticise Heath's policy of 'confrontation', as seen in the Industrial Relations Act, it can also be argued that the unions behaved in a selfish way and were over-ready to use strike action.

Any assessment of the years 1970–3 should also take into account that, despite the picture created in the media (and later exploited for political gain in the Thatcher years), strike activity was actually restricted to only 2 per cent of manufacturing establishments, the majority of conflicts lasted less than three days and only around 5 per cent of disputes received official backing. The problems were mainly confined to the coal, docking and car industries, all of which had their own particular reasons for complaint.

Heath's premiership was so overshadowed by the problem of industrial relations that it is easy to forget the other measures that took place under his leadership. Britain's membership of the EEC in 1973, the raising of the school leaving age to 16 the same year, currency reform in 1972 (following the initial decision to **go decimal** under Wilson in 1965), the availability of the pill on the NHS, the reorganisation of local government, and the setting up of regional and area boards to run the NHS were among Heath's achievements. Heath, like Wilson, was a planner, even if not all of his plans succeeded.

Labour's return

The results of the February and October 1974 elections can be seen in Table 2 on page 99. Wilson resumed office in March and the miners' strike was promptly ended on the basis of an agreement reached by Heath just before the election. A pay board was set up to investigate the miners' claims and the miners returned to work with a 29 per cent pay rise. A national plan for coal, including big investment in new coalfields such as Selby in return for increased production, was agreed.

Wilson revoked the Industrial Relations Act, set up the Advisory Conciliation and Arbitration Service (ACAS) and persuaded the unions to moderate wage claims in return for legislation to increase social and legal rights. Although there was a nurses' strike in May, Wilson's tactics appeared promising and he called the October election to strengthen his position. From 1974–5, the number of days lost through strikes halved and they were to halve again the following year. In September 1975, the TUC promised there would be a voluntary wage restraint and by 1976 the situation seemed calmer.

Key term

Go decimal: in 1966 the Decimal Currency Board was created to prepare for the introduction of a new British currency replacing the old 144 pence with 100 new pence in a pound. The traditional 12 pence in a shilling and 20 shillings in a pound would become obsolete. The new system was designed to put Britain more in line with the rest of Europe, which used a system based on tens and hundreds.

However, when Wilson retired at 60 in 1976, Britain's economic problems and industrial relations were far from solved. The Labour government had been forced to introduce high taxation (83 per cent at the top rate and 98 per cent for unearned income) and there was talk of further controls and selective nationalisation. The long boom was over and from 1974 living standards would go into decline. The problem of unemployment was back and the optimism that had bred the 'Swinging 60s' had gone.

 Summary question

'Edward Heath promised voters a lot but achieved very little.' Explain why you agree or disagree with this view of Heath's premiership between 1970 and 1973.

AQA Examiner's tip

Begin by making a list of Heath's promises of 1970 and alongside each promise write down whether it was wholly achieved, partly achieved or not achieved and give some examples. (Look at Sources 3, 6 and 7 for quotations to use in support of your ideas.) In your answer, consider where Heath tried to carry out his promises and why he succeeded or failed.

Your conclusion might provide an explanatory overview. For example, if you feel Heath failed to live up to his promises, was this because he was fundamentally dishonest or were there other reasons?

10

Widening opportunities

In this chapter you will learn about:

- the extent to which women had improved their position and gained greater equality with men by 1975

- new ideas on education and the development of comprehensive schools in the late 1960s/early 1970s

- the reasons for and results of the expansion of higher education and the inauguration of the Open University.

Fig. 1 *The Conservative Party leader, Margaret Thatcher, had to juggle the demands of being a wife and a mother with her burgeoning political career*

Fig. 2 *Female emancipation?*

Activity

Revision exercise

You have already seen how the position of women changed during the 1960s. Before reading this chapter, jot down as many of the changes that you can remember that altered the position of women. You may like to look back to Chapters 3 and 8 to help you with this.

Progress towards equality for women

Table 1 *Acts of parliament affecting the position of women, with reference to changes in property and divorce law, equal pay and sex discrimination*

Year	Act	Details
1964	Married Women's Property Act	Allowed women to retain half the money they saved from any housekeeping
1967	Matrimonial Homes Act	Gave husband and wife the same right of occupation of the family home
1969	Divorce Reform Act	Allowed irretrievable breakdown of a marriage as sufficient grounds for divorce (from 1971)
1970	Matrimonial Property Act	Recognised that a wife's work – inside or outside the home – made a financial contribution to married life and should be taken into account when dividing up the property in a divorce case
1970 (Labour)	Equal Pay Act	Ruled that men and women should receive the same pay for the same job (but implementation was delayed to allow employers time to prepare their payroll adjustments)
1972	Criminal Justice Act	Ended the property qualification for jury service enabling more women to serve on juries
1973	Guardianship of Children Act	Gave mothers equal rights with fathers in bringing up children
1973	Domicile and Matrimonial Proceedings Act	Enabled a married woman living apart from her husband to have a legal domicile of her own
1975	Sex Discrimination Act	Enforced the Equal Pay Act of 1970

Women's work

Table 2 *Women in paid employment, 1951–71*

	1951	1961	1971
As % of total labour force	31	33	37
As % of women aged 20–64	36	42	52
Part-time as % of total labour force	12	26	35
% of all married women aged 15–59 in labour force	26	35	49

Jane Lewis, **Women in Britain Since 1945***, 1992*

The statistics in Table 2 demonstrate the growing trend towards paid female employment, which accelerated in the 1970s as a new lifestyle pattern began to emerge with far more women returning to work after the birth of their children and taking minimal 'time out'. Yet women still remained disproportionately concentrated in lower-status occupations and employment varied by region with far more females working in the affluent south and east in comparison with less prosperous areas such as Wales. The numbers in professional jobs still rose only slowly and women remained massively under-represented in parliament, the police and the armed forces. Nevertheless, women were gradually beginning to break into new areas of work from bus drivers and jockeys to RSPCA inspectors.

Equal pay and the Sex Discrimination Act

Although women formed about 35 per cent of the workforce by 1970, a report established that average pay rates were only 63.1 per cent of men's. The 1970 Equal Pay Act attempted to address this disparity and established the principle of equal rates of pay for the same work or work rated as equivalent.

However, compliance was left as voluntary until 1975. The act brought a marked increase in women's relative earnings, but the gap did not disappear and some women resorted to taking their cases to the European Court, highlighting the need for further action. One concern was the act's failure to address bars to female promotion, a matter remedied by the Sex Discrimination Act 1975.

Under the terms of the Sex Discrimination Act it became unlawful to:

- ■ discriminate on grounds of sex in the field of employment and in the provision of educational facilities, housing, goods, services and opportunities
- ■ discriminate in adverts in the above-mentioned areas.

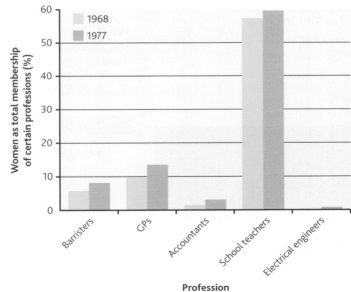

Fig. 3 *Women in certain professions, 1968 and 1977*

Fig. 4 *The campaign for equal pay for women was a long hard battle*

The Equal Opportunities Commission was also established to administer and monitor the act, with powers to investigate discrimination and issue orders that had the force of law.

This was not a final victory but it did mean that by 1980 women's wage levels had reached 73.5 per cent of men's and, significantly, more women were entering business and professional occupations.

Pressure for equality did, of course, cut both ways. For some, like the female machinists at the Dagenham Ford plant on whose behalf Barbara Castle intervened to bring their wages in line with the men's in 1968, or the female MPs whose pension status was made equal to men's the same year, it improved their lot. However, some female sportswomen found the media asking whether women should continue to have their own championships, while in the street, deference to women and other manly courtesies seemed to be on the wane.

As with so many changes, the quest for equality also produced some extremist ideas. Some feminists suggested that the English language should be rewritten and words like 'mankind' removed, while the Labour Party was the first to introduce the term 'chair person' rather than chairman at party gatherings. Certainly the early 1970s had seen some gains, but these were far outweighed by the inequalities and discrimination that remained. Sexual harassment remained a problem and issues like rape and domestic violence were taken up by feminist groups.

The appointment of Margaret Thatcher

One victory in the onward march of women towards greater equality came with the election of Margaret Thatcher as the Conservative Party leader in 1975. Women had been eligible as parliamentary candidates since 1918 but they had remained oddities before the Second World War and even in 1945 there had only been 24 women MPs (21 of these sitting as Labour MPs). Between 1950 and 1979, the number of women standing for election remained around 40 for Labour and 30 for the Conservatives and, in 1966, just 26 female MPs had been elected.

Margaret Thatcher had been one of only seven women (as opposed to 246 men) on the Conservative benches in 1966 and she had only got there by fighting the prejudices of selection committees, who thought she would be unable to mix work as an MP and mother, as well as those of male colleagues anxious not to be overshadowed by a woman.

Key profile

Margaret Thatcher

Margaret Thatcher (born 1925) was the daughter of a grocer from Grantham, Lincolnshire. She attended the local grammar school and went to Oxford University. She married Denis Thatcher, a businessman, and entered parliament for Finchley in 1959. She joined Heath's cabinet as Education Minister in 1970 and in February 1975 stood against Heath in the leadership contest, defeating him by 130 votes to 119. She went on to become the first female prime minister in 1979.

Fig. 5 *Margaret Thatcher became the first female Prime Minister of Britain in 1979*

That a female should have made it to the top of the Conservative Party, and one from the middle classes too, shows just how far that party had come since 1970. It was a cause for much female celebration. Yet, even Margaret Thatcher's rise should not be seen as an all-out women's victory. She had been able to advance herself because she had married a wealthy businessman. Without Denis's money, connections and support, she might never have been able to raise a family and achieve a parliamentary seat. Making her way in a man's world had not been easy and it had taken someone of her particular determination to do this. In parliament, she was patronised and sneered at as opposition leader and yet her resilience proved an example to women fighting their own lesser battles. As a leader, she tried to turn her position as a woman into an asset. Her handbag became a personal trademark and when the Russians dubbed her the Iron Lady she took it as a compliment. However, some might say that she simply 'acted the man'; she indulged in 'power dressing' and even learnt to lower the pitch of her voice.

■ Question

'Women were still regarded as second-class citizens in 1975.' Explain why you agree or disagree with this view.

■ Education and comprehensive schools

Fig. 6 *Holland Park School in London, seen here in 1961, was one of the new generation of modern comprehensive schools*

Following the **Butler Act** 1944, most British children sat an eleven plus exam in their last year at primary school. From this, they were selected for grammar school, technical school (although the numbers here were very small) or a secondary modern. This system had led to a social division between those pupils who attended the grammar schools, took examinations and generally pursued higher education and those who were sent to the more practical secondary schools where students left at 15, without qualifications. By the 1960s, the idea that the different types of secondary school were equal in status had long since passed. The secondary modern pupils were seen as

Key term

Butler Act: passed in 1944, this act tried to provide 'secondary education for all', allowing for the development of different types of secondary school. By 1960, two out of every three state-educated children went to secondary modern schools.

eleven plus failures and the whole system appeared socially divisive with the majority of grammar school places going to those from a middle-class background.

Studies proved that IQ testing could be influenced by upbringing and coaching and that the system discriminated against working-class children. Even when they made it to a grammar school, they could find the experience difficult. They might lose friends or contact with their neighbourhood or even parents. A working-class girl from Huddersfield recalled:

> My old friends dwindled away until they only included those from the [grammar] school and the church I attended. Quarrels with my parents came from the fact that other children were earning their living at my age – 'Why couldn't I be more thoughtful?' I'd reply, 'You sent me to grammar school. I can't help you because of my homework.' Grammar school taught me to read widely, yet at the expense of my parents. I thought an evening could not be spent in a pleasanter way than doing my homework and then reading – and not joining in conversation.

1   *Adapted from Ross McKibbin, **Classes and Cultures**, 1998*

Key term

Comprehensive school: one which provides secondary education for all the children in a given area. It does not select its pupils.

Under the Butler Act, local education authorities were given responsibility for schools and in some areas, for example Labour-controlled Greater London, they had established **comprehensive schools**. In such schools, every child had, in theory at least, the same opportunities to learn at their own pace and sit exams according to their own abilities in each subject.

By 1964, 1 in 10 pupils was being educated in a comprehensive School (10 times as many as in 1951) but it was still only a small minority. Labour's election victory in 1964 and the advent of Tony Crosland as Minister of Education from 1965 accelerated this process. Although Wilson had promised in 1963 that grammar schools would only be abolished 'over my dead body', Crosland's views had always been more extreme. His name will long be associated with this memorable declaration to his wife:

Did you know?

Scotland has a separate education system and was therefore beyond Crosland's control.

> If it's the last thing I do, I'm going to destroy every last f– – – – – – grammar school in England. And Wales. And Northern Ireland.

2   *The words of Tony Crosland, recalled by his wife, Susan*

In July 1965, Tony Crosland issued Circular 10/65 to local education authorities (LEAs):

> It is the Government's declared objective to end selection at eleven plus and to eliminate separatism in secondary education. The Government's policy has been endorsed by the House of Commons in a motion passed on 21st January 1965:
>
> 'That this House, conscious of the need to raise educational standards at all levels, and regretting that the realisation of this objective is impeded by the separation of children into different types of secondary

schools, notes with approval the efforts of local authorities to reorganise secondary education on comprehensive lines which will preserve all that is valuable in grammar school education for those children who now receive it and make it available to more children; This House believes that the time is now ripe for a declaration of national policy.'

The Secretary of State accordingly requests local education authorities, if they have not already done so, to prepare and submit to him plans for reorganising secondary education in their areas on comprehensive lines.

| 3 | *Tony Crosland, Circular 10/65, 12 July 1965* |

Although this circular was not a statutory requirement, many authorities responded. In 1966, the government made money for new school buildings conditional on the drawing up of plans for comprehensive schools and by 1970 only eight authorities had failed to do so. By 1970, there were 1,145 comprehensive schools catering for one in three of all state-educated secondary school pupils.

This growth continued despite the arrival of a Conservative government in 1970 and Margaret Thatcher as Minister of Education from 1970 to 1974. The Conservatives withdrew Labour's 1965 circular but otherwise left the matter in the hands of the local education authorities, which generally continued with plans for comprehensive schools as they could save money by merging existing girls' and boys' schools. By 1974, there were 2,000 comprehensives catering for almost two in three secondary school pupils. Only when a forceful case was put forward by interested parties were local authority plans to comprehensivise stopped.

Dame Hornsby-Smith successfully took up the case against one comprehensive school:

> I defy any educationalist to prove that this scheme [to merge Bexley Grammar School with Westwood Secondary Modern] provides better education and opportunities for the children in my constituency. It can only reduce the education which is successfully pursued in first- class schools with devoted staff. These proposals are opposed by the schools concerned and by hundreds of parents. I can say without fear of contradiction that the schools are well above average. I ask the Minister to ensure that in any new scheme this provision is not reduced, and that opportunities for children are not and shall not be destroyed.

| 4 | *Dame Patricia Hornsby-Smith, MP for Chistlehurst Heath* |

Margaret Thatcher rejected the Bexley proposals as 'educationally unsound'. However, Edward Heath was later to write in his autobiography:

> All too few schools followed Bexley's example and Margaret Thatcher felt able to reject only 326 out of 3,612 proposals to end selection that were submitted to her. I do wish in retrospect that the many supporters of selection had all campaigned more vigorously before it was too late.

| 5 | *Edward Heath, **The Course of My Life**, 1998* |

Key term

Direct grant schools: mostly old, endowed grammar schools that admitted a substantial proportion of pupils on scholarships from the LEAs. They catered for around 2 per cent of secondary school pupils. Some 80 per cent of those pupils stayed until 18 and half their leavers went to universities. These were phased out from 1976.

Exploring the detail

The Plowden Report

Lady Plowden's report of 1967 followed a long investigation into English primary education and the transition to secondary education. It began, 'At the heart of the educational process lies the child' and it emphasised the need to see children as individuals. It approved the abolition of secondary selection and recommended greater flexibility in the curriculum, for example 'learning by discovery'.

Activity

Source analysis

Explain how far the views in Source 7 differ from those in Source 6 in relation to the impact of educational change in the 1960s.

It is hard to say how successful these new comprehensives were. The mergers and changes in status for schools caused considerable disruption in the early days. Wilson justified them by claiming that comprehensives meant a 'grammar school education for all', but many middle-class parents remained unconvinced. Some turned to the **direct grant schools** (which were allowed to continue) and independent schools, which meant that the idea of a truly 'comprehensive' system was flawed from the start. Opponents argued that comprehensives downgraded standards and were only as good as the area in which they were situated. In Sheffield, the local authority attempted to create a social mix by bussing children from one residential area to another, but this had to be abandoned after parental protests. Unfortunately, the coincidence of the development of the comprehensives with the Plowden Report of 1967, which favoured mixed-ability classes and child-centred learning, created the misleading impression that comprehensive schooling meant the abandonment of traditional styles of learning.

> The destruction of the selective state schools of England merely drove more of the middle class to the private sector, thus improving the prospects and profits of the fee-charging public schools that Labour's radicals so despised. Other parents who could afford it bought a home in a 'good' school district, leaving the children of the poor at the mercy of the weakest schools and the worst teachers and with a much reduced prospect of upward educational mobility. The 'comprehensivisation' of British secondary education was the most socially retrograde piece of legislation in post-war Britain.

6

*Tony Judt, **Post-war: A History of Europe Since 1945**, 2007*

> The belief which drove politicians like Tony Crosland was a passionate conviction that all children, from whatever background, are alike in their capacity to reason, to imagine, to aspire to a successful and rewarding life and to achieve their full potential. In the 1960s this meant rejecting the flawed science and blatant injustice of the eleven plus and it also demanded structural change. Comprehensive schools played a vital role in overcoming the inherent injustices of the post-war system. For some they were the springboard to opportunity.

7

A speech to the Fabian Society by Ruth Kelly, 30 March 2005

Ruth Kelly went on to make some criticism of the developments in education in the 1960s:

- First, the focus was almost entirely on children of secondary school age, and mostly on ending the 11 plus.
- Second, there was little agreement on what it meant to provide a high quality education once children were inside the school gate. As long as people were not selected this was good enough for some.

■ Third, schools tended to take on a single model, with little scope for innovative leadership or the ability to develop a distinctive character or ethos.

■ Fourth, too often poverty became an excuse for poor performance. In too many areas comprehensive schools divided into 'good' middle-class and 'bad' working-class schools with children in the latter not getting the education they deserved.

■ And fifth, users – parents and pupils – were not placed at the heart of reform. Crosland's famous circular 10/65 – requesting that local authorities embrace comprehensive principles – did not even mention consulting parents on such significant changes.

| 8 | *A speech to the Fabian Society by Ruth Kelly, 30 March 2005* |

■ **Activity**

Talking point

Divide into five pairs or small groups and take one of Ruth Kelly's points each. Within your group, debate what she meant, whether she was correct, how this problem might have been avoided and why a different approach might have been better.

The expansion of higher education and the inauguration of the Open University

A good many times I have been present at gatherings of people who are thought highly educated and once or twice I have been provoked, and have asked the company how many of them could describe the Second Law of Thermodynamics. The response was always cold: it was also negative. Yet I was asking something which is the scientific equivalent of: 'Have you read a work by Shakespeare?'

I now believe that if I had asked an even simpler question, such as, 'What do you mean by mass', or 'acceleration', which is the scientific equivalent of saying, 'Can you read?' – not more than one in ten of the highly educated would have felt that I was speaking the same language. The majority of the cleverest people in the western world have about as much insight into modern physics as their neolithic ancestors would have had.

| 9 | *C. P. Snow, **The Two Cultures**, 1993* |

■ **Exploring the detail**

C. P. Snow

The words in Source 9 were first given as part of a Cambridge lecture by C. P. Snow (1905–80), who, as a trained scientist and successful novelist, was well qualified to address what he saw as a breakdown of communication between the 'two cultures' of modern society: the sciences and the humanities. He believed this was a major hindrance to solving the world's problems. Although heavily criticised by F. R. Leavis in the *Spectator,* who dismissed Snow as a 'public relations man' for the scientific establishment, his work was nevertheless very influential at the time of Wilson's government (1964–70) when science was seen as essential for the future.

Fig. 7 *The students' common room in the new University of Sussex in 1964*

Fig. 8 *The spread of universities in the 1960s*

The 30 universities in existence in 1962 comprised both the 'ancient universities' of Oxford, Cambridge, Durham, London (and in Scotland, St Andrews, Glasgow, Aberdeen and Edinburgh); the 'redbrick universities' such as Manchester, Birmingham, University of Wales (with various offshoots), Bristol, Leeds, Liverpool and Sheffield; and the more recent Nottingham, Southampton, Hull, Exeter and Leicester.
New universities of the 1960s included Sussex, York, Kent, Warwick, Lancaster, East Anglia, Stirling and Essex.

The Robbins Report

In 1960, Lord Robbins was commissioned to look into Britain's provision of higher education. There was considerable concern that Britain was lagging behind its continental neighbours in the provision of university places and that there were far too few students engaged in the study of science and technology. His report of 1963 confirmed such fears, revealing that just 4 per cent of the relevant age group attended Britain's 30 universities and that most followed arts-related courses.

Following the recommendations of the report:

■ Quasi-university status was given to leading colleges of technology, which were renamed polytechnics. Their focus was to be on applied education for work and science.

■ The Council for National Academic Awards (CNAA) was set up to award polytechnic degrees. This broke with the tradition of universities awarding their own degrees.

■ Polytechnics would offer a broad range of courses and focus on teaching rather than research.

■ Nine colleges of advanced technology became full universities and the Royal College of Science in Scotland became Strathclyde University.

■ 'New' universities were founded (and charters given to some, like Sussex which had recently been established).

■ Many colleges – particularly those of art and design – were upgraded and teacher training colleges were renamed colleges of education offering four-year courses.

The results of the Robbins Report

By 1968, there were 30 polytechnics and 56 universities, and some of the older ones such as London were expanding. New institutions brought new courses and it became possible, for example, to take a degree in town planning or architecture. The new polytechnics and universities opened up higher education for many whose families had never attended a university, although middle-class children still dominated. Furthermore, while Oxbridge still attracted a large public school intake, some polytechnics struggled with split sites and financial worries, so it was hard to persuade anyone of the parity of opportunity.

Nevertheless, the total number of students grew steadily (Figure 9) and more were attracted to study science, although this still ranked considerably below the numbers studying the arts, particlarly among females. It was also the case that a boy was twice as likely as a girl to get a university place, with three males to every two females in 1975. It was not until the 1980s that female entries surpassed 40 per cent.

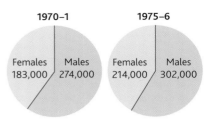

1970–1		1975–6	
Females 183,000	Males 274,000	Females 214,000	Males 302,000

Fig. 9 *Number of students in higher education in the UK in the early 1970s*

The Open University

Harold Wilson was later to say that he most wanted to be remembered for the creation of the Open University. It combined his enthusiasms for equal opportunities in education, modernisation and the 'white heat of technology' by attempting to offer high-quality degree-level learning to people who had never had the opportunity to attend campus universities.

The idea was not new. In 1926, the educationalist J. C. Stobart had advocated a 'wireless university', but it was not until the early 1960s that the idea was revived. In March 1963, a Labour Party study group proposed an experiment on radio and television to be called the University of the Air but initially Wilson was uncertain of how to proceed. Following his election success in 1964, he appointed Jennie Lee to consider the project and it was her commitment that saw it through.

Fig. 10 *Professor Maxim Bruckheimer, Dean of the Maths Faculty of the Open University, records a television programme*

■ Key profile

Jennie Lee

Jennie Lee (1904–88) came from a working-class family and was only able to attend Edinburgh university with support from a trust that agreed to pay half her fees. During the General Strike of 1926, she gave some of her bursary money to her family, as her father, a union activist, lost his job. She was first elected to parliament in 1929 and in 1964 was appointed Arts Minister. She retired in 1970 and was created Baroness Lee of Asheridge.

I knew it had to be a university with no concessions, right from the very beginning. After all, I had gone through the mill myself, taking my own degree, even though it was a long time ago. I knew the conservatism and vested interests of the academic world. I didn't believe we could get it through if we lowered our standards. I hated the term 'University of the Air' because of all the nonsense in the press about sitting in front of the telly to get a degree.

10 *Jennie Lee, commenting on the history of the O.U.*

Jennie Lee established an advisory committee, which led to a White Paper published in February 1966. The *Times Educational Supplement* said of this:

> A pipe dream; just the sort of cosy scheme that shows the socialists at their most endearing but impractical worst.

| 11 | *The **Times Educational Supplement**, 4 March 1966* |

Nevertheless, after Labour's success in that year's election, a crucial cabinet decision was made in September 1967, to set up a planning committee 'to work out a comprehensive plan for an open university'. The university was duly launched and received its first charter in 1969.

Professor Walter Perry was appointed as the Open University's first Vice-Chancellor.

> I came to the Open University from a wholly traditional background, having spent most of my working life at Edinburgh University. I had no experience of any of the new universities, nor had I ever been involved in adult education. I had heard about the University of the Air, but I regarded it as a political gimmick. It wasn't until my son read out the advertisement for the post of Vice-Chancellor that I began to think seriously about the proposal. It wasn't that I had any deep-seated urge to mitigate the miseries of the depressed adult; it was that I was persuaded that the standard of teaching in conventional universities was pretty deplorable. It suddenly struck me that if you could use the media and devise course materials that would work for students all by themselves, then inevitably you were bound to affect – for good – the standard of teaching in conventional universities. I believed that to be so important that it overrode almost everything else. And that is what I said in my application.

| 12 | *From Walter Perry's memoirs* |

In September 1969, the Open University's headquarters were established in Milton Keynes and by the middle of 1970 there had been enough applications for the first students to begin their studies in January 1971. Although it attracted some criticism – Ian Macleod MP, for example, described it as 'blithering nonsense' – it became a rapid success. The university used radio and television in innovative forms of distance learning and recruited largely part-time students with a totally different social profile from traditional ones. It attracted the mature, women and the disadvantaged and it helped raise the esteem of those who had previously regarded themselves as educational failures.

The university required commitment though. In the early days, students had to tune into BBC broadcasts when the channel was not providing public broadcasting, often at night. The arrival of audio cassettes made life a little easier for students, but it took considerable devotion to stay the course. Nevertheless increasing numbers enrolled. By 1980, there were 70,000 students and the Open University was awarding more degrees than Oxford and Cambridge combined.

Activity

Source analysis

Use Sources 10, 11 and 12 and your own knowledge.

How far was the Open University motivated by genuinely educational reasons?

Activity

Thinking point

'The educational changes of the 1960s and early 1970s were a great success.' Explain why you agree or disagree with this view.

Activity

Try to see Willy Russell's play/ film, *Educating Rita*. It concerns Rita, a 26-year-old hairdresser from Liverpool who enrols at the Open University because she wants to be a different person. The play describes the trials and transformations that she goes through.

Learning outcomes

In this section you have looked at the ways in which governments intervened to help bring about the modernisation of society from 1964. You have examined the successes and failures of both the Labour and Conservative governments of this period and have seen how legislation contributed to the widening of opportunities for women, children and students. To complete your understanding of 1960s society, you need to study the final section of this book that addresses issues of immigration and race.

 Examination-style questions

(a) Explain why the Sex Discrimination Act was passed in 1975. *(12 marks)*

 Try to identify both the short- and the longer-term reasons for change. The inadequacy of the Equal Pay Act in 1970 will need mentioning, as will issues arising from the growth in female employment.

(b) 'Government-led change ensured a great improvement in education between 1964 and 1975'. Explain why you agree or disagree with this view. *(24 marks)*

 This quotation invites a challenge. There were certainly changes in education between 1964 and 1975 but did these bring 'great improvements'? You should debate changes in both the provision of secondary school and of higher education. Remember that the examiner will be looking for a balanced answer.

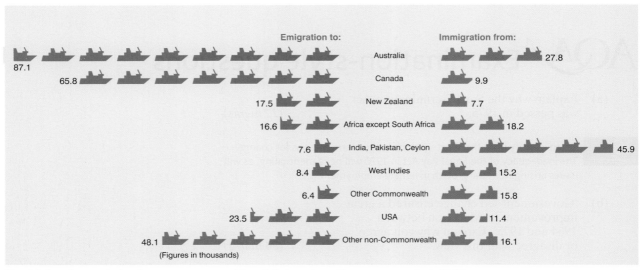

Emigration to: | Immigration from:

87.1 — Australia — 27.8

65.8 — Canada — 9.9

17.5 — New Zealand — 7.7

16.6 — Africa except South Africa — 18.2

7.6 — India, Pakistan, Ceylon — 45.9

8.4 — West Indies — 15.2

6.4 — Other Commonwealth — 15.8

23.5 — USA — 11.4

48.1 — Other non-Commonwealth — 16.1

(Figures in thousands)

Fig. 1 *Migration graph showing movement to and from Britain and non-European countries in 1967*

In this chapter you will learn about:

- the extent of immigration from the New Commonwealth by the 1960s

- the response of ethnic Britons, trades unions and the mass media to the issues posed by immigration and settlement

- the political response to issues of nationality, and the legislation passed to curb immigration and deal with the issue of race relations.

Activity

Statistical analysis

Before reading further, examine Figure 1 and note down what you can learn from it about immigration in 1967.

New Commonwealth immigration

The abolition of Empire Day (24 May) in 1962 confirmed a movement that had been gathering pace since the Second World War. From the declaration of independence for India in 1947 to the ceding of Hong Kong to China in 1997, 64 nations had ceased to be ruled by the British and, of these, 37 were given up between 1960 and 1973. Nevertheless, Britain still clung to the idea of a British Commonwealth of Nations (set up in 1926) and 51 of the former imperial states remained Commonwealth members.

Despite its break-up, British governments proved reluctant to cast aside the legacy of empire. Although foreign immigration into Britain had been restricted since 1905, there was a long-established belief that Britain should act differently towards its former colonial dependents. This was seen at its strongest in 1948 when, in recognition of the Commonwealth's wartime contribution, the British Nationality Act 1948 was passed by the Labour government. This gave full British citizenship, including the right of free entry into Britain, to every inhabitant of the Commonwealth. The Labour Prime Minister, Clement Attlee, declared in July 1948:

> It is traditional that British subjects, whether of dominion or colonial origin (and of whatever race or colour), should be freely admissible to the UK. That tradition is not, in my view, to be lightly discarded, particularly at a time when we are importing foreign labour in large numbers.

1 *Clement Attlee, 1948*

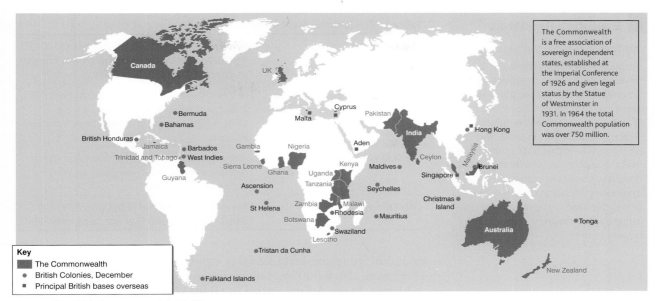

Fig. 2 *The British Commonwealth, 1967*

In the 1950s and early 1960s escalating numbers of people from the New Commonwealth, particularly black people, started coming to Britain. The earliest arrivals came from the West Indies, but they were soon followed by others from India, Africa and Hong Kong. They were attracted, in part, by their own romanticised picture of Britain as the land of opportunity and, in particular, by the plentiful job opportunities and good wages that were on offer. As the British economy recovered from its wartime dislocation, there was plentiful work for the unskilled in Britain's booming factories and the wages on offer were higher than most immigrants could ever dream of in their own countries. As word travelled back to their friends and families, the number of immigrants increased. Not all planned to stay permanently though. Indeed, in the 1950s, it was more often the case that young men came and went according to fluctuations in the trade cycle. Most arrived in the hope of staying long enough to repay their passage (often loaned by a recruiting firm), send money home to the family, and then return themselves, with wealth to live on.

The British government actively encouraged immigration in the 1950s. Posters appeared in the Caribbean showing an attractive female native smiling from the footplate of a London bus and exhorting others to join her. There were successful recruitment drives to encourage unskilled workers to take up a range of low-paid jobs, particularly in public transport and the NHS, and in 1956 London Transport took on nearly 4,000 new employees – mostly from Barbados. Some of these chose to put down roots and sent for their wives, children and girlfriends to join them. Since there was plenty of work available, no action was taken to limit immigration, although, equally, none was taken to help migrants settle or find decent accommodation.

According to Home Office estimates, numbers from the Commonwealth living and working in Britain by 1958 were still relatively small, but growing. The 1951 census had shown 100,000 born in the New Commonwealth; by 1958 there were some 205,000, three-quarters of them male.

Most of the immigrants settled in poorer parts of towns, forming the nucleus of subsequent immigrant communities. Nearly half, particularly West Indians, lived in London while the 25,000 in and

Did you know?

The day 24 May was chosen in 1916 as Empire Day in honour of the birthday of Queen Victoria during whose reign (1837–1901) the British Empire had reached its height. The idea was that it would 'remind children that they formed part of the British Empire, and that they might think with others in lands across the sea, what it meant to be sons and daughters of such a glorious Empire'. Schools across the empire saluted the Union flag, sang patriotic songs like 'God Save the Queen' and listened to inspirational speeches. The highlight was leaving school early in order to take part in marches, maypole dances, concerts and parties.

Exploring the detail

Immigrants from Jamaica

Although not strictly the first immigrants, the first to attract media interest were the 492 mostly male Jamaican passengers who arrived on the steamship *Empire Windrush* at Tilbury, East London, in 1948. This ship arrived without prior notification and the authorities were hastily forced to house the immigrants in a temporary shelter at Clapham. These immigrants led to the creation of the subsequent immigrant community in nearby Brixton.

Table 1 *New Commonwealth immigrants, 1958*

c115,000 West Indians	An increase from 17,500 West Indians in 1951. By 1959, West Indian immigration was running at about 16,000 people per year
c55,000 Indians and Pakistanis	In 1949, there had only been 100 Indians in Birmingham but, by 1959, there were to be 3,000 immigrant arrivals from India and Pakistan
c25,000 West Africans	A drift, mostly of students, from West Africa had begun in the inter-war years and this accelerated after 1945
c10,000 Cypriots	Most of these had fled in the war of 1955–9 and, in 1959, 25,000 Cypriots came to Britain

around Birmingham included large numbers of Indians and Pakistanis. There were also 8,000 in Manchester and 6,000 each in Liverpool and Leeds. Many Asians settled in Oldham and Bradford where the declining textile industries were desperate for cheap unskilled labour.

Fig. 3 *By 1958, nurseries were providing amenities for the children of immigrants who had come to Britain to work*

As Britain entered the 1960s, the number of immigrants grew sharply. In 1961, 130,000 had entered the UK; a total equivalent to the previous five years put together. This took the total number of immigrants to four times that of 1951 and in the three-year period from 1960 to 1962 more immigrants arrived in Britain than in the whole of the 20th century up to that point. Most were from the New Commonwealth, with increasing numbers from India and Pakistan and, with the spread of direct flights, from Hong Kong. In 1951, there had been just 5,000 Chinese, mainly living in British ports but, by 1971, their numbers had increased to 50,000. There were also waves of crisis-driven immigration. In 1967, Kenyatta's policies of enforced Africanisation drove many Asian Kenyans with British passports to Britain, while in 1971 the accession of the ruthless dictator, Idi Amin, provided a further influx of Asian Ugandans. Immigration ran at just over 50,000 a year between 1962 and 1965, and by the late 1960s the size of Britain's ethnic population had reached around 1 million, although non-whites still made up only 3 per cent of the British population in 1976 and of these 40 per cent had been born in Britain.

■ Issues of settlement and nationality

Given the need for cheap labour, there was limited racial controversy over immigrants who arrived in the early 1950s and the newcomers were almost treated as 'novelties'. Beryl Gilroy, Britain's first black headmistress, gave an interview to *Woman's Hour* in January 1960:

I had come as a teacher from British Guiana and found my new class very chatty. I was asked 'Why are you made of chocolate?' When I explained that I came from a hot country, I was asked, 'Why did you sit in the sun for such a long time then?' Another said 'May we feel your hair?' Soon a score of fingers were racing over my head. Then came the remark 'Me Mum says them black people's 'air must feel the same as a fibre mat – bristly like. But it ain't true.'

2   *Beryl Gilroy, talking on Woman's Hour,*
                                        January 1960

Key profile

Beryl Gilroy

Beryl Gilroy (1924–2001) came to the UK from British Guiana in the West Indies in 1951. She was one of a small group of pioneering black teachers and rose to become Britain's first black headmistress in 1969, at Beckford primary school. She was an academic, psychologist and writer. In 1976, she published an autobiography *Black Teacher*. Her novels include *Frangipani* (1986) and *Steadman and Joanna* (1996), which addressed issues of slavery.

Exploring the detail

Kenyatta and Amin

Kenyatta was the first Prime Minister (1963–4) and then President (1964–78) of Kenya, following its independence from British rule. He initially supported the white settlers, but in the later 1960s became increasingly authoritarian. He wanted Kenya to be a purely African state and pressurised Asian settlers (many of whom held British passports) to leave. Idi Amin came to power in Uganda in a military coup in 1971. He wanted to free Uganda from all foreign influence, expelling members of other ethnic groups, religious leaders, journalists, professionals and foreign nationals – including many British Asians. Estimates of the number of people killed as a result of his regime range from 80,000 to 500,000.

Curiosity was mingled with uncertainty, and indifference was more frequently encountered than intolerance. However, as the post-war boom slackened, the prejudice and anxieties that were never far below the surface grew. Worries about the dilution of British cultural and national identity were coupled with a concern to protect houses and jobs. A local shopkeeper was quoted in the *Birmingham Mail* in November 1961:

We were very kind to them when they first came, but now I just get in my car at the weekends and drive to where I cannot see a black face. Some of them are very decent folk, but others have this inferiority complex and they try to make up for it. They are rude and cheeky.

3   *Birmingham Mail,*
                                        28 November 1961

Increasingly, immigrants found life in Britain failed to live up to expectations. When it came to jobs, it was the immigrants who bore the brunt of redundancies and the employers who had been so keen to recruit them were just as happy to dispose of their labour and send them to the dole queues when hard times struck. Those who found and kept jobs

Fig. 4 *Immigrants were not always welcomed, but here London students are trying to demonstrate goodwill to immigrants in 1961*

were usually placed at the bottom end of the pay scale while, within their communities, immigrants generally obtained the poorest houses in the least desirable parts of the area.

Balraj Khanna, an Indian painter who arrived in 1960, later wrote:

> I used to cry in my little room at night. I used to say to myself, why the hell did I come here? Why don't I go back? But that would have been a moral defeat. I remained through pride.

4   *Balraj Khanna, personal reminiscences*

It did not take much to turn discrimination into aggression. The first indicators of trouble came in the summer of 1958 when the 'Teddy Boys' began attacking blacks and Oswald Mosley set up his Union Movement campaign. Violent riots between local whites and black immigrants broke out in Notting Hill, London and in Nottingham. The police arrested 177 people and Mr Justice Salmon gave the judgement that 'men must be able to walk the Queen's highway in peace and without fear'. Nevertheless, although this view was widely supported and mostly endorsed by the press, there were still those who blamed the victims, the black immigrants, for causing conflict by living in these areas in the first place.

Faced with increasing prejudice, immigrant communities began to band together in self-defence. In 1959, Kelso Cochrane, a 32-year-old Antiguan carpenter from Notting Hill, was stabbed to death by a gang of six white youths. Over 1,000 West Indians, most of whom had never known him, turned out to line his funeral route. This display of immigrant solidarity increased the concerns of the resident community. In a survey in 1962, 90 per cent of the population supported legislation to curb immigration and 80 per cent agreed that there were too many immigrants in Britain already.

A survey in North London in 1965 showed that one in five objected to working with blacks or Asians, half said they would refuse to live next door to a black person and nine out of ten disapproved of mixed marriages. However, such attitudes were mild compared with the more extreme racists – characterised by Alf Garnett in the hit TV series *Till Death Us Do Part*. His constant swearing about 'bloody coons' won him a cult following and sadly struck a chord with many, even though the writer's intention had been to satirise ignorant bigotry. Bob Whitfield's experiences as a young RAF cadet showed that there were some extreme racial opinions around.

> Growing up in the south of England in an all-white environment I hardly met any black people. My first encounter with unashamedly racist attitudes was when I was on a cadets' visit to an RAF base. While waiting for an opportunity to fly in a trainer aircraft, the Flight Sergeant, who had previously served in Aden and had developed what can only be called a complete hatred for Arabs and black people, subjected each cadet to his views on race and immigration, including his extraordinary proposal that Britain should 'Kill a wog a day'. That was 1963.

5   *Bob Whitfield, personal reminiscence, 2007*

In the later 1960s, racial tension became more acute under the influence of Powell's rabble rousing and the formation of the **National Front (NF)** in 1967. Racist attitudes were strongest among those working-class

Exploring the detail

Mosley and the Union Movement

Oswald Mosley, former leader of the British Union of Fascists, founded the Union Movement (UM) in 1948. Mosley stood as a candidate in the 1959 election in Kensington North (which included Notting Hill) and made immigration his campaign issue. He ran an intense campaign with pamphlets provocatively featuring blacks with spears entering Britain and slogans such as 'Stop coloured immigration' and 'Houses for White people'. He called for assisted repatriation and spread scare stories regarding the criminality and bad behaviour of immigrants. Although he received only 8.1 per cent of the vote, his campaigns increased white extremism.

Cross-reference

Details of **Enoch Powell's** inflammatory speeches and his demands for an end to immigration are found on pages 128–30.

Key term

National Front (NF): an extreme right-wing political party founded in 1967. It was formed from a merger of the League of Empire Loyalists and the British National Party. The NF believed in the repatriation of black immigrants and national autonomy. At its strongest, the NF won about 3 per cent of the vote in national elections in the 1970s.

communities that found themselves living in or near predominantly immigrant communities. In the East End of London, the Bengalis who had settled in some of the city's poorest housing were subjected to campaigns of violence that rendered certain streets 'no go' areas, especially at night. Girls were kicked going to school, stones flung, and eggs and tomatoes hurled. It was not even safe to wait at a bus stop or go shopping. Nor was this the only area. From Bradford to Luton 'Paki-bashing', which referred to physical or verbal attacks on anyone perceived to be Pakistani, became an all-too-common occurrence.

In 1963, a Southall residents' association was formed in west London. White residents were alarmed by the fall in property values that they believed to be because of the immigrant Punjabi community. They decided to take matters into their own hands and demanded segregated schools and property sales to whites only. The association said:

> Our whole way of life is threatened and endangered by a flood of immigrants who are generally illiterate, dirty and completely unsuited and unused to our way of life. They overcrowd their properties to an alarming degree, create slums, endanger public health and subject their neighbours to a life of misery, annoyance and bitterness.

6

Fig. 5 *Black boys often grew up with low expectations and underachieved at school*

Racist views were also found in the trades unions and among grass—roots labour organisations. The unions had not been happy at offers of jobs to immigrants in the 1950s. The Transport and General Workers' Union (TGWU) had threatened a strike if forced to take on West Indians, and in 1947 the General Secretary of the National Union of Agricultural Workers had famously said:

> We appreciate of course that these people are human beings but it would seem evident that to bring coloured labour into the British countryside would be a most unwise and unfortunate act.

7
General Secretary of the National Union of Agricultural Workers, 1947

Fig. 6 *Crowds block Cannon Street, Middlesbrough, the centre of the town's black quarter, following race riots in the city in 1961*

In the General Post Office, where a substantial proportion of Caribbeans worked, the union was dominated, until the end of the 1960s, by right-wing nationalist politicians and year after year branch officials were elected who openly advocated the racist policies of Mosley and Powell. As the employment position got worse, trades union attitudes hardened and the dockers turned out en masse to support Powell's demands for an end to immigration.

It was a shrewd move when Cousins, former General Secretary of the TUC, was appointed to head the new Community Relations Commission in 1968 under the Labour government.

Activity

Source analysis

Study Sources 2 to 7. How far might immigrants into Britain expect to be welcomed and assimilated into British communities in the 1950s and early 1960s?

Political responses

Increasingly, a body of political opinion built up in favour of restrictions on immigration. The argument was actually more about the type of immigrants than immigration itself, as Britain was losing more citizens than it gained. Although 'black' immigration was actually quite limited in real terms, campaigns to 'keep Britain white' grew in the tense period that followed the Notting Hill race riots. A group of Conservative MPs

Fig. 7 *There was a last-minute rush of Commonwealth immigrants before the Commonwealth Immigrants Act 1962 came into effect. What do you notice about these immigrants?*

from the West Midlands, encouraged by pressure groups such as the Birmingham Immigration Control Association formed in 1960, began pushing for political action. They argued that, unless something was done, Britain would cease to be a European nation and become a mixed African-Asian society.

Activity

Thinking point

The government's attempts to address the problems associated with immigration and race relations are explained in this chapter. As you read through the rest of this section, complete the table below and consider the impact of the important developments and legislation described.

Date	Party in power	Details of act or event	Impact – positive	Impact – negative
1948				
1962				
1965				
1965				
1968				
1968				
1971				

The Commonwealth Immigrants Act 1962 (Conservative)

The Commonwealth Immigrants Act ended free immigration for former colonial subjects, even when they held a British passport. Instead, a work permit (voucher) scheme was put in place. Although this did not explicitly discriminate against black workers, it had the same effect. The Irish were exempt and most white immigrants had skills that enabled them to obtain vouchers. The unskilled black applicants, however, were made to wait their turn and in the 12 months following the act only 34,500 arrived in Britain, many of these within the six months prior to the act becoming law. The act was both unfair and difficult to operate, but it received massive public support (opinion polls suggested 70 per cent).

The act soon ran into problems as massive queues for entry built up and, by 1964, there were 330,000 voucher applications pending. Furthermore, it had the effect of encouraging immigrants to put down roots in Britain, for fear they would be unable to return. Increasing numbers sent for their families (which was still permissible) and, although in 1961 only a sixth of immigrants were women and there were very few children, by 1971 these groups made up three-quarters of the total number of immgrants.

Issues of immigration featured strongly in the 1964 general election campaign. In Smethwick, which had some 6,000 recent immigrants in its population of 70,000, giving it the highest concentration of immigrants in any county borough in England, Peter Griffiths (Conservative) managed to win the seat from Patrick Gordon Walker (then the Labour Shadow Foreign Secretary) by using the slogan 'If you want a nigger for a neighbour, vote Labour'. Harold Wilson, the new Labour Prime Minister, called such campaigning a 'disgrace to British democracy', but it was clear that many voters shared Griffiths's view, forcing the new government to take note.

Exploring the detail

The Commonwealth Immigrants Act

This act divided would-be immigrants into three groups:

A Those with employment in the UK already arranged.

B Those with skills or qualifications that were in short supply in the UK.

C All others who were placed on a waiting list, with ex-servicemen at the top.

A system of quotas was drawn up whereby a limited number of entry vouchers would be issued annually, starting with categories A and B and so limiting the numbers in the C category.

The 'Immigration from the Commonwealth' White Paper 1965 (Labour)

The new Labour government reduced the number of work vouchers to 8,500 a year, with a proviso that no more than 15 per cent were to be granted to any one country. Children over 16 were barred from entering as family members, while those under 16 could join only parents not other relatives.

A Gallup poll suggested that 9 out of 10 Britons approved these measures. Richard Crossman, Minister for Housing and Local Government, wrote in his diary in 1965:

> This has been one of the most difficult and unpleasant jobs the government has had to do. We have become illiberal and lowered the quotas at a time when we have an acute shortage of labour. No wonder all the weekend liberal papers have been bitterly attacking us. Nevertheless I am convinced that if we hadn't done all this we would have been faced with certain electoral defeat in the Midlands and the South-East. Politically, fear of immigration is a most powerful force today.

8   *Richard Crossman, diary entry, 1965*

The Race Relations Act 1965 (Labour)

This cross-party act forbade discrimination in public places 'on the grounds of colour, race or ethnic or national origins'. However, discrimination in housing and employment were excluded and incitement to race hatred was not made a criminal offence. Complaints were to be referred to the Race Relations Board whose job was to conciliate between the two sides.

By 1967, the racial issue had become even more acute. The National Front (NF) was campaigning to end to all 'black' immigration and to force the expulsion of immigrants already in England, while the same year saw the unexpected influx of Kenyan Asians. In the first two months of the year, 13,000 arrived in an attempt to beat any decision by the British government to impose restrictions.

The government prepared an emergency bill that was rushed through both Houses of Parliament and became the Commonwealth Immigrants Act 1968.

The Commonwealth Immigrants Act 1968 (Labour)

This act restricted UK citizenship to those who had at least one British parent or grandparent, born, adopted or naturalised in the UK. Again, this meant that most white immigrants could come to Britain but Kenyan Asians could not. There was much argument over the act and 35 Labour MPs, 15 Conservatives and all Liberals voted against it. To balance the heavy criticism, a further Race Relations Bill was introduced.

The Race Relations Act 1968 (Labour)

This act banned racial discrimination in housing, employment, insurance and other services. The Race Relations Board was given stronger powers and a new Community Relations Commission set up, initially headed by Frank Cousins (TUC leader), to promote 'harmonious community relations'. However, there were still loopholes. Employers could discriminate against non-whites in the interests of 'racial balance' and complaints against the police were excluded from the law. Furthermore,

---

■ **Exploring the detail**

The Race Relations Board

The Race Relations Board was set up to consider discrimination complaints and take part in publicity, research, finance and other aspects of race relations. It compiled statistics and produced reports on the numbers of immigrants, the problems they faced and the types of discrimination they were subjected to. However, the board could not compel witnesses to attend hearings and although it handled 982 complaints in its first year, 734 were dismissed through lack of evidence. Over half of those upheld were about racial stereotypes in advertising rather than direct examples of discrimination.

■ Cross-reference

The issue of **Kenyan Asians** was presented earlier in this chapter on pages 120–1.

It was during debate on the Race Relations Bill 1968 that **Enoch Powell** (Conservative) stirred up violent racial sentiment. This is discussed on pages 128–30.

the Race Relations Board upheld only 10 per cent of the 1,241 complaints it received about discriminatory employment to January 1972 and the number of complaints remained low because victims had little faith in getting effective redress.

The Immigration Act 1971 (Conservative)

With the return of a Conservative government, a new tough measure incorporating voluntary repatriation and restricting immigration to those with at least one grandparent born in the UK became law. Other would-be immigrants had to possess work permits with a guaranteed job for at least a year and even then applicants would have to wait at least five years before they could gain permanent residence. Special powers were also taken to deal with illegal immigrants.

The act made it difficult for anyone from the New Commonwealth to gain entry unless they already had close relatives in Britain, and even this loophole was to be closed in the 1980s.

In 1971, an exception was made to permit some 28,000 Ugandan Asians to settle in Britain, but generally, after 1971, Britain operated some of the toughest immigration controls in the world and immigration ceased to be a major political issue.

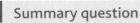

Summary question

Explain why so many measures were taken to curb immigration in the 1960s.

In this chapter you will learn about:

■ the political controversies that stemmed from the views of Enoch Powell

■ the extent of racial prejudice in Britain in the late 1960s and early 1970s

■ the degree to which immigrant communities had been assimilated into British society by 1975

■ how far Britain had gone along the road to multiculturalism by 1975.

In 15 or 20 years, on present trends, there will be in this country three and a half million Commonwealth immigrants and their descendants. Whole areas, towns and parts of towns across England will be occupied by sections of the immigrant and immigrant-descended population.

Britain must be mad, literally mad, as a nation to be permitting the annual inflow of some 50,000 dependants, who are for the most part the material of the future growth of the immigrant-descended population. It is like watching a nation busily engaged in heaping up its own funeral pyre.

The effect of this immigration has been to make Britons feel strangers in their own country, their wives unable to obtain hospital beds in childbirth, their children unable to obtain school places, their homes and neighbourhoods changed beyond recognition, their plans and prospects for the future defeated.

As I look ahead, I am filled with foreboding. Like the Roman, I seem to see the River Tiber foaming with much blood.

1   _Adapted from a speech by Enoch Powell, front-bench Tory MP for Wolverhampton to a meeting of Conservatives in Birmingham on 20 April 1968_

Enoch Powell

Powell's speech of 1968 caused a media furore. His final sentence, based on a reference to the classical poet Virgil, led the press to refer to this as the 'Rivers of Blood' speech. Powell continued with the story of a woman from his own constituency who, he said, had written to him about her experience of living in a street 'taken over' by immigrants.

Fig. 1 _Enoch Powell provoked racial controversy with his speeches on immigration in 1968_

Windows are broken. She finds excreta pushed through her letter box. When she goes to the shops, she is followed by children, charming, wide-grinning piccaninnies. They cannot speak English, but one word they know, 'Racialist', they chant. When the new Race Relations Bill is passed, this woman is convinced she will go to prison. And is she so wrong? I begin to wonder.

2   _Adapted from a speech by Enoch Powell in Birmingham, 20 April 1968_

Powell's speech met with an enthusiastic reception in Birmingham but the Conservative leader, Edward Heath, sacked him from the Shadow Cabinet the next day:

The content of the speech was deplorable enough, coming from someone who boasted of his scholarship, but the fictitious statistics and references to alleged letters from constituents who could not be traced afterwards* were deceitful and disgraceful. The tone was still worse. At a time when all responsible politicians were trying to deal with a regrettable and delicate situation, here was a front-bencher setting citizens of his own country against each other.

3   *Edward Heath, **The Course of My Life**, 1998*

[* The media sent reporters to find the woman referred to in Source 2 but never did so. It is probable she did not exist.]

Powell was seen as a hero among the wider public for having the courage to speak out and some claimed his sacking was an invasion of free speech. The *News of the World* predicted that most people would come to agree with Powell and many letters to the press were in Powell's favour. A poll at the end of April showed 74 per cent of respondents agreed with him. Seven out of ten thought Heath wrong to sack him and eight out of ten wanted stricter immigration controls.

As the Commons prepared to vote on the 1968 Race Relations Bill, thousands of dockers marched to Westminster in Powell's support. This was the first time such a body of men had shown sympathy for a Tory. They carried placards saying 'Don't Knock Enoch' and 'Back Britain Not Black Britain' and sang 'Bye Bye Blackbird' outside Westminster. Meat porters also staged walkouts and there were other copycat strikes as far afield as Southampton,

Fig. 2 *Dockers turn out to support Powell and march past the Houses of Parliament, 1968*

Norwich, Coventry and Gateshead. By the beginning of May, Powell had received more than 43,000 letters and 700 telegrams of support (with only 4 telegrams and 800 letters disagreeing with him). The National Front chanted 'Powell for PM'.

It is difficult to be precise about the effect of the speech. The 'macho' skinhead culture that developed in the later 1960s obviously owed something to the racial bigotry that Powell helped stir up, but this movement was the product or other factors too. Powell's speech should be seen in context. It was probably the more potent because it came at a time when British optimism and self-confidence were beginning to wane and the Black Power movement in America appeared to show the consequences of mixed-race communities. It certainly encouraged others to bring their prejudices out into the open but it did not necessarily create those prejudices. This is not to belittle his influence. In a 1969 gallup poll, he was voted the most admired man in Britain.

Did you know?

Powell quoted Home Office statistics which projected that immigrants and their children would make up 3 million people by the end of the 1980s and added his own prediction that by 2000 this would be 5 to 7 million. This latter figure in the event proved to be only 2 per cent out, although it was considered to be scaremongering at the time.

Powell wanted to halt all further non-white immigration and have a scheme for voluntary repatriation for those already in Britain; this involved providing public funds and a free passage for Africans, West Indians and Asians wishing to return to their countries of origin.

Cross-reference

The **skinhead movement** is introduced on pages 69–70.

Exploring the detail

The Black Power Movement

Black Power arose in the USA in the mid-1960s. It was a political movement that sought to express a new racial consciousness among the blacks and to lead the struggle against racism and imperialism in the United States. The movement stemmed from earlier civil rights movements but supporters wanted to develop African-American communities rather than fight for integration with whites. While Malcolm X provided leadership, musicians like James Brown produced slogans such as 'Say it loud, I'm Black and I'm proud'.

Activity

Source analysis

Use Sources 1 to 5 and your own knowledge.

1. How far do the views expressed in Source 5 differ from those expressed in Source 4 in relation to Enoch Powell's anti-immigrant speeches?

2. How far should Enoch Powell be blamed for racist behaviour in the late 1960s?

He was motivated by his intense patriotism. In Powell's view national identity was built on the long continuity of England's history, culture and institutions. It was based on the continuous life of a united people in its island home, on parliaments and the monarchy. This romantic notion could not encompass newcomers from very different cultures because in Powell's view they had no stake in English history and could never be properly assimilated.

4 *Dominic Sandbrook, **White Heat 1964–1970**, 2006*

Fig. 3 *Enoch Powell received a flood of mail, most of it in support of his views*

Powell became intoxicated by the favourable response to his stand by some extremists. He revealed his true thinking when he told a journalist, in an interview not published until after his enforced departure, 'I deliberately include at least one startling assertion in every speech in order to attract enough attention to give me a power base within the Conservative Party. Provided I keep this going, Ted Heath can never sack me from the Shadow Cabinet.'

5 *Edward Heath, **The Course of My Life**, 1998*

A multicultural society?

Roy Jenkins, Labour Home Secretary from 1965 to 1968, defined racial integration as (Source 6):

…not a flattening process of assimilation but equal opportunity accompanied by cultural diversity in an atmosphere of mutual tolerance.

6 *Roy Jenkin*

By 1975, racial integration of the type Roy Jenkins describes was far from complete. **Assimilation** was under way. A second generation of

Key term

Assimilation: involves the acceptance and integration of outsiders into a community.

immigrants who had known no other homeland, was growing up in Britain. Immigrant communities were becoming more established and British systems were adapting to accommodate the settlers. However, equal opportunity was still a far distant goal, despite the inroads made by legislation. Furthermore, the positive benefits of cultural diversity, while certainly growing, still tended to be swamped, in the public mind, by its negative aspects. Mutual tolerance was spoken of rather than acted upon. While few would admit to racist ideas and the National Front remained a politically insignificant right-wing party, nevertheless black prejudice remained in many walks of life.

Assimilation

Assimilation, which had proved so difficult in the 1950s and early 1960s, was almost bound to become easier as a new generation grew up speaking English, attending British schools, watching British television and being, of necessity, immersed in British ways of life. The debate that had taken place in the 1960s as to whether or not it was possible to 'become a Briton' seemed to have answered itself. While first generation immigrants – particularly Muslim Pakistanis or Hindu Indians – might not feel or wish to feel 'British', their children often did. Indeed, they seemed more likely to think and act like Americans, just as their young white contemporaries did.

This did not necessarily breed harmony though. Mixed in with racial issues came new tensions. Intergenerational divides exacerbated problems as some youngsters tried to challenge or break free from their parents' religious or cultural heritage. This was particularly true in Muslim communities where the Islamic way of life, for example keeping women and girls inside the house and arranging marriages according to family connections, was at odds with traditional British practices.

It is difficult to assess the degree of assimilation of immigrant communities because the immigrants were so varied in type. West Indians, who were English-speaking and shared the predominant Christian religious background of the native British, were generally more easily assimilated, although their perceived 'brashness' contrasted with traditional British reserve. Indians and Pakistanis, on the other hand, who were often very hard-working and whose children frequently became higher achievers in school, were nevertheless regarded as more alien. Some cultural traditions did not easily fit in a country that had, pre-war, been almost exclusively Christian, and the British tradition of toleration and freedom of expression was subject to a variety of challenges.

Tensions were never far away. Although different races might be mixing more in schools and the workplace, they might clash over issues as diverse as what was acceptable behaviour, how, when and what they should eat and how much it mattered to them to maintain the rituals of religious observance. Cultural differences could keep communities apart. To cite just one example, the Islamic interdict on the consumption of alcohol kept Muslims out of local pubs and yet these were very often the centre of white British working-class culture in the neighbourhood.

Other factors also prevented the full assimilation of immigrant communities. These included was the physical separation of immigrant communities from their white 'neighbours' within cities; poverty and poor housing, which could isolate immigrants; barriers of language, particularly among the older generations; disparities in education and employment; the unfair application of the justice system.

Fig. 4 *Second-generation immigrants often adopted the ways of their white counterparts*

Did you know?

In a survey in Nottingham in the early 1960s, Robert Davison found that 87 per cent of the Jamaicans said they felt 'British' before they came to England and 86 percent were happy for their children to feel 'English'. However, among the Indians and Pakistanis only 2 per cent felt 'British' before arrival and only 6 per cent wanted their children to feel 'English'.

Activity

Thinking point

Is it important to 'feel British' if you live in Britain? What might prevent individuals from feeling British?

131

Nevertheless, there were growing signs of acceptance from the ethnic British community. Cardiff City Corporation, for example, built a mosque, at public expense, for its Islamic inhabitants and schools adjusted their teaching to provide for children for whom English was not a first language. Civic campaigners and community activists worked with immigrants to try to resolve specific problems and health care and social services were expanded. Although it was not easy for immigrants to rise through their adopted community, some individuals showed that it was possible.

Activity

Revision exercise

Complete the following table to show the forces that were helping to assimilate immigrant communities in Britain and those that were preventing assimilation.

The state of Britain's immigrant communities c.1975	
Forces helping assimilation	**Forces preventing assimilation**

AQA Examiner's tip

You will need to consider factors such as family (home, aspirations, income), education and contacts, predominant social attitudes, legal status and employment prospects, and should reflect on how these affected the life chances of both young blacks and whites. Remember people are affected by internal factors such as personal expectations, confidence and determination, as well as by their background, those they meet and the circumstances they find themselves in. Finally, be wary of treating all youngsters, black or white, as though they all felt and behaved in the same way.

Question

Explain why the life chances of young blacks brought up in Britain in the early 1970s were much inferior to those of whites.

Key profiles

Learie Constantine

Learie Constantine (1901–71) was a cricketer from Trinidad who had moved to England in 1929. When he was refused service in a British hotel because of his colour, he prosecuted and won. A friend said, 'He revolted against his first class status as a cricketer and his third class status as a man.' He went on to become High Commissioner in London for Trinidad and Tobago (1962–4), Governor of the BBC and a member of both the Race Relations Board and the Sports Council. In 1969, Constantine became the first black person to gain a life peerage.

John Sentamu

John Sentamu (born 1949) came from Uganda. He was the sixth of 13 children and walked 20 km (12 miles) to school each day until a missionary provided a bicycle. He trained in law but left his country in 1974 when Idi Amin began to violate human rights. He studied theology at Cambridge and entered the Church, becoming Bishop of Stepney and the first black member of the General Synod of the Church of England. While driving his episcopal car he was stopped and questioned by the police. He became Britain's first black archbishop when he was appointed to York in 2005.

Vijay Patel

Vijay Patel (born 1952) and his brother Bhikhu were brought up in poverty in Kenya. Vijay came to Britain aged 16 in 1968. He worked his way through sixth form and the College of Pharmacy in Leicester and with a loan opened his first pharmacy in Leigh-on-Sea, Essex in 1975. This grew into a chain of 21 pharmacies and a medical wholesaler – Waymade Healthcare. In 1982, he was joined by Bhikhu and in 2001 the brothers were named joint entrepreneurs of the year with a fortune of over £250 million.

Activity

Thinking point

What do these immigrant 'high flyers' have in common?

Cultural diversity

The arrival of immigrants had a more positive side, in that they proved a force for the enrichment of British culture. For example, Notting Hill developed as a vibrant multicultural community and the Notting Hill Carnival with its colourful processions and steel bands became an attraction for all races and particularly for younger people.

A closer look

The Notting Hill Carnival

The Notting Hill Carnival began as a local festival, set up by the West Indian immigrants of the area. After the racial tensions of the late 1950s, dances were organised in halls in North London to try to improve community relations and encourage people to mix socially. At the same time, steel band music performed by immigrant Trinidadians was becoming more popular in local pubs in the Earls Court area. From this, the idea developed of using the steel band to help create a street festival in Notting Hill to encourage children of all races and colours to come on to the streets and express themselves socially as well

Fig. 5 *The Notting Hill Carnival has become an established attraction for people of all races and colours and takes place over the August bank holiday weekend. This photograph was taken in 1996*

as artistically. The first carnival first took place in 1964 and was a huge success. The festival has since evolved as a regular attraction on August bank holiday, with spectacular floats and steel bands playing traditional Trinidadian calypso music. The carnival features bright, outlandish costumes, imaginative floats and dancing on the streets. It is accompanied by stalls serving typical Caribbean food, particularly jerk chicken, rice and peas and rum punch.

One West Indian pensioner said:

> We done a lot for Britain. We bring life to them, no matter what they say. We give all our energy and our strength and all the riches that we can get. We give them another culture and background that they didn't have before.

7 *Tony Kushner's personal reminiscences*

Exploring the detail

Caribbean Voices

The BBC radio programme *Caribbean Voices* was set up in 1946 by Henry Swanzy and ran until 1991. It was a weekly programme that focused on the literary output of the Caribbean region. It helped authors find publishers, assisted them when they arrived in Britain, and provided them with work as readers. In the 1960s, it featured other migrant writers too.

Immigrant communities also began to play a role in the mass media. Following the appearance of the newspaper *West Indian World* in the early 1970s, a number of ethnic papers appeared celebrating Britain's different cultures. Such papers were particularly proud to report the achievements of individual immigrants, especially in the realms of sport where 'blacks' were able to compete more equally than in other spheres with native 'white' Britons. On the radio, *Caribbean Voices* spread information about immigrant authors, while on television black characters began appearing in popular TV dramas like *Emergency Ward 10* and *Z Cars*. The black children's television presenter Floella Benjamin became a well-known figure and the BBC documentary series *Black Man in Britain* (1972) traced the history of black settlement.

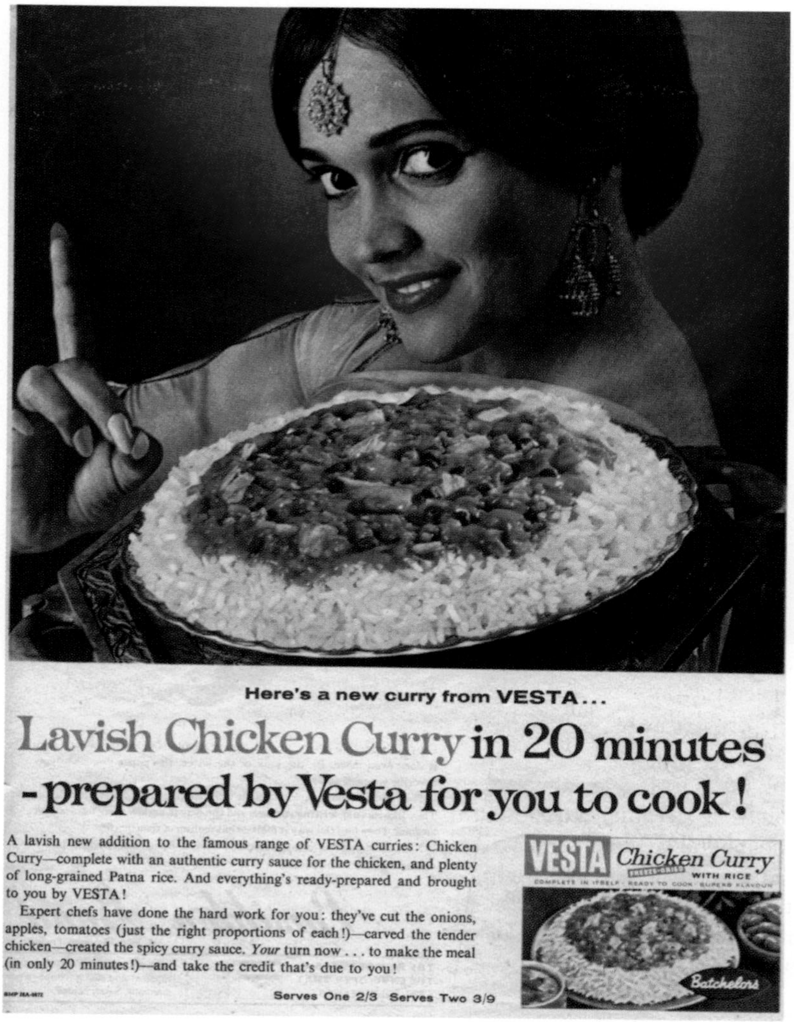

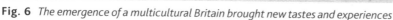

Here's a new curry from VESTA...
Lavish Chicken Curry in 20 minutes -prepared by Vesta for you to cook!
A lavish new addition to the famous range of VESTA curries: Chicken Curry—complete with an authentic curry sauce for the chicken, and plenty of long-grained Patna rice. And everything's ready-prepared and brought to you by VESTA!
Expert chefs have done the hard work for you: they've cut the onions, apples, tomatoes (just the right proportions of each!)—carved the tender chicken—created the spicy curry sauce. Your turn now . . . to make the meal (in only 20 minutes!)—and take the credit that's due to you!
Serves One 2/3 Serves Two 3/9
VESTA
Chicken Curry
WITH RICE
Batchelors

Fig. 6 *The emergence of a multicultural Britain brought new tastes and experiences*

The Christian Caribbean settlers even had an influence on religious services in Britain, introducing more informal music, with gospel choirs and pianos or guitars taking the place of a church organ. In some churches, participants were encouraged to testify their faith in God or to relate their personal troubles and this style of worship was copied by some of the evangelical churches in Britain.

Food shops and restaurants transformed traditional British tastes. The appearance of Asian corner shops and Chinese takeaways were indications that other cultural groups were in Britain to stay. Indeed, immigrants not only introduced new foodstuffs, they also encouraged new means of cooking including curries and tikka masala from India and sweet and sour cuisine (first popularised in a cookbook edited by Jill Norman in 1972) from Asia.

Youth culture also drew from the ethnic communities in music, fashion and street life. The white, middle-class, young hippies of the late 1960s romanticised 'black urban cool' by wearing Indian and African cottons, kaftans, Arabian pants, Indian scarves and ethnic beads. Some enjoyed West Indian styles of music, jazz and ska and accompanied it with a liking for marijuana. Others were attracted by Eastern ways and customs and followed

the Beatles' 'conversion' under the guidance of the Maharaja Mahesh Yogi to meditation, yoga, 'love and peace'.

As immigrant communities came to be respected more for what they could give rather than for what they took from the surrounding area, there was a greater willingness to involve them in local politics. There were a growing number of black councillors elected in the 1970s and they helped develop schemes of urban regeneration, improving housing and job opportunities, as well as supporting cross-cultural activities. However, it took until 1987 before a black MP entered parliament.

Clearly the idea of a 'cultural exchange' was slow to emerge and, for most of the 1960s, this perspective was hardly in evidence at all. It was certainly missing from the attitudes of those who framed the race legislation and whose concern was only to keep certain foreign groups 'out'. Whatever newer immigrants might have to offer, there was little attempt to promote and, at times, even to tolerate alternative cultural ideas on a wider scale.

Activity

Challenge your thinking

Either: In groups, make a list of the ways in which you feel immigrant communities have 'enriched' British culture since the 1960s. Try to refer to as many areas as possible including music, sport and literature. Different members of the group may like to pursue different themes and prepare an illustrated class presentation.

Or: Using the internet, or by talking to individuals within your community, find an individual whose family came to Britain as immigrants in the 1950s or 1960s and make a case study. Ask the following questions:

- What was it like in the country of origin and why did the family in your case study choose to move to Britain?
- What was that family's experience of arriving, settling and finding work in Britain?
- How does that person feel about their (or their parents') country of origin?

Mutual tolerance

A number of issues made integration frustratingly slow and discontinuous. The Campaign against Racial Discrimination (1964), the Race Relations Board and the Community Relations Commission (1968) played their part in curbing prejudice, but their control was weak and discrimination certainly continued. Most worrying was the mistrust felt between immigrant communities and the police. The police were known to be more likely to stop a black person than a white person and constant harassment embittered relations. Sometimes the mere presence of the police provoked violence, although there were also genuine attempts at fraternisation, for example during the Notting Hill Carnivals.

It has been suggested that racial prejudice had become a 'normal' feature of British culture by the mid-1970s and that, because it was so well entrenched among those responsible for running the country, it became acceptable at all levels of society. In a series of interviews with West Indians living in London in the mid-1970s (published 1978), a sociologist, Thomas Cottle, recorded this outburst from a 13-year-old:

Cross-reference

The **Race Relations Board** and **Community Relations Commission**, as well as legislation on **immigration** and **discrimination**, are discussed on pages 126–7.

When's anything going to change for us? We ain't moving at all man. My father can't find work over here, work he's fitted for, something he can do well. Are they keeping him from the good jobs because he's black? I'd say yes, sure they are. But how you going to prove it? You can't prove these things to anybody. Board people work for the government. They don't make their own rules. The law says everybody has an equal chance, but anybody can see that's a lie.

8   *A 13 year old's views from the findings of Thomas Cottle, 1978*

The State's policy of trying to keep black people out of the country was seen to legitimise racism. It seemed as though the black people themselves, not racism, were regarded as the cause of problems and there were no doubt many British people, encouraged by the media, who held the lingering belief that Powell had been right. However, the extreme racial violence and destruction predicted by Powell did not occur. Despite the troubles and tensions in the West Midlands and parts of London such as Southall and Brixton, perhaps most Britons did what they are always so good at and simply buried their heads in the sand on racial issues.

Britain in 1975

Britain was a multicultural society by 1975, if only by virtue of the fact that many different cultures co-existed within the British Isles. However, the broader definition of multiculturalism–where people not only have their own cultural beliefs but also work together and serve to enrich one another while bound by a common core of interests–was less in evidence.

In some respects, the picture of Britain in the mid-1970s looked bleak, with race having replaced class as the most significant and dangerous divide in British society. How to reconcile different racial groups and ensure future harmony exercised the brains of the politicians and provided fuel for the journalists.

Some argued that ethnic minorities needed to assimilate more fully into British ways before they could become part of British society; others felt that it was ethnic British prejudice that needed breaking down and that positive discrimination was the only way to create a truly multicultural society. Some argued that British traditional culture should be seen as just one among many and should not be given a pride of place; others that minority cultures should be respected but not seen as central. The Kenyan, Dr John Sentamu, now Archbishop of York, said:

Multiculturalism has seemed to imply, wrongly for me, let other cultures be allowed to express themselves but do not let the majority culture at all tell us its glories, its struggles, its joys, its pains.

9   *John Sentamu in 'Multiculturalism has Betrayed the English', 22 November 2006*

The clash between attempts to preserve alternative cultures and to engender a sense of 'Britishness' is one that beset society in the mid-1970s and remains a burning issue today.

Activity

Talking point

Hold a class debate on the motion: 'Racial harmony will only become possible when immigrant communities are fully assimilated into a British way of life.'

Divide your class into two groups and decide which group will support and which will oppose the motion. Every member of each group should help prepare a speech, but only one need be chosen – by a throw of the dice – to deliver the speech in a lesson. The rest should ask questions of the speakers on both sides.

Learning outcomes

In this section you have gained an insight into a different aspect of British society in the 1960s and early 1970s – namely the implications of immigration from the former colonies and what this has meant for native British people and the British way of life. You have studied the way different politicians reacted to the challenge posed by immigration as well as discovering something about the attitudes of those at grass-roots level who found themselves living in a developing multicultural society. It is to be hoped that by studying how issues were addressed at the time and by considering the questions that contemporaries debated, you will have been inspired to think for yourself and to draw your own conclusions on matters that remain burning issues in 21st-century Britain.

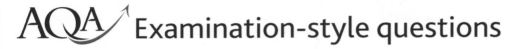

AQA Examination-style questions

Read Sources A, B and C below and answer the questions that follow.

I came to the UK in 1960 to join my sister in Huddersfield. I wanted to get a better life. It was easy to get jobs, but the pay was very poor. I took work in a factory, then a garage and finally finished up in a foundry. It wasn't difficult to adapt to British life although the food seemed odd. When I first came I heard people talking about fish and chips so I went and bought some but I had to throw it away. It took me a long time to eat Yorkshire Pudding too, and I'm still not a great fan. I'm still living in the house I first bought and have a year or so of mortgage to pay.

A　　　　　　　　　　*Adapted from the reminiscences of Eustace Ford,*
a West Indian immigrant

I came to England when I was 14 in 1966. My father had arrived in 1958 and settled in Bradford where he knew some Indians. He worked in the woollen industry where the dirty jobs were left for the foreigners. At school, the teacher called me, 'you brown one', no one understood prayer time, and at lunch time I struggled to avoid meat. I ate fish and chips until I learnt they were fried in fat, so then I had to avoid them. In 1968 we bought a house. Mortgages were not allowed as paying interest was forbidden. We lived alongside other Indians. The white people didn't want us in their areas.

B　　　　　　　　　　*Adapted from the reminiscences of Abdul Aslam,*
an Asian immigrant

In Great Britain there is too little discussion of racial matters; too much avoiding the matter in everyday discourse. To listen to some people is to believe there are no racial problems in the United Kingdom. To listen to others is to hear the problem called minor and easily resolved. No one who speaks with West Indian, Pakistani, Indian and Mauritian families living in England would call their circumstances minor or exaggerated.

Adapted from Thomas Cottle's survey of Britain in the 1970s, published in 1978

(a) Explain how far the views in Source B differ from those in Source A in relation to the experiences of immigrants settling in Britain in the 1960s.

(12 marks)

Examiner's tip You will need to look closely at the information and feelings expressed in Sources A and B. Make a short list of the ways in which they differ and another of the similarities shown. This will enable you to address 'how far' the experiences of the West Indian and Asian are different. Your answer should provide a developed comparison of the views in the sources and should incorporate some of your own knowledge to demonstrate your contextual understanding of the issues they raise.

(b) Use Sources A, B and C and your own knowledge. How far had a multicultural society emerged in Britain by 1975?

(24 marks)

Examiner's tip This question requires you to advance an argument that provides a supported view on the degree to which a multicultural society had emerged in Britain by 1975. Obviously, you need first to decide what your argument will be and you should plan your answer accordingly, advancing your view through your various paragraphs. Don't forget to support your ideas with factual information and wherever possible with source references. You must include all three sources to obtain good marks and you should also show that you are aware of differing opinions and interpretations.

6 Conclusion

Fig. 1 *What were the 1960s all about?*

The 1960s have acquired a reputation as a watershed decade; providing a gulf between a rather drab, conventional and conformist society and one that is diverse, liberal in attitude and 'modernist' in outlook. It is often said that there is a world of difference between those who grew up before The Beatles and those who came after them. To put this another way, anyone reaching adulthood before the 1960s is likely to have been moulded by a very different set of experiences and values from the generations that have followed. Although this may also be true of other decades, for a variety of reasons, the 1960s seem to have had a particularly profound social impact.

Anyone growing up in the pre-1960s era would have been affected, in one way or another, by the experience of the Second World War. Many would have been born well before that war and would also have experienced the lean years of the 1930s and indeed the impact and aftermath of the earlier conflagration of 1914–18. They would have known what it meant to 'scrimp and save' and they would have learnt to value hard work and family support. They would have been raised in a class-dominated society, in which each individual knew his or her place and they would have grown up in a predominantly 'white' Britain whose laws and customs were moulded by a Christian morality and an unwritten code that condemned anything deemed 'permissive'. At the risk of generalisation, pre-1960s society in Britain still carried the marks of the Victorian era and, while the experience of war had helped to bring some 'social levelling', there was a belief, encouraged by leaders such as Churchill, that such 'British attitudes' had made Britain 'great' and had helped gird the country for victory.

The 1950s had certainly seen changes occur. By 1959, as the 1960s dawned, the age of consumerism had already arrived in Britain. Post-war Britain enjoyed a buoyant labour market with shops teeming with goods and advertising hoardings tempting those who still remembered wartime austerity to go out and buy. The TV had arrived (at least in black and white), as had the motor car for the better off. Rising incomes gave people the chance to participate in new forms of leisure, particularly holidays at a coastal resort. For most of the population, the 1950s were an optimistic decade, and justifiably so, since average living standards were rising and, in some cases, rising fast, despite a slowing of Britain's growth rate in comparison with other European countries and America.

However, no big breakthroughs in social attitudes had yet occurred and certain aspects of life remained more akin to the 1940s and than the 1970s. The family unit remained strong and conventional morality prevailed. Most women gave up work on marriage and accepted a housewife's role. The class structure was perpetuated and although education was more inclusive than it had been before the war, it was strongly linked to wealth and status, with the governing clique educated in the top public schools and a predominantly middle-class intake filling the grammar schools. Most of the country remained white, and although there were pockets, mainly in London, where New Commonwealth immigrants had started to flow into the country, for most people, their family and community-orientated lives may have been more comfortable, but were otherwise little changed.

By 1975, at the end of the era often known as the 'long 1960s', the outlook may have seemed rather more gloomy, after a spate of crippling strikes and dire forecasts about Britain's economic future; and yet standards of living had continued their inexorable rise and most people were living in comfort, with a colour TV in the lounge and a car in the garage. There was a good chance of a family enjoying a holiday abroad and eating out from time to time. Many more women were in work and certainly far more were benefiting from increased educational opportunities and rising through the professions. Comprehensive schools had largely replaced the 'grammars' and although public schools continued there was a much broader spread of backgrounds in governing circles. There was also greater ethnic diversity, although non-whites still only made up 3 per cent of the population.

Such a rise in living standards might well have been predicted in the mid-1950s, but the accompanying change in social and moral attitudes would have been less easy to forecast. By 1975, one-parent families, illegitimacy and divorce had become far more acceptable in society. The pill was widely available – to unmarried as well as to married women – and abortion and homosexuality were legal. Literature and the theatre were no longer curbed by rigorous censorship and the TV broadcast into homes material of an explicit and sometimes intimate nature. Experimentation with drugs and the alternative lifestyles of the hippy culture had rather passed their peak by 1975 but the legacy of the heady 'years of youth' remained. A distinctive 'youth culture' had been born and would not go away. Young people were no longer lost somewhere between the realms of childhood and adulthood and had become a potent social force in their own right. Outlooks too had broadened. As more people travelled abroad or mixed with people of different races, they were forced to question long-held beliefs about religion, behaviour and customs.

The change was not all gain. The 1960s saw an increase in family breakdown, mental illness and drug addiction. There was a coarsening in standards and debate raged as to what constituted 'decency' or even 'good manners' and civility. Authority was placed under question – from parents to the police and the governing authorities – and some were left wondering what there was to believe in or by what moral code they should lead their lives. There were race riots, student demonstrations and industrial strife. The 1960s may have bred a greater open-mindedness, but they also brought more insecurity and uncertainty.

The 1960s are usually defined as a period of 'liberation' but they might equally, although rather more long-windedly, be described as the time when society responded to the impact of affluence. The continuity with the 1950s is obvious. As the era of austerity and want gradually gave way to an age of abundance, many people found that they had both the money and time for other priorities. Only in an era of plenty could youngsters indulge their search for identity or could women have the luxury of being able to think for themselves. It was the coming of the consumer society that helped break down class barriers, challenge traditions and make old customs obsolete. The 1960s demonstrate, without doubt, the power which economic developments exercise over society.

Just as the social developments of the 1960s may be seen as the logical outcome of the 1950s, it would be wrong to place too much stress on the extent of those developments and their impact on the mass of people living at the time. 'Many people' always leaves aside those who did not benefit from greater wealth and whom the 1960s left untouched. There were also large numbers of people who, although not totally unaffected, experienced nothing that could be deemed worthy of the description 'revolutionary' change'. 'Pot, psychedelic happenings and Carnaby Street' were always minority concerns. Feminism, homosexuality and teenage promiscuity did, by their very nature, only affect certain groups within the population.

Attitudes, tastes and behaviour did not change overnight and Mr and Mrs Average were predictably conventional, law-abiding citizens. They tutted at the antics of those whom the press seized upon as examples of 'what this country has come to', and marvelled at the lives of the supposed beneficiaries of the 'swinging London' phenomenon. They were suspicious of many things foreign or 'new' and liked to watch *The Black and White Minstrel Show* on television, without perceiving anything untoward in this. In 1967, they helped propel Engelbert Humperdinck's ballad *Release Me*, rather the Beatles' *Strawberry Fields/Penny Lane*, to the No. 1 spot in the hit parade and they queued up to watch *Carry On Doctor* rather than rushing out to see Antonioni's *Blow up*.

It takes time for long-established conventions to die and for changes to embed themselves in society and even by 1975, particularly in the less-developed parts of Britain, some of those changes were only just beginning to be felt. However, once they arrived, there was no back-tracking. The liberating, self-expressive and anti-authoritarian developments of the 1960s were to stay and they have continued to influence society ever since. The '1960s' did not stop in 1969 nor even in 1975, which has been taken as the finishing date for this study. Just as the 1960s were born of the 1950s, so the 1970s and beyond have built on 1960s change.

At the beginning of this book, you were invited to consider the extent to which the changes of the 1960s warranted the title 'a social revolution'. It is now time to try to address that question and to reflect on exactly what changes had taken place. Look back over the material provided in this book and draw up your own 'before' and 'after' comparisons and use your findings to try to assess the degree, the speed, the quality, the desirability and the impact of the change that occurred.

It is unlikely that you will have reached the end of this study without someone quoting to you the famous adage – 'if you can remember the 1960s you weren't there' – in a reference to the dope-smoking haze in which the 1960s are reputed to have been passed. For most readers of this book, the 1960s are history, but it is hoped that by talking to those who were there and through debate on the themes and issues raised in these pages, they will now have a far more balanced view of the '1960s social revolution'.

Glossary

babydoll dress: a short flowing dress, often with a ribbon or bow across the chest (occasionally even smocking) and short puff sleeves. Some might have a rounded white collar and such dresses would usually be of a light fabric, such as cotton, and printed with a small floral pattern. They represented 'innocence' and mirrored the clothes worn by a baby. Sometimes they were worn with frilly pants – rather like those worn by baby girls over their nappies.

by-election: this occurs between general elections (which are held at a maximum every five years) when a serving MP dies or resigns from his position. An election is held within that MP's constituency to elect a new MP to replace him. By-elections are sometimes thought to reflect the public's opinion of the serving government – supporting it, by electing its representative; or showing displeasure, by turning to a different party.

C

charter flights: under the strict regulations imposed in the 1960s, it was only possible to offer discounted flights to passengers who belonged to a group such as 'bird-watchers'. Furthermore, the purpose of the group could not be travel. Entrepreneurs therefore arranged for flights to be 'chartered' or booked by such a society (sometimes a completely bogus group) and then sold its seats to individuals who sought cheap travel. These flights often left from the smaller airports at odd times and were 'no frills' services.

Confederation of British Industry (CBI): the main employers' organisation in the UK. The CBI was formed in 1965 through the merger of the Federation of British Industries, the British Employers' Confederation and the National Association of British Manufacturers. Its members come from industry, commerce, retailing, finance, mining, construction, transport and the nationalised industries. It acts as a pressure group for those whom it represents.

consumerism: consumer goods are things that can be bought, ranging from clothes and food to household articles, TVs and cars. Consumerism is the desire to buy such goods, which sets up a demand, which in turn increases supply. In a consumer society a substantial proportion of manufacturing production is directed towards satisfying consumer wants.

D

decriminalisation: someone convicted of a serious criminal offence may be prosecuted in a criminal court in front of a jury (while less serious cases are heard by magistrates) and, if convicted, fined or imprisoned. When something is decriminalised, such prosecutions no longer take place.

depression: a time of slump marked by a collapse in trade and mass unemployment. Depression had hit Britain in the 1930s and, although the effects were varied and the north suffered more than the south, making ends meet was a constant struggle for the working-class. Many households, particularly those with families to support, had to learn to be frugal.

discotheque: the 1960s update of the dance hall and usually quite small and crowded, with live groups or loud recorded music and a DJ. There would be drink and dancing rather than food, and often coloured 'whacky' lighting effects (and, from the later 1960s, sometimes psychedelic effects).

dole: the 'dole' is a slang term for unemployment benefit. Being 'on the dole', means being unemployed and forced to live off State support.

E

Establishment, the: a network of holders of influence unified by a common social background and attitudes. The term became more widely used after the journalist Henry Fairlie wrote an article in the *Spectator* in 1955, in which he alleged that the social elite had tried to cover up the treachery of the Soviet spies, Burgess and Maclean. Members of the Establishment would normally have had a public school education, be Oxbridge graduates and hold positions in prominent institutions such as the civil service, judiciary, Church, government, boards of major companies and the BBC.

expert witness: an expert witness might be called to give evidence in cases such as a trial or when a parliamentary committee is considering legislation, when it is considered helpful to have some professional knowledge. Professionals with particular expertise in their subject matter can help make the position clear to others who are required to give a judgement.

F

Female Eunuch, The: an influential book by the Australian feminist Germaine Greer, written in 1970. Greer's theme was female oppression and in her book she claimed that traditional sex roles were learned not natural and that the differences between the sexes had historically been exaggerated. The first six chapters of *The Female Eunuch* were devoted to an examination of the female body in order to support these claims, while the remainder of the book examined the processes by which girls were conditioned to conform to a female stereotype and their struggles against it. Greer believed 'romantic love' and the happy family were myths. She claimed that most women led miserably unfulfilled lives.

fraternity: a fraternity is literally a 'brotherhood'. It suggests a group of like-minded people whose lifestyles and behaviour are similar and who are loyal to one another and go around together.

G

Gallup poll: this is a method of assessing public opinion by questioning a representative sample of the population. The idea came from America where it was first developed in the 1930s but it was not adopted in the UK until the 1960s. It proved unreliable in the 1970 general election, when it gave the Labour Party a 7 per cent lead in the last week of the campaigning, prior to a Conservative victory.

H

hire purchase restrictions: hire purchase is a system of buying goods by borrowing a large sum of money with which to make a purchase and then paying that money back (with interest) over a period of time. Freely available hire purchase facilities encourage consumers to buy more, encouraging economic growth, but this can also lead to inflation as high demand pushes up prices. One way of trying to curb inflation is to make it more difficult for people to buy goods under hire purchase schemes by raising interest rates and restricting the amount of money that can be borrowed.

House of Commons: this is the 'lower' of the two Houses that make up the British parliament (the Commons and the Lords). Its members are directly elected for a maximum of five years. Its main functions are to pass legislation, authorise government expenditure, scrutinise government policy and debate political issues. The government is formed from the group (usually a single political party) that can command a majority in the House of Commons.

L

Lord Chamberlain: the Lord Chamberlain's Office is a department of the Queen's Household. Since the 17th century, playwrights had been required to submit their plays to the Lord Chamberlain's Office at St James's Palace so that any inappropriate material or vulgar language could be removed.

LP: long-playing vinyl gramophone records were first introduced in 1948. They remained the normal way in which to release recordings for about 30 years from the late 1950s until they were replaced by compact discs (CDs) in the late 1980s. They were usually 25 cm (10 in) in diameter and played at $33\frac{1}{3}$ rpm (revolutions per minute) for around 45 to 60 minutes, divided over two sides.

LSD: a powerful hallucinogenic drug invented in 1938 by the Swiss chemist Albert Hoffman, who was searching for new medicines and saw potential therapeutic uses for LSD. Since it possesses hallucinatory properties, LSD was widely adopted by the hippy culture of the 1960s, who claimed it led to higher states of consciousness and helped them search for 'enlightenment'. The Beatles even wrote a song 'Lucy in the Sky with Diamonds' about the psychedelic effects of LSD but after a number of fatal accidents such as people under the influence of LSD jumping to their deaths off high buildings thinking they could fly, it was banned in 1971.

M

McCarthyism: used to describe the intense anti-communist suspicion that developed in the United States between the late 1940s and the late 1950s when fears about the intentions of the USSR were at their height. US Senator Joseph McCarthy led a witch-hunt against communist sympathisers with the slogan 'better dead than red'. Since Britain was closely allied to the USA, its effects had repercussions across the Atlantic too, breeding suspicion and concern for Britain's future.

Marxist: ideas derived from the writings of the 19th-century German revolutionary socialist, Karl Marx, whose work, *Das Kapital* had criticised capitalist society and had promoted socialism and Communism in which all members of society would be equal, with wealth according to their needs. The British Labour Party had committed itself to a socialist objective with – 'public ownership of the means of production' (Clause Four) in 1918. After losing office in 1951, the Labour Party experienced faction-fighting between the left-wing 'Bevanites' who wanted to keep this commitment and the right-wing followers of Hugh Gaitskell, the elected leader from 1955, who tried unsuccessfully to persuade the party conference to abandon Clause Four in 1959.

N

nationalisation: taking privately-owned industries or other activities into public ownership by acquiring their assets in order to create State-owned monopolies. In 1945–51, Labour governments nationalised large sections of industry and services.

Night of the Long Knives: refers to the occasion when Macmillan removed more than a third of his cabinet ministers from their jobs in July 1962. Among those dismissed was his close friend, Selwyn Lloyd who, after an unpopular budget, lost his post as Chancellor of the Exchequer. The name Night of the Long Knives echoed the occasion in 1934 when Hitler disposed of his 'loyal' followers, Ernst Roehm, and the SA. The difference, however, was marked. Hitler executed his enemies and relished the occasion. Macmillan merely dismissed, and did so with a heavy heart.

O

Old Bailey: the building housing, and thus popular name for, the Central Criminal Court of Justice in the city in London.

old school tie network: *see* the Establishment. This refers to the connection between members of the Establishment who had attended similar public schools and whose old boys' ties acted as a mark of 'belonging'.

P

package holiday: an inclusive holiday incorporating flights, transfers (usually by coach), accommodation, meals and often entertainment too. At a time when foreign holidays were regarded as a wildly adventurous form of travel, the opportunity to have everything arranged by a 'package company' proved very appealing.

peerage: the formal name given to titled aristocrats who had a right to sit in the House of Lords, along with those given life peerages introduced in 1958.

public school: a senior independent school normally belonging to the Headmasters' Conference, the Governing Bodies Association or the Governing Bodies of Girls' Schools Association. Although now much changed, traditionally most public schools were single-sex boarding schools that charged high fees for the education they provided.

R

radicalism: a 'radical' is a person who challenges established views and who wants change. While 'rebellion' is used of all resistance to authority, radicalism suggests extremely liberal political ideas. So, while most mods and rockers were simply rebels, student activists in the universities were radicals.

reggae: music based on an off-beat rhythm, with accents on the 2nd and 4th beat of each 4-beat bar. Reggae was a musical genre developed in Jamaica in the 1960s. Its origins lie in the music of Africa and the Caribbean. Reggae song lyrics deal with many subjects including faith, love and social issues.

S

satire boom: political satire enjoyed a vogue in the years after the Second World War and ranged from biting newspaper cartoons to the 'mocking' magazine *Private Eye* (edited by Richard Ingrams) to new-style shows on radio, in the theatre and on TV, like *The Goon Show*, *Beyond the Fringe* and *Monty Python's Flying Circus*. The roots were in public school humour and two of the most inspiring exponents were Peter Cook and Spike Milligan. In February 1962, the Queen saw *Beyond the Fringe* in London's Fortune Theatre, where some outraged individuals had walked out of the lampooning of Macmillan, the serving Prime Minister. The Queen laughed, and so helped the cause of 1960s satire. In 1961, Peter Cook opened the Establishment Club in Soho as a centre for satire and David Frost also gained celebrity status for *That Was The Week That Was*, which ran on TV between 1962 and 1963.

secular: the opposite of 'sacred' and refers to things that are worldly and not religious. A secular society is one that pays little heed to religious teaching.

social services: systems set up by the State to support those in need and so protecting individuals from the worst consequences of ill-health, poverty, old age or the death of a spouse. The basis of the system was laid down in the National Insurance Act 1946, which was, in turn, based on the Beveridge Report of 1942. Benefits can either be contributory, paid through National Insurance contributions or non-contributory. Non-contributory benefits are sometimes known as welfare benefits.

stalwart: a person of strong and determined views who does not easily give in. The CND stalwarts were committed and hardened campaigners who kept up the fight for the cause even after it had become less fashionable and support had begun to fall off.

stereo: refers to stereophonic sound, which is the reproduction of sound using two or more independent audio channels, so that different loudspeakers will give the impression of sound from various directions, as in natural hearing. It came to replace monophonic (or mono) sound, which uses only one channel, in the later 1960s. The first stereo records were actually produced by Pye in Britain in 1958, but the technique remained too expensive for common use.

stigmatisation: branding a person or a group as 'bad' for no well-supported reason. This could include speaking badly of people because of the way they dress or because of their general attitude. 'Negative stereotyping' is a similar irrational way of seeing a particular group in a poor light, without making any exceptions or looking into individual circumstances.

T

trades union: *see* Trades Union Congress (TUC).

Trades Union Congress (TUC): originally founded in 1868, this represents workers' unions which, in turn, are representative bodies for different trades. The TUC may be consulted by governments on a wide range of social and economic issues.

transistor radios: by replacing the vacuum tubes in the amplifier of a radio with transistors, the American pioneers of the mid-1950s were able to produce a much smaller, lighter and more efficient radio. With a transistor, sound was heard immediately because there were no filaments to heat up and, because large batteries to heat the tube filaments and power the cathode and other circuitry were unnecessary, small transistor radios powered by a single compact 9V battery became possible. The first British transistor radio was manufactured by Pye in June 1956, but it was not until the end of the decade that UK manufacturers were able to produce high quality transistorised receivers.

U

unanimity: the British jury system whereby a 12-member (or, in Scotland, 15-member) jury of random members of the public decides the verdict in a trial. This practice had been established by Magna Carta in 1215 but, until 1967, every member of the jury had to be in agreement for a conviction to be brought. However, this had led to increasing numbers of perpetrators escaping punishment because of one lone voice. Therefore, Roy Jenkins introduced majority verdicts (at the discretion of the judge), provided there were no more than two dissenters.

Bibliography

Resources

Broad coverage

Donnelly, M. (2005) *Sixties Britain*, Pearson/Longman.

Moynahan, B. (1997) *The British Century*, Random House.

Sandbrook, D. (2006) *Never Had It So Good 1956–1963*, Abacus.

—(2006) *White Heat 1964–1970*, Little Brown.

Others

Cawthorne, N. (1999) *Sixties Source Book*, Quantum Grange Books.

Grant, R. (1993) *The Day Kennedy Died: A Snapshot of the Sixties*, Dial Press.

Macmillan, J. (1985) *The Way It Changed 1951–1975*, William Kimber.

Marwick, A (1998) *The Sixties*, Oxford University Press.

Masters, B. (1985) *The Swinging Sixties*, Constable.

Powell, P. and Peel, L. (1994) *Fifties and Sixties Style*, Quantum Grange Books.

General histories of Britain

Black, J. (2007) *The Making of Modern Britain*, Sutton Publishing.

Boxer, A. (1996) *The Conservative Governments 1951–1964*, Longman.

—(1996) *The Modern Historian*, Longman.

Childs, D. (1997) *Britain Since 1945*, Routledge.

Clarke, P. (1997) *Hope and Glory: Britain 1900–1990*, Penguin Books.

Garnett, M. and Weight, R (2004) *Modern British History*, Pimlico.

Judt, T. (2007) *Post-war: A History of Europe Since 1945*, Pimlico.

Marr, A. (2007) *A History of Modern Britain*, Macmillan.

Marwick, A. (1984) *Britain in Our Century: Images and Controversies*, Thames and Hudson.

Morgan, K. (1991) *The People's Peace*, Oxford University Press.

Sked, A. and Cook, C. (1984) *Post-war Britain*, Penguin.

Thompson, A. (1971) *The Day Before Yesterday*, Sidgwick and Jackson.

Tiratsoo, N. (ed.) (1998) *From Blitz to Blair*, Phoenix.

Biographies

There are many excellent biographies and autobiographies of people who lived through the 1960s. Particularly useful are the political biographies of the following prime ministers: Harold Macmillan (1957–63), Alec Douglas-Home (1963–4), Harold Wilson (1964–70 and 1974–6) and Edward Heath (1970–4). There are also good autobiographies by political figures such as Tony Benn, Richard Crossman and Barbara Castle.

Benn, T. (1995) *The Benn Diaries 1940–1990*, Hutchinson/Arrow.

Heath, E. (1998) *The Course of My Life*, Hodder and Stoughton.

Also look out for biographies of cult figures such as pop stars, models, broadcasters and celebrities. Sometimes you will also find useful sections on the childhood or teenage years of those who later became celebrities.

Social and cultural context

Johnson, P. (ed.) (1994) *Twentieth Century Britain: Economic, Social and Cultural Change*, Longman.

Levin, B. (2003) *The Pendulum Years: Britain in the Sixties*, Icon Books.

Marwick, A. (1982) *British Society Since 1945*, Penguin.

—(2002) *The Arts in the West Since 1945*, Oxford University Press.

—(1991) *Culture in Britain Since 1945*, Blackwell Publishers.

Popular culture, TV and pop music

Inglis, I. (ed.) (2000) *The Beatles, Popular Music and Society*, Macmillan.

Kureishi, H. and Savage, J. (eds.) (1995) *The Faber Book of Pop*, Faber and Faber.

Macdonald, I. (1995) *Revolution in the Head: The Beatles, Records and the Sixties*, Pimlico.

Melly, G. (1970) *Revolt into Style: Pop Arts in Britain*, Allen Lane.

Miles, B. (1997) *Paul McCartney: Many Years from Now*, Secker & Warburg.

Try to listen to the music of 1960s pop stars and read the lyrics on the internet. The early 1960s were dominated by singers like Tommy Steele, Cliff Richards, Billy Fury, the Shadows and the Tornadoes. This can be compared with the 'Merseybeat pop' epitomised by the Beatles and the 'blues rock' of the Rolling Stones.

Also try to listen to:

Brian Poole and the Tremeloes

Cilla Black

Cream

The Dave Clark Five

Donovan

Dusty Springfield

Freddie and the Dreamers

Gerry and the Pacemakers

Helen Shapiro

The Kinks

Lulu

Sandie Shaw

The Small Faces

The Supremes

The Who

Youth and protest

Ali, T. (1987) *Street Fighting Years: An Autobiography of the Sixties*, Fontana/Collins.

—and Watkins, S. (1998) *1968 Marching in the Streets*, The Free Press.

Green, J. (1998) *All Dressed Up: The Sixties and the Counterculture*, Jonathan Cape.

Neville, R. (1995) *Hippie Hippie Shake*, Bloomsbury Publishing (also a documentary drama).

Osgerby, B. (1997) *Youth Culture in Post-war Britain*, Blackwell.

Literature, theatre, cinema and the press

Murphy, R. (ed.) (1992) *Sixties British Cinema*, BFI Publishing.

Strong, R. (1997) *The Roy Strong Diaries 1967–1987*, Weidenfeld & Nicholson.

Try to see or read some of the plays of the 'angry young men' of the late 1950s, especially John Osborne's *Look Back in Anger* (1956) and *The Entertainer* (1957). Also look out for Harold Pinter's plays: *The Birthday Party* (1957), *The Caretaker* (1959), *The Homecoming* (1964) and other Royal Court productions that give some of the flavour of the 1960s.

■ Films and DVDs

Alfie (1966)

Blow-Up (1966)

A Clockwork Orange (1971)

Dr Strangelove (1963)

Easy Rider (1969)

The Graduate (1967)

A Hard Day's Night (1964) – the first Beatles film

Help! (1965)

If ... (1968)

Magical Mystery Tour (1967)

Performance (1970)

Poor Cow (1967)

The Rolling Stones Rock and Roll Circus (1968)

Saturday Night and Sunday Morning (1960)

Scandal (1988)

A Taste of Honey (1961)

Tonight Let's All Make Love in London (1967)

Up the Junction (1967)

Woodstock (1970)

■ Archive TV programmes

Steptoe and Son (BBC 1962–5)

That Was The Week That Was (BBC 1962–3)

Till Death Us Do Part (BBC 1966–8, 1972 & 1974–5)

■ Websites

www.bbc.co.uk/onthisday

www.psr.keele.ac.uk (party election manifestos)

www.retrowow.co.uk (populist but useful general information)

www.sixtiescity.com

Use an internet search engine to seek out past articles/editorials on the main media/press websites, e.g. www.guardian.co.uk

Obituaries are often a source of rich information

■ Novels

Amis, K. (1970) *Lucky Jim*, Penguin Books.

Bradbury, M. (1962) *Eating People is Wrong*, Penguin Books.

—(1975) *The History Man*, Secker & Warburg.

Braine, J. (1957) *Room at the Top*, Eyre & Spottiswoode (also a film)

Byatt, A. S. (2003) *The Frederica Quartet*, Vintage.

Delaney, S. (1992) *A Taste of Honey*, Heinemann Educational Publishers (also a film).

Dunn, N. (1988) *Up the Junction*, Virago Press.

—(1988) *Poor Cow*, Virago Press.

Fleming, I. The *James Bond* novels.

Heller, J. (1994) *Catch 22*, Vintage.

Le Carré, J. (1992) *Call for the Dead*, Hodder & Stoughton (and other spy novels).

Lodge, D. (1969) *The British Museum is Falling Down*, Panther.

MacInnes, C. (2001) *Absolute Beginners*, Allison & Busby.

—(1986) *City of Spades*, Penguin.

Moorcock, M. (2004) *The Cornelius Quartet*, Four Walls Eight Windows.

Plath, S. (2001) *The Bell Jar*, Faber and Faber.

Sillitoe, A. (1990) *Saturday Night and Sunday Morning*, Flamingo (also a film).

Storey, D. (1960) *This Sporting Life*, Longman.

■ Women

Greer, G. (1970) *The Female Eunuch*, MacGibbon & Kee.

Murray, J. (ed.) (2006) *Woman's Hour – Celebrating 60 Years of Women's Lives*, John Murray/Hodder Headline.

Rowbotham, S. (2000) *Promise of a Dream: Remembering the Sixties*, Allen Lane/Penguin.

■ Race and immigration

Winder, R. (2004) *Bloody Foreigners*, Little Brown.

■ Oral history

Ask family and older friends

Listen out for radio and TV programmes

Look for newspaper articles that reflect back on the 1960s

Acknowledgements

Author acknowledgements:

Thanks to my husband, who has been amazingly supportive during my writing of the book; to my Mother, Mollie Golding, colleague, Bob Whitfield, and friend, Sally Carewe, all of whom supplied personal reminiscences for sources used in the book.

The author and publisher would like to thank the following for permission to reproduce material:

Source texts:

p10 Harold MacMillan, 20 July 1957. Quoted in M. J. Cohen and John Major, *History in Quotations*, Cassell, 2004; p12 From the 'Conservative Campaign Guide, 1964' – referring to the later 1950s. David Childs, *Britain Since 1945*, Routledge, 1997; p15 Adapted from party election manifestos for 1959, www.psr.keele.ac.uk/area/uk/man.htm; p17–8 Alan Thompson, *The Day Before Yesterday*, Sidgwick and Jackson, 1971; p20 Quoted in Nick Tiratsoo (ed.), *From Blitz to Blair*, Phoenix, 1998; p20 Quoted in Mark Garnett and Richard Weight, *Modern British History*, Pimlico, 2004; p26 From *The Times*, 'It's a moral issue', 11 June 1963. Andrew Boxer, *The Modern Historian*, Longman, 1996; p26 Andrew Boxer, *The Modern Historian*, Longman, 1996; p27 Adapted from Andrew Marr, *A History of Modern Britain*, Macmillan, 2007; p31 Tony Judt, *Post-war: A History of Europe Since 1945*, Pimlico, 2007; p31 I. MacDonald, *Revolution in the Head: The Beatles, Records and the Sixties*, Pimlico, 1995; p32 Adapted from an article by Bulent Yusuf, *The Observer*, Sunday 6 July 2003; p33 From a speech at the Labour Party Conference by Harold Wilson, 1 October 1963. Dominic Sandbrook, *White Heat 1964–1970*, Little Brown, 2006; p34 Tony Benn, The *Benn Diaries 1940–1990*, Hutchinson/Arrow, 1995; p34 Bernard Levin, *The Pendulum Years: Britain in the Sixties*, Icon Books, 2003; p37 *Woman's Hour*, 'In my opinion' broadcast, 1960. Jenni Murray, *Woman's Hour*, John Murray/Hodder Headline, 2006; p37 Jenni Murray (ed.), *Woman's Hour – Celebrating 60 Years of Women's Lives*, John Murray/Hodder Headline, 2006; p40 Mark Donnelly, *Sixties Britain*, Pearson/Longman, 2005; p40 Sir William Haley, Director-General of the BBC (1942–52). Policy statement, 1949. Quoted in Asa Briggs, *Sound and Vision: History of Broadcasting in the United Kingdom, vol. IV*, Oxford University Press, 1979; p40 Hugh Greene, Director-General of the BBC (1960–9). Hugh Greene, 'The Conscience of the Programme Director', 1965, quoted from www.terramedia.co.uk/quotations; p41 Adapted from articles on the BBC website that can be viewed at www.bbc.co.uk/cult/classic/bbc2. Quoted from 'The Launch Night that Never Was' by Caroline Briggs, 2004; p44 Tony Benn, *The Benn Diaries 1940–1990*, Hutchinson/Arrow, 1995; p44 *The Sun*, 15 September 1964, quoted in Dominic Sandbrook, *White Heat 1964–1970*, Little Brown, 2006; p45 Tony Judt, *Post-war: A History of Europe Since 1945*, Pimlico, 2007; p45 Arthur Marwick, *The Sixties*, Oxford University Press, 1998; p47 Original source from Mollie Golding (aged 85 years) recalling holidays in the 1960s when she lived in Essex; p50 Quoted in Mark Garnett and Richard Weight, *Modern British History*, Pimlico, 2004; p50 A Cornishman's recollections. From Dominic Sandbrook, *Never Had It So Good 1956–1963*, Abacus, 2006; p51 From the foreword to the Beeching Report www.beechingreport.info; p57 From a report by a young man living in Coventry in the early 1960s. Quoted in Dominic Sandbrook, *Never Had It So Good 1956–1963*, Abacus, 2006; p57 Colin MacInnes, *Absolute Beginners*, Allison & Busby, 2001; p57 Bill Osgerby, 'The Teenage Revolution', from A. Briggs and P. Cobley (eds.), *The Media: An Introduction*, Longman, 1998; p59 Colin MacInnes, *Absolute Beginners*, Allison & Busby, 2001; p59 S. Hattenstone, *The Best of Times*, Guardian Books, 2006; p60 Jonathan Aitken, journalist. Quoted in Dominic Sandbrook, *White Heat 1964–1970*, Little Brown, 2006; p63 www.twiggylawson.co.uk/fashion.html; p64 Mary Quant, quoted in Dominic Sandbrook, *White Heat 1964–1970*, Little Brown, 2006; p64 From 'London, the Most Exciting City in the World', article by John Crosby in *Weekend Telegraph*, 16 April 1965; p64 Robert Murphy (historian) quoted in Dominic Sandbrook, *White Heat 1964–1970*, Little Brown, 2006; p66 Andrew Marr, *A History of Modern Britain*, Macmillan, 2007; p68 Tony Judt, *Post-war: A History of Europe Since 1945*, Pimlico, 2007; p69 David Loshak writing in *The Daily Telegraph*, May 1964. Christopher Howse (ed.) 'How We Saw it', *The Daily Telegraph 1955–2005*, Bertrams, 2004; p69 Dr George Simpson, Chairman of the Margate Bench, prosecuting youths charged with disturbances, 1964. Christopher Howse (ed.), 'How We Saw it', *The Daily Telegraph 1955–2005*, Bertrams, 2004; p70 Ferdinand Zweig, who conducted a survey of students at Oxford and Manchester in 1962 – The Student in an Age of Anxiety, 1963. Quoted in Arthur Marwick, *The Sixties*, Oxford University Press, 1998; p71 David Childs, *Britain Since 1945*, Routledge, 1997; p72 Sally Carewe, young CND supporter (personal reminiscence); p72 A.J.P. Taylor, *Personal History*, Hamilton, 1983; p74 Independent TV report, quoted in Arthur Marwick (ed.), *Britain in Our Century: Images and Controversies*, Thames and Hudson, 1984; p74 Quoted in Arthur Marwick, *The Sixties*, Oxford University Press, 1998; p75 Editorial in the *Wood Green*,

Southgate and Palmers Green Weekly Herald. Quoted in Arthur Marwick, *The Sixties*, Oxford University Press, 1998; p77 Adapted from Roy Jenkins, *The Labour Case*, Penguin, 1959; p79 Christopher Howse (ed.) 'How We Saw it', *The Daily Telegraph* 1955–2005, Bertrams, 2004; p80 W. A. Darlington, *The Daily Telegraph*, 28 September 1968. Quoted in Christopher Howse (ed.), 'How We Saw it', *The Daily Telegraph* 1955–2005, Bertrams, 2004; p85 Harry Hopkins in 'The New Look', 1964. Quoted in Dominic Sandbrook, *White Heat 1964–1970*, Little Brown, 2006; p86 Margaret Thatcher interviewed by *Woman's Hour* in 1976. Jenni Murray (ed.), *Woman's Hour – Celebrating 60 Years of Women's Lives*, John Murray/Hodder Headline, 2006; p87 Jenni Murray (ed.), *Woman's Hour – Celebrating 60 Years of Women's Lives*, John Murray/Hodder Headline, 2006; p88 Excerpt from 'This Be The Verse' from *Collected Poems* by Philip Larkin. Copyright © 1988, 2003 by the Estate of Philip Larkin. Reprinted by permission of Farrar, Strauss and Giroux, LLC; p89 Quoted in Bernard Levin, *The Pendulum Years: Britain in the Sixties*, Icon Books, 2003; p89 From the Encyclical Humanae Vitae 25 July 1968 www.vatican.va/holy_father/paul_vi/encyclicals; p90 Adapted from a speech by Mary Whitehouse, 5 May 1964. Parts of this speech can be found in 'Forty years of achievement-filled campaigning', 5 May 2004, at www.mediawatchuk.org.uk; p91 Michael Grade, Director-General of the BBC (2001), from 'Whitehouse Kept TV on its Toes', BBC Obituary, Friday 23 November, 2001; p91 Richard Hoggart, journalist (2001), from 'Valid Arguments Lost in an Obsession over Sex', article by Richard Hoggart in the Guardian, 24 November 2001; p92 Quoted in the *Sunday Times*, 20 July 1969; p93 Letter published in the *Glasgow Herald*, 22 August 1982 from Mary Whitehouse and headed 'Permissive Jenkins'; p93 Mark Donnelly, *Sixties Britain*, Pearson/Longman, 2005; p94 Quoted in Reg Grant, *The Day Kennedy Died: A Snapshot of the Sixties*, Dial Press, 1993; p97 Harold Wilson, TV broadcast, quoted in Dominic Sandbrook, *White Heat 1964–1970*, Little Brown, 2006; p103 Edward Heath election address (paper), Enoch Powell (Conservative MP), Mr Joe Gormley, leader of the NUM – Sources 3–5 from bbc.co.uk 'On This Day', 7 February 1974 news.bbc.co.uk/onthisday/hi/dates/stories/february/7; p103 Nick Tiratsoo (ed.), *From Blitz to Blair*, Phoenix, 1998; p104 Andrew Marr, *A History of Modern Britain*, Macmillan, 2007; p110 Adapted from Ross McKibbin, *Classes and Cultures*, Oxford University Press, 1998; p110 Susan Crosland, *Tony Crosland*, Jonathan Cape, 1982; p110 Tony Crosland, Circular 10/65, 12 July 1965 www.oldmonovians.com/comprehensive/circular1065.htm; p111 Dame Patricia Hornsby-Smith for Chistlehurst Heath, quoted in Edward Heath, *The Course of My Life*, Hodder and Stoughton, 1998; p111 Edward Heath, *The Course of My Life*, Hodder and Stoughton, 1998; p112 Tony Judt, *Post-war: A History of Europe Since 1945*, Pimlico, 2007; p112 A speech to the Fabian Society by Ruth Kelly, 30 March 2005; p113 C. P. Snow, *The Two Cultures*, Cambridge University Press, 1993; p115 Jennie Lee, quoted in 'The History of the OU'; p116 *The Times*

Educational Supplement, 4 March 1966; p116 Walter Perry, quoted in 'The History of the OU' www.open.ac.uk/about/ou/p3.shtml; p118 Quoted in Peter Clarke, *Hope and Glory: Britain 1900–1990*, Penguin Books, 1997; p121 Jenni Murray (ed.), *Woman's Hour – Celebrating 60 Years of Women's Lives*, John Murray/Hodder Headline, 2006; p121 Birmingham Mail, 28 November 1961. Quoted in Nick Tiratsoo (ed.), *From Blitz to Blair*, Phoenix, 1998; p122 Quoted in Robert Winder, *Bloody Foreigners*, Little Brown, 2004; p122 Bob Whitfield, personal reminiscence, 2007; p123 Dominic Sandbrook, *White Heat 1964–1970*, Little Brown, 2006; p123 Robert Winder, *Bloody Foreigners*, Little Brown, 2004; p126 Quoted in Mark Donnelly, *Sixties Britain*, Pearson/Longman, 2005; p128 (both) Adapted from a speech by John Enoch Powell, Tory MP for Wolverhampton and Conservative Front Bench spokesman for Defence, to a meeting of Conservatives in Birmingham on 20 April 1968; p128 Edward Heath, *The Course of My Life*, Hodder and Stoughton, 1998; p130 Dominic Sandbrook, *White Heat 1964–1970*, Little Brown, 2006; p130 Edward Heath, *The Course of My Life*, Hodder and Stoughton, 1998; p130 Arthur Marwick, *British Society Since 1945*, Penguin, 1982; p134 Tony Kushner, 'Immigration and Race Relations', in Paul Johnson (ed.), *Twentieth Century Britain: Economic, Social and Cultural Change*, Longman, 1994; p135 Arthur Marwick, *British Society Since 1945*, Penguin, 1982; p136 'Multiculturalism has Betrayed the English', 22 November 2006, www.timesonline.co.uk/tol/news/uk/article592693.ece; p137 Migration from Jamaica to Huddersfield – Eustace Ford, 1960–9; p137 Migration From Kashmir to Bradford – Abdul Aslam, 1950–69; p138 Adapted from Thomas Cottle's survey of Britain in the 1970s, published in 1978 as Black Testimony. Quoted in Arthur Marwick, *British Society Since 1945*, Penguin, 1982.

Photographs courtesy of:

Central Press/Getty Images 2 and 17; Getty Images iv and 113; HMSO WHA 97; Photos12 Jean-Marie Périer 66; Photo by John Downing/Daily Express/Getty Images 123; Public Domain 59; Spectrum Colour Library/HIP/Topfoto 70; The Advertising Archives 35, 36 top, 39, 46, 48 top, 52, 134; Topfoto 4, 5, 10, 11 left and right, 14 left and right, 20, 22–5, 28, 31, 33, 38, 43, 45, 47, 48 bottom, 50, 53, 56, 58, 63, 65, 68, 71, 73, 76, 78 top and bottom, 82, 83, 85, 89, 94, 95, 99, 100, 106 top and bottom, 108 top and bottom, 109, 115, 120, 121, 124 top, 128–131, 133; Topfoto/HIP 139; Topfoto/The Image Works 36 bottom; Vicky [Victor Weisz], courtesy of the Evening Standard and the British Cartoon Archive at the University of Kent 19

Cover photograph: courtesy of Corbis/Image Source

For further information concerning any pictures appearing in this book, please email samuel@uniquedimension.com

Photo research by Unique Dimension Limited

Special thanks to Topfoto

Index